# Worlds in Common?

Television discourse in a changing Europe

Kay Richardson and
Ulrike H. Meinhof

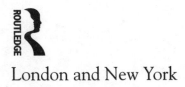

London and New York

First published 1999
by Routledge
11 New Fetter Lane, London EC4P 4EE

Simultaneously published in the USA and Canada
by Routledge
29 West 35th Street, New York, NY 10001

Typeset in Goudy by Routledge
Printed and bound in Great Britain by Clays Ltd, St. Ives PLC

*British Library Cataloguing in Publication Data*
A catalogue record for this book is available from the British Library

*Library of Congress Cataloging in Publication Data*
Richardson, Kay, 1955–
Worlds in Common?: Television discourses in a changing Europe/
Kay Richardson and Ulrike Hanna Meinhof.
p. cm.
Includes bibliographical references.
1. Television broadcasting–Europe. 2. Television–Semiotics.
3. Cable television–Europe. 4. Direct broadcasr satellite televison–Europe.
I. Meinhof, Ulrike H., 1947– II. Title.
PN1992.3.E78R5 1999          98–30279
302.23'45' 094–dc21  CIP

ISBN 0–415–14060–9 (hbk)
ISBN 0–415–14061–7 (pbk)

# Contents

# Acknowledgements

We would like to acknowledge the contributions of the following people in the production of this volume, and to give them our sincere thanks.

We are grateful to Julia Hall, who initially commissioned the book for Routledge. John Corner, Gunther Kress and Paddy Scannell provided constructive commentary upon draft versions, and we have benefited considerably from their advice. Thanks are due too to Frank Gloversmith, who gave considerable assistance with the proof-reading, and also to Ursula Meinhof, Cornelie Meinhof, Amrei Meinhof and Giovanni Bisoli who supplied photographs of German and Italian satellite dishes for the cover design. We would also like to mention Louisa Semlyen, Miranda Filbee and Stephanie Rogers at Routledge, who guided the book into production.

# Introduction

This book has been written as a cross-cultural contribution to the emerging literature concerned with the changing character of television broadcasting in the 1990s and into the next decade. Its rationale is exploratory – our goal is to provide readings from within the Western European media environment with relevance for current debates about the future of television and its contribution, for good or ill, to the cultural lives of viewers. Its approach is the textual/semiotic analysis of programmes, genres and channels which are distinctive, foregrounded or emergent in the new era. And its substantive focus is upon British and German strands of European television programming.

The present introductory chapter sets out the framework for the book, under four main headings. We begin with a section on *context*, characterising the changing nature of European television broadcasting in its global economic, political and cultural context. Under the heading of *rationale*, we give an account of our own interest in this changing environment with particular reference to our thematic focus upon time, space and quality in the chapters which follow. A section on *methodology* allows us to explain the approach we have taken in choosing and analysing the selected material, including some theoretical propositions about the assumptions behind our textual analysis. The introduction concludes with a section on *history*, comparing the broadcasting regimes of the UK and of Germany in order to establish both the similarities and the differences between these regions of the European audiovisual space as they pass into the era of transition and on to the world of post-traditional television.

## Context

The period during which this book was researched and written has been an era of transition. There has been much speculation about the future of television, along with real changes in the regimes of broadcasting which characterised what some have called its Second Age – the era of terrestrial, rationed television:

> The first two ages of British broadcasting each lasted about thirty years. The first age, that of radio domination, began in 1922 and ended in 1953, when the pageantry of the Coronation triggered a transfer of power and of popularity

from radio to the infant television. The second age, from 1953 to today, has been the Golden Age of Rationed Television. BBC-1, then ITV, then BBC-2 have been fashioned into a programme service of flexibility and of force, deliberately but delicately regulated by the BBC and the IBA in accordance with the wishes of the Parliaments of the time. But now, just around the corner, lie the twin developments of increased picture transmission by satellite and by cable. Just how, and how quickly, they will be allowed and encouraged to develop is a matter for open speculation, but there can be no doubt that the end of rationing that they imply will administer drastic shocks to the traditional mechanisms of broadcast production, distribution and exchange and to the regulatory arrangements that have sustained them.

(Wenham 1982: 15)

Wenham is writing from a British perspective, but similar stories could be told from within other Western European countries. His account provides a valuable starting point not just for its felicitous periodisation of the history of broadcasting, but because Wenham's own futurology was such a perceptive anticipation of the TV world of the late 1990s. Wenham foresaw the fights over the right to broadcast key sporting events; the 'dumbing down' debates; niche broadcasting, pay-per-view arrangements and 24-hour news, amongst other features which have become a reality in the years since his book was published.

The first and second age of broadcasting each in their turn had to achieve stability, as regimes for the production and consumption of familiar kinds of cultural material. Each needed to achieve a balance between novelty and consistency which ensured the continuity of the medium and of the institutions responsible for the output. The third age of broadcasting has yet to achieve its own distinctive stability, although patterns are emerging. Just as the shift from sound broadcasting to audiovisual transmission took place at varying speeds in different countries (even now there are countries where radio reaches more people than television does), so the same unevenness of development is occurring in respect of the shift to the age of multi-channel television. As regards the programming itself, we may note that, just as the era of terrestrial television inherited practices and routines from the radio era which preceded it, so the era of multi-channel television inherits traditions from the terrestrial era. The basis of the novelty at this key juncture (from few to many channels) is less fundamental than the introduction of broadcast moving images at the earlier moment. Some functions, such as continuity announcements, are as old as broadcasting, despite changes in the styling of such material in different phases of the history. Important studies have been undertaken showing that conventions now taken for granted and naturalised had first to be invented by practitioners (see Scannell and Cardiff 1991: 153–78 on the development of radio talk as a one-to-one speech event). Multi-channel broadcasting has required the development of new conventions, such as those surrounding the appropriate formatting for 24-hour news channels, and channels mixing locally originated programming with national material (see Chapters 2 and 6 below).

Within this perspective, upon television in an era of transition, it is important to ask about the changing experience of the viewers. At the end of the twentieth century television is undoubtedly, in developed countries, a permanent and taken-for-granted component of cultural life. The regulation of the industry is predicated upon this ubiquity of a medium which, more than any which preceded it, connects and integrates the domains of the personal, domestic, private, with those of the external world. It is not likely that the technological/industrial changes now in progress will significantly undermine this relation between the lived experience of the viewer and the mediations available to her via television. Television, in the West, will continue to be ubiquitous. It will also continue to be a domestic medium, 'consumed' in the home, even if it does become more interactive and develops new functions through integration with Internet services. It will continue to be the most important experiential basis for 'intimacy-at-a-distance' with public figures, celebrities whose images are pervasively displayed upon the TV screen and integrated into the imaginative lives of the viewers (Horton and Wohl 1993). Television will continue to occupy a key role as provider of symbolic material through its myriad textual forms and representations.

Nevertheless, there are, or there will be, important changes in the relation between television and its audiences which are worthy of examination during this period of transition. The background picture concerns the properties of that relation which developed during the 'second age' of broadcasting and which underpinned the various national ecologies of viewing in societies making significant use of television as a medium. Broadly speaking, Western Europeans, unlike Americans, have been used to ecologies wherein public-service traditions have dominated over those of the marketplace. Public-service goals always formed an important basis for discussion of the merits of television, even in countries like Britain which accommodated commercial production from an early stage (ITV broadcasting began in 1955). But scholars, in general, agree that the general tendency is away from public-service traditions and towards a more commercial structure. Public-service channels survive; in some countries they even continue to be the dominant channels – yet even they are 'commercialising' in the face of competition from privately funded channels (C. Barker 1997: 31–48; Coleman and Rollet 1997: 5–20; Weymouth and Lamizet 1996).

Other, more specific changes in viewing possibilities are more to do with the particular uses to which the new European broadcasting potential is being put. One such 'new' use is the rise of the 24-hour news channels, first CNN, in its 'international' variant (which remained however obviously American in ethos), then the more regional newcomers: Sky News (addressing principally the British market, in English), n.tv (addressing principally the German market, in German) and, most recent of all, the BBC's own satellite news channel, News 24, currently licence-fee-funded (also intended primarily for the British market). These are the channels which purport to satisfy the viewers' need for 'news on demand'. Shopping channels, too, did not exist in the 'traditional' TV era. The discourse of the Shopping Channel is intended to initiate acts of consumption on the part of viewers – consumption which is transacted by tele-phone and which is quite compatible, it seems, with uninterrupted television viewing. Hour by hour there is discursive evidence of this complex social rela-tion, as 'successful' consumers telephone the show and are heard to talk about their pleasures in the purchase.

In the late 1990s, the primary context for the re-evaluation of television is that of globalisation. Whether the focus is economic (i.e. upon the corporations with significant media interests), political (i.e. upon the regulation of television and its market) or cultural/social (i.e. upon the viewers and viewing contexts), it is no longer sufficient to focus upon particular national systems without refer-ence to global considerations. Large amounts of programming are made with the international as well as the national market in mind (see Cunningham and Jacka 1996, on Australia as an exporting country). Many 'national' systems rely heavily on bought-in material which is dubbed or subtitled for the national audience if necessary. The geographic 'reach' of satellite transmission ensures simultaneous transmission across several countries, language areas and time zones.

Trans-national relations between broadcasting institutions as well as broad-casting audiences are very much in focus in such works as C. Barker (1997), Sreberny-Mohammadi *et al.* (1997) and Mowlana (1997):

> While there have always been grounds for exploring the economic and cultural significance of television, the case is particularly acute at present because of changes in the patterns of global communications and global culture. Since the mid 1980s there has been a significant rise in transna-tional television both in terms of global ownership and in the use of the distribution technologies of satellite and cable to open up new markets. In turn, the globalization of the institutions of television raises crucial ques-tions about culture and cultural identities, for television is a major disseminator of cultural maps of meaning and a resource for identity construction.
>
> (C. Barker 1997: 3)

The semantics of 'global' suggest something more than merely trans-national. There is a McLuhanesque vision here of the world as a single media system with bonding elements of no geographic specificity. It remains no more than a vision (see Ferguson 1990). The 'widest' broadcasters (CNN, Star TV, MTV) have been forced to narrow their output to a regional level. Straubhaar (1997) in particular has argued for the importance of the trans-national region, for geocul-tural rather than global markets, in understanding how television is distributed worldwide:

> Geo-cultural markets are unified by language (even though different accents and dialects may divide countries somewhat). However, they go beyond language to include history, religion, ethnicity (in some cases), and

culture in several senses; shared identity, gestures and non-verbal communication; what is considered funny or serious or even sacred; clothing styles; living patterns; climate influences and other relationships with the environment. Geo-cultural markets are often centred in a geographic region, hence the tendency to call them regional markets, but they have also been spread globally by colonisation, slavery, and migration.

(Straubhaar 1997: 291)[1]

'Regions', thus identified, may in many cases be trans-national but the importance of a shared language remains strong, for obvious reasons. In addition, as Straubhaar also acknowledges, the power of cultural tradition, along with broadcasting tradition itself, acts to ensure the continuing power of the *national* voice in television. Viewers prefer, so the evidence suggests, to watch programmes made 'for them', where 'they' (we) are consciously French, German, British. . . There is demand too for the truly 'local', i.e. the sub-national, in broadcast output, despite technological and cultural difficulties in constructing appropriate localities.

Straubhaar identifies seven major geocultural markets, of which the US-dominated Anglophone market is by far the largest. In addition, he draws attention to:

> Western Europe, where the European Community has been trying to create a region-wide cultural market; Latin America, linked also to other 'Latin'-based language markets in Italy and France: a Francophone market linking France and its former colonies: an Arabic world market; a Chinese market: and a Hindi or South Asian market.

(Straubhaar 1997: 285)

Geocultural markets in this sense do not develop accidentally, nor can they be constructed *ab initio* through deliberate political or commercial policy. They must founded upon pre-existing cultural realities of considerable historical depth.

Within this perspective, 'Europe' is obviously problematic. Gifreu (1996), for one, talks about the specific problem of language within post-Maastricht Europe, focusing upon the linguistic diversity, not only within the continent, but also within the countries which belong to the Union. Schlesinger (1993) discusses the issues raised by the EU attempts to construct a European audiovisual space. Despite the undeniable levels of shared history and culture in Europe, it is a history which includes profound internal cultural conflict and insurmountable degrees of linguistic difference. Furthermore, the position of the two English-speaking countries, Ireland and the UK, locates them firmly and securely within the US-dominated Anglophone television market – Ireland principally as an importer, but the UK also as a crucial exporter. The result is an irony:

> ...bearing in mind the strength of national preferences both for national styles and contents in television consumption patterns, it could fairly be

said that the real common currency of the European audiovisual space is actually *American* television's output, for the U.S. produces the moving images that most easily traverse *any* European national barriers. By contrast, European-produced programs apparently offer much more limited scope for audience identification and do not travel too well beyond their national confines or, English-language ones excepted, their language area.

(Schlesinger 1993: 72)

Other researchers with reservations about the mythology of television globalisation have emphasised the importance of audience research demonstrating the scope for diverse interpretations of the same media texts. The key reference here is still the work of Tamar Liebes and Elihu Katz (see Liebes and Katz 1989), on the cross-cultural reception of *Dallas*. On the basis of this and other research, important claims have been made stressing what a mistake it would be to equate globalisation with homogenisation. Hence the neologisms 'glocal' and 'glocalisation'. These terms were evidently first coined within marketing discourse. Robertson (1995) discusses their origins, and is responsible for introducing these terms into the vocabulary of cultural studies, the point being that marketing, undertaken at a global level, nevertheless has to attend to particularities of local context and to plan its strategies accordingly:

The global and the local are relative terms, the idea of the local, specifically what is considered local, is produced within and by a globalizing discourse, which includes capitalist marketing and its increasing orientation to differentiated local markets. As Robertson suggests, diversity sells so that ethnicity is commodified and sold, sometimes as nostalgia, sometimes as a sign of cosmopolitanism. In any case, an emphasis on particularity and diversity can be regarded as an increasingly global and universalistic discourse ... *glocalisation* [expresses] the global production of the local and the localisation of the global.

(C. Barker 1997: 205)

It is important to bear in mind this *specific* origin and use of the term, because in the absence of this specificity there is a tendency for phrases such as 'the localisation of the global' and 'the globalisation of the local' to degenerate into mere slogans, and for the conceptual content to attenuate, to the point where it is hard to understand what kind of *causality* we are meant to attend to (or, indeed, whether there really is an underlying causal argument).

## Rationale

There are two important questions of a general kind, which lie behind the present research:

- In the European context, how will the television experience of the next decade or so compare with that of the late twentieth century?
- Should we regard that future optimistically or pessimistically?

It is these questions which have given the book its overall shape and character, and which have been privileged over questions about the changing institutional context of television production and regulation.[2] They provide a rationale not just for our attention to new kinds of programming in the multi-channel environment, and the explicitly evaluative perspective which we have allowed ourselves, but also for the specific choice of themes – time, space, quality – for each of the sections in the book itself.

Television's cultural/symbolic order has been 'unsettled' by recent changes. Television still makes sense, but sometimes requires more work, sometimes different work, from its viewers before that sense is vouchsafed. Despite the large amounts of recycled material on the new channels, there has been a wave of televisual novelty effects rippling through our societies. People have stories to tell about the first time they saw CNN; or MTV; or the Shopping Channel; or Jerry Springer; or topless darts; or financial news read by a woman steadily removing all her clothing. This book belongs entirely to the moment of novelty – we have written it understanding that much of what we wanted to write about will not yet have been seen by many of our readers.

Any characterisation of the new instability presupposes a prior stability (though not a homogeneity – television has always been characterised by variety in its output). Previous researchers have stressed stabilities of *time*; specifically, the grounding of TV discourse in a 'live' moment, shared by broadcaster and viewer. They have also stressed stabilities of *space*; specifically, the strong preference for a *national* orientation in programming discourse. Some have attached considerable phenomenological importance to these stabilities, using them in arguments about the experience of modern life as citizens, consumers and individuals.

The significance of *quality*, our third theme, is similar. Here, we have drawn attention to developments which push 'quality' further than before in directions already inscribed in traditional television practice. New programme types move TV discourses further towards 'high-quality' television as well as further towards 'low quality' television. The benchmark for these judgements is the cultural logic of the medium as we have come to understand it, knowing not only what goes out and when, but also how it is spoken and written about.

### The semiotics of time in the third age of broadcasting

Our point of departure in this section is a set of arguments respecting the role of television (and radio) as clock and as calendar. Traditional television can be regarded as an institution whose practices have become essential in the regulation of time for its viewers at a number of different levels. The stability of the 'normal' day and the 'normal' week in modernity derives substantially not from television but from paid labour – due allowance being made for groups whose orientation to the labour market derives not from their own participation in it but from that of 'significant others' in their lives – partners, children, parents. Within that context, the routines of broadcasting began by orienting themselves to these pre-existing forms of temporal order – as they still do. The workday still has a normative status in Western European societies, and broadcasting's collusion in this respect is an important mechanism in maintaining that normative status. At the same time, the frameworks constructed in order to deliver the output of the channels have introduced a further layering of routines and continuities with their own specificity and their own claims upon the time of viewers. Television's routines have temporal significance at many different levels, ranging from the importance of the 'time-check', through the requirements of scheduling on a day-to-day, week-to-week, season-to-season, year-to-year basis, and on to the long-running dramas in which characters age at the same rate as their viewers.

This is what television has been in the lives of its viewers (see Scannell 1996), certainly in Western European countries, which, unlike the USA and Canada, do not have to take account of different time zones in the planning of schedules. A slogan from 1960s Britain captures much of this:

> It's Friday!
> It's five to five!
> And it's *Crackerjack!*
> (Loud cheers from studio audience)

Thus were British children, home from school with a weekend ahead, invited into the spirit of a variety-type show with its own very distinctive ethos and personalities, popular and long-running, however 'naff' it may seem in retrospect.

Does television still accept this time-maintaining function in the era of transition? Will it continue to do so in the post-traditional era? Foregrounded in Part I is our case study of the routines of the new, 24-hour news channels. The significance of 24-hour scheduling is the potential it offers to *reject* the temporalities of the normative lived day of its viewers. Technology does not require 'down time'; neither does economics – there are resources enough to fill the screens around the clock. The nature of the output (live or near-live reportage of current events *worldwide)* has no necessary temporal structure, since, while national news can be oriented to the framework of the normative day (stories timed to 'hit' at just the right moment for the early-evening or mid-evening bulletin), global news must in principle find these to be 'provincial' specificities, whatever the country of origin.

In practice, the times of the viewing audience are still privileged over other times – but with somewhat less insistence than in the traditional regimes. 24-hour news channels address the 'need' for TV news-on-demand, and thus break with the tradition which ties news programming to specific times of day. This is one aspect of changes in scheduling practice which arguably give a different kind of basis for the temporal relations between TV and its audiences. Television becomes less important than heretofore in constructing 'dailiness' on the basis of predictably different 'mornings', 'afternoons' and 'evenings' – an experiential construction of time. In place of the rhythms of the (working) day, 24-hour news foregrounds its hourly cycles of repetition. This is a more formal and mechanical construction of time, perhaps more liberating in a world where work routines are less uniform than before (see Chapter 2).

## The semiotics of space in the third age of broadcasting

As indicated above, our point of departure here is the preference for national TV programming in most countries (including those which nevertheless are obliged on cost grounds to fill the schedules with large amounts of imported material). National programme speaks to the national audience, about national celebrities, customs, experiences and events. There is little evidence that television nationalism in this sense is likely to come to an end, in the short or medium term. Britons have seen powerful corroborating evidence of that in 1997, as we watched the invocation of 'national experience' in the drama of the death and funeral of Diana, Princess of Wales. Although this was an event which evoked a global response of the same proportions as the Kennedy assassination, it was in Britain that Diana was constructed as 'our' princess, and the loss as one which was 'personal' for millions of people who had no acquaintance with the princess beyond familiarity with her media image.

National specificity can be regarded positively, where it fosters an inclusive sense of community. There are fault lines in this cultural geography, which lead to justified complaints from minorities regarding themselves as underrepresented, stereotyped or scapegoated in traditional programming. Free-market remedies may be a possibility in the new broadcasting regimes, for minorities with resources enough to take advantage of channel abundance. But the market, unlike the State, accepts no obligation to minorities, and sceptics will continue, on those grounds, to argue for the continuation of public-service principles, used imaginatively to meet the needs of the whole community.

The benign face of national programming is at its strongest in relation to the 'public sphere' functions of television. TV may not always live up to its best civic goals, but it has embraced them: to give citizens some access to their political leaders, to make representatives accountable for their actions and decisions, to involve us all in the political process. It is therefore important to assess the possible future of national television, through a consideration of the extent to which the TV experience of the future will offer alternatives. On the one hand there lies fragmentation, dislocation, spatial incongruity – the end of community, at least in so far as community depends upon recognising itself in televisual representation. On the other hand lie the other kinds of bounding locations which are, or could become, important in the sense of identity and community. Cities in Europe are now capable of supporting television services, via cable delivery systems, speaking to their local audiences. Large question marks remain over the power of such programming to usurp the time viewers devote to better-funded national shows. The large footprints of the new satellites have made Europe-wide distribution technologically possible, and some development of European broadcasting institutions has been encouraged from Brussels. Commercial interests are less convinced, and cultural resistance to 'Europeanisation' of television remains strong.

These are issues which are of considerable importance to policy makers and to those responsible for the provision of television services. Our own interest is in the 'textualisation' of spatial relations between broadcasters and their audiences: in the evidence offered by the programmes and channels themselves that a different kind of spatial 'order' may take over from the one we have regarded as natural in the television world. We have examined television discourses which eschew national address in favour of either a European one or something more localised. The point of our analysis is to assess the extent and significance of the divergence from traditional television. Nor have we ignored the possibility that 'grounded' television discourse, firmly located somewhere – the continent, the country, the region, the city – is itself a phenomenon of its time, and vulnerable to a de-spatialisation in which it is no longer possible or desirable to know where the programming comes from in order to make sense of it.

## Questions of value

In Part III we turn our attention to the projection of value in the new regimes of broadcasting; the biggest fear for the future being the absolute decline in 'quality', and the greatest hope being the provision of television channels for every taste, every hobby, every minority group. In one scenario, the elusive 'quality' disappears because the resources to support it are spread too thinly. In another scenario, 'quality' is equated with diversity (see C. Barker 1997).

> Two of the most influential groups thinking about television have been inclined to see quality as something between a figleaf and a figment. For the liberal economists it is of far less interest than market structure and efficiency or for that matter, the freedom to buy, sell and publish. For them, most arguments about quality are little better than the special pleading of vested interest, fearful that their restrictive cartels are soon to be burst open. Meanwhile for many of the television academics, particularly those influenced by semiotics, postmodernism and the new schools of cultural studies, quality is a non-issue for another reason: namely, that it is just another legitimation of the old hierarchies of judgement, a concept drained of meaning by years of (ab)use by those in power.
>
> (Mulgan 1997: 14)

Despite the influence of semiotics on our own work, we agree with Mulgan about the importance of trying to identify criteria of value to work with in assessing television's contribution to cultural, social and political life, while recognising the difficulties involved when confronting this task in a multicultural and hierarchical society, with deep and multifaceted conflicts of interest. Mulgan himself discusses the quality of television under seven headings:

- producer quality and professionalism
- consumer quality and the market
- television's aesthetic
- television as ritual and communion
- television and the person
- the televisual ecology
- quality and diversity.

We have touched upon more than one of these themes in the course of this volume, on television and the person in relation to the idea of a European identity, on television as ritual and communion in relation to the rhythms of 24-hour news, and on television as diversity in relation to multi-channel programming as such.

The market looks for popularity. General channels, insofar as they are market-driven, want programmes which will maximise audiences. But even 'niche market' channels must find audiences big enough to support their activities. In February 1998 the Country Music Channel stopped broadcasting in Europe. Evidently, there are insufficient country music fans in Europe to convince advertisers to buy space on the channel.

Popularity has traditionally been a suspect source of value in the public service model (Mulgan 1997; Corner 1997; Eide *et al.* 1997; C. Barker 1997). 'Good' programmes may attract small audiences for a variety of reasons: because they appeal to taste segments which are narrow; because they offer instruction when the mass audience prefers entertainment and escapism; because they require more effort of understanding than the usual fare. Less good programmes may attract large audiences because their form of appeal is more general, their entertainment value prioritised, their accessibility straightforward. Positively 'bad' programmes may be successful enough to allow them into the schedules. Popularity cannot be the (only) yardstick of value, but neither can 'quality' be attributed *without argument* to programmes of particular types.

The coming of the multi-channel environment certainly affects the nature of this debate. From one perspective it solves the debate, or at least offers the best kind of solution that is affordable in the context of a multicultural, hierarchical society with conflicts of interest and of taste. The tastes of the opera fan and the rock music fan can be satisfied simultaneously and painlessly. Force of numbers decides that opera and rock are different but equal, and that country music (in Europe) is inferior. It is a partial solution, provided that we can accept as a consequence that opera fans remain ignorant of rock, and vice versa. 'Tastes' do not just happen: they are *constructed*, in particular times and places for particular groups and individuals. The notion of fully formed taste cultures to which television makes no difference except in 'satisfying' those existing tastes is a peculiar one. It may – just – work for music, but it is much less adequate as an understanding of other cultural expression, particularly drama. Furthermore, what counts as 'good' in terms of journalism, documentary, current affairs can't be resolved quite so easily in terms of taste preferences.

The citizens of 1990s Europe are inheritors of 'traditional' taste hierarchies (see Bourdieu 1990) which have become problematic because of the demonstrable disjuncture between 'popularity' and 'quality', defined in terms of those hierarchies. Perhaps the hierarchies (at least in certain domains) have moved, in Raymond Williams's (1976) terms, from 'dominant culture' to 'residual culture', and broadcasting has been an instrument of their relegation. Individuals whose loyalty to tradition is strong may never have found much for them in the world of television. If this is the case it isn't surprising that 'high culture' has a niche market in the multi-channel environment: for example, the English-language Performance Channel – and (arguably) the Franco-German channel ARTE (see Chapter 8).

But a high-culture niche market preserves one layer of the hierarchy, not the hierarchy itself. In that sense, far from challenging the relegation of the hierarchy, 'culture' channels express that relegation. In any event, the existence of particular kinds of channel and programme is only part of the story. The rest of the story will depend upon examination of the textual structures and strategies employed by programming which continues broadcasting's commitment to 'culture' and 'the arts'. Textual analysis will help us to understand better what is becoming of the old taste hierarchies in the new broadcasting dispensation.

One way of depicting the present configuration is to describe it thus. There is a residual culture which clings to a clear taste hierarchy and has a preference for cultural forms and practices at the higher end of that hierarchy. This residual culture is catered for, as a well-defined but minority market, within a dominant culture which is awkwardly relativistic: not everything can be defended/ celebrated, but diversity is itself to be valued, and differences of taste respected. The dominant culture takes its cultural liberalism as far as it can: its limits are tested at one level by pornography as both pleasure-giving and (arguably) harmful to its consumers, and at another level by 'vulgarity'. The concept of vulgarity derives its force from the residual culture, since it expresses a sensibility which aligns class and taste. To the extent that dominant culture has, with pleasure, made room for working-class leisure activities, it has rejected the older judgements. But it makes room for these activities on its own terms. Sometimes the result is to 'sanitise' vulgarity (televised soccer versus the view from the terraces), which makes it more acceptable to a heterogeneous audience. Sometimes the result is to replace it with less problematic (because less authentic) 'spectacular' forms. In a multi-channel environment, where channels have smaller and less heterogeneous audiences, there is scope for less sanitised presentations. In the case of the US talk shows the depicted vulgarity does not represent unqualified commitment to working-class expression, but rather a spectacular form of that expression produced for mass consumption, in which vulgarity is not sanitised but *heightened*, and which caters for voyeuristic pleasures.

# Methodology

Our plan throughout this book has been to focus upon some of the more interesting and important themes in current media research, as indicated above, and to follow up these issues through a focus upon the textual forms and strategies of particular programmes and channels. In pursuing this objective, we have developed a series of case studies, which are of variable length and depth depending on the nature of the argument in any particular chapter and the type of exegesis which it required. This section begins with a brief survey of research which is relevant to the present study, before introducing some observations of a more theoretical kind.

Research on cable and satellite broadcasting is not new. These recent developments in the television industry have been monitored by scholars from the outset (see, for example, Wenham 1982; Collins 1992, 1994; Negrine and Papathanassopoulos 1991). However, within this literature the principal focus to date has been upon the questions of policy which arise in relation to the funding and the control of the industry. It is difficult for academic scholarship to keep abreast of the changes within the industry, and it is very much the case that a lot of the published research in this area is now out of date as regards specific facts and figures, for example, on cable and satellite penetration of different national markets; on the ownership of media companies; on the latest regulatory measures at local, national and European levels; on the channels which are actually available to viewers. Fortunately, detail of this kind is not essential to the present project. In addition there is a small amount of academic research which looks at the spread of satellite technology from the viewer's end. This includes an article by Charlotte Brunsdon about the 'taste' issues which developed in the British press in relation to the siting of actual satellite dishes on the outer walls of receiving homes – a form of 'blot on the landscape' in neighbours' eyes (Brunsdon 1991).

More recently, Moores (1996) undertook an ethnographic research project on homes within socially distinctive neighbourhoods in South Wales which had invested in satellite technology (DBS – Direct Broadcasting by Satellite). By talking to all members of the households with satellite dishes Moores was able to investigate their motivations. This was a project which very much addressed itself to the construction of social identity. Moores wanted to show that satellite technology was variably used, within different homes and different neighbourhoods, while drawing attention to some similar dimensions in the construction of social identity. For example, he found that satellite television was important to the construction of generational difference within the home. He also found that, while some viewers associated the resources of satellite with 'America' and took pleasure in it because of that association – more like being in America than with the TV they were used to – others identified it with 'Europe' and in doing so claimed for themselves a European identity. Jensen (1995) is another important contribution to research on multi-channel television – this research included a study of the frequency with which different groups of people did actually change channel while watching TV.

What is missing in much of this research, a gap which the present volume seeks to fill, is any very detailed attention to the programming which satellite and television services make available. There are signs that this may be changing. Apart from Jensen, we should draw attention to MacGregor (1997), who pays close attention to the programming available on 24-hour news channels, in comparison with terrestrial channels, although with an emphasis different from our own. And Chris Barker (1997) has a section which focuses specifically upon news and upon soap opera, though in both cases what he does is to take the existing research on these television forms and contextualise this within his concerns for the current state of 'global' television. Nevertheless, the kind of close analysis that we have attempted to produce for our various case studies, drawing upon traditions of discourse analysis, applied linguistics and social semiotics, does make the present volume distinctive.

There is of course a valuable strand of media research which is concerned with textual form and meaning (see, for example, Corner 1995). We have drawn from this research as appropriate throughout the present volume. Particularly relevant here are such edited collections as those of Allen (1992) and Mellencamp (1990).

Another relevant point of reference is the work undertaken by scholars whose background is in language study rather than media studies. The best-known texts are those of van Dijk (1988), Bell (1991) and Fowler (1991). In relation to television discourse, a key text is that of Fairclough (1995). Bell and Garrett (1998) is the most recent collection of work in this area, some of it concerned with the press and some with television. There is a concern in some of this work with questions of 'ideology' and its reproduction. If we have ignored this theme in the present volume, it is not because we regard the power of the mass media as unimportant. We have concentrated upon other topics and issues partly to offer something distinctive and partly because, within the intellectual context of the 1990s, a focus upon ideology runs the risk of foreclosing around a range of texts and issues which are narrower than we wished to explore. It was the intellectual context of the 1970s and 1980s which gave the concept of ideology its 'bite' (along with related concepts such as that of 'hegemony'). These concepts still have their descriptive value, but not as the keystones of definitive theoretical frameworks, in an era of much greater scepticism towards totalising theory.

A long tradition in sociology, going back to the work of Berger and Luckman (1967), represents the relation between discourse (sometimes called language) and social reality as a constructive one. Constructivists view the reality of social life as sustained, in whole or in part, through discourse: it is the concepts and propositions adopted in our talk and our writings which form the basis of intersubjectively shared realities. Some versions of this argument, such as that of the ethnomethodologists, give a privileged place to the role of *talk* in this process. For them it is in face-to-face spoken interaction where the greatest power resides, because in talk we can inspect the ongoing *processes* of reality-construction, as well as the terms upon which these are a matter of local management or negotiation between participants. Other versions seek to understand the emergence of social structures which transcend the local social relations negotiated in talk. Social institutions such as 'the family'; 'Parliament' and even 'the BBC' may be discursive constructions, but they are constructions underpinned by substantial power relations and sedimented deep within the social order. In such cases it may be the constructive power of written discourses which is more significant.

Broadcasting occupies an interesting position in relation to these perspectives. On the one hand a substantial amount of broadcast output takes the form of 'talk'. Constructivist arguments have set great store by interactive, dialogic talk and broadcast talk is not essentially dialogic. It very rarely involves the fully fledged interactivity of non-mediated talk (though even the interactivity of non-mediated talk can be exaggerated, since it is not all types of talk which possess this property). Against this we may observe that there are many forms of broadcast talk which require on-screen participants to engage one another dialogically, for the benefit of the overhearing audience; further, even monologic broadcast discourse is partially mimetic of face-to-face interaction. Thus, though broadcast talk may lack the *particular* kind of reality-confirming/creating power possessed by face-to-face interaction, it may nevertheless have a distinctive power of its own, combining on the one hand, in a second-order way, the solidarity relations generated in (certain kinds of) face-to-face talk, with the authority relations generated by the ubiquitous *presence* of broadcasting. To this must be added, in the case of television, the contribution of the visual forms of television in the construction of social reality. There is a convention on television as a visual medium that depicted entities and scenes have a reality which is independent of the viewing process, and that the viewing of the screen image is a viewing of that reality. It is because of this convention that we can speak of a 'transparency effect'; the sense of watching, not a mediation of reality, but reality itself.

The forms of analysis adopted in this book depend upon approaching texts as codifications of the social of different kinds, and at different levels. So, for example, there are semiotic practices in television which classify time as 'now' and 'not-now' as well as practices which classify space as 'here' and 'not-here', and classify here as 'Liverpool', 'Britain', 'Europe'. It is indeed important to take seriously the argument that the classificatory practices of discourse give substance to the realities they encode. We must not, however, forget that television discourse is a contribution to the lived experience of viewers. Viewers' lives are touched by many discourses besides those of broadcast programming, and we have not fallen into the trap of deducing the character of the experiential world from that of the texts which feed into it. There is no reception analysis in this study, but we are very conscious that the forms of textual study represented here raise important questions about the viewers and their susceptibilities. It would no doubt be instructive, for example, to examine the 'Europeanisation' of the viewers, alongside and in relation to the attempt to produce a 'European' channel for them to enjoy.

The case-study material offered below covers the following material, some of which has been subjected to very little discussion in previous media research:

- 24-hour news channels (NBC and Sky News), with special reference to a day in the life of the beef crisis story
- Live TV, the channel owned by Mirror Group newspapers
- EuroNews
- Local TV channels in Liverpool (Liverpool Live and Channel One) and mdr, a regional channel in Germany
- QVC, the Shopping Channel
- American talk shows
- ARTE, the Franco-German 'culture' channel.

The principles underlying this selection are further explained within the appropriate chapters, but we can give an indication here of how they fit in with our chosen themes.

In Part I of the book, the most intensively developed case study focuses upon the 24-hour news channels, Sky News and n.tv. These are important because they point towards a different way of connecting broadcasting time with viewing time from the arrangements which have previously prevailed and which still prevail upon traditional channels with a news remit. In particular we have used these channels to focus on the nature of the news cycle, and on the construction of 'live' news. Another chapter in Part I focuses upon the early months of Live TV. The texts analysed here (in less depth than those of the news channels) are of interest with respect to the channel's attempt to make 'liveness' or 'immediacy' the foundation of its aesthetic, relating this to broadcasting's tradition of liveness.

Part II of the book, on 'space', has as its first chapter a case study of EuroNews. This is a news channel supported by the European Union which attempts to speak to its audience as 'Europeans', via the Eutelsat (Hot Bird) satellite. We have attempted in Chapter 4 to provide a critical account of how EuroNews imagines and constructs 'Europeanness', reinforcing through textual analysis a point about the artificiality of the European cultural identity which other commentators have been at pains to argue in general terms – against the logic of the policy discourse originating within the committees of the EU. The case studies in Chapter 5 are shorter ones. The focus here is upon different sorts of local channels, some Liverpool cable channels, expressing/promoting local identity, and mdr, a channel in Germany which, although regional in address, nevertheless is watched by a substantial national and trans-national audience. Finally, in Part II, we include a discussion of the Shopping Channel, QVC. The interest of QVC lies not in its difference from the characteristics of terrestrial television, but in its intensification of certain tendencies present throughout the terrestrial era. QVC has very little to work with in order to sustain the sociability it requires between itself and its audience. Restricted as those resources are, it nevertheless manages through its use of space and its discursive routines to sustain an ethos which is familiar and pleasurable.

Part III comprises two complementary case studies. One of these looks at the American talk shows which have provided material for new TV channels (Granada Talk, UK Living, Sky One) for some time and look likely to be increasingly part of the schedules on traditional channels, too. These shows stand for the 'debasement' of television programming, at least for some critics, and our analysis examines the terms of the criticism as well as the character of the discourse they offer. Conversely, the channel ARTE stands for the preservation of taste and culture on our TV screens: the case study in Chapter 8 examines the terms of that preservation and the extent to which 'high culture' now interpenetrates with popular culture in this domain.

It has been our aim to characterise, through textual analysis, particular types of programme and particular channels. As is common in such work, this came down to a matter of selecting particular broadcasts, to represent the programme type or channel in which we were interested. The selection process was straight-forward enough: after ensuring, through repeated viewing, that we were familiar with the general characteristics of what we wished to examine, we made tape collections over an appropriate period of time (one day in the case of Sky News and n.tv; three weeks in the case of talk shows). From this material we selected examples which we deemed to be representative of the type, based upon our expertise as viewers. These examples were subjected to analysis, and this is reported below in the relevant chapters. After analysis, any further concerns we had respecting the typicality of our extracts were dealt with by further viewing of relevant channels. We are confident that we have not chosen untypical days, or untypical texts, in any of the chapters. Any readers who doubt that this is so have an easy way of checking, since, with one exception, we have focused on material which anyone with a satellite dish or cable connection can access. The exception is the discussion of Live TV in Chapter 3. Although Live TV still broadcasts via cable it has changed considerably since the early days, and in particular it has not attempted to sustain the particular experiment with news language which we looked at in that chapter.

The analyses attempted are undoubtedly selective, and this is deliberate. We have given primary attention to language, though in no case have we over-looked or slighted the contribution of the visual dimension to the construction of meaning. In general, it is meaning rather than form which has been our main concern, and it is because of that emphasis we would wish to characterise our endeavour as an essentially social-semiotic one. There are some differences from other work within the social-semiotic paradigm – notably, the grounding we have given it in concerns and issues which derive from media studies – and thus from outside semiotic or linguistic theory as such.

More specifically, we have approached the task of exegesis as analysts of *discourse* – intending thereby to indicate a primary interest in textual form/meaning at a generic level. We have also attempted to make use of linguistic tools and concepts appropriate for the analysis at hand. This is most evident in Part II on television and its spatial relations, which includes for the benefit of readers unfamiliar with this literature a discussion of linguistic deixis as this has previously been theorised.

## History

In the history section, we attempt a brief historical overview of broadcasting in the two countries we have concentrated upon in the present volume – Britain and Germany. This history forms the background for the case-study chapters to follow and, as such, it is more descriptive than the preceding discussion. For more extensive accounts, see Humphreys (1990) and the chapters by Sandford and Swales in Coleman and Rollet (1997).

Multi-channel broadcasting has become possible on a large scale in Europe because of the advent of DBS technology, allowing anyone with a dish receiver and appropriate set-top decoders to receive satellite transmissions, as well as broad-band cable systems (allowing television programming to be 'piped in' to individual homes from head stations, gathering their material from video-cassettes, from terrestrial broadcast signals, and from satellite broadcast signals). Digital transmission will further complicate this picture in respect of technological infrastructure, but the result as far as the viewers are concerned will be the same – a larger number of channels than in the terrestrial television era. Germany and Britain have accommodated to the new era in distinctively different ways, as the following summaries indicate.

### British television broadcasting

Terrestrial British television broadcasting began in 1936, though it closed down during the war and recommenced in 1946. The monopoly of the BBC was ended in 1955 when the first commercial channel (ITV) went on the air. A second public channel (BBC2) was introduced in 1964 and a second commercial channel (Channel 4) started in 1982. The third commercial channel is Channel 5, which began broadcasting in 1997. Not all homes can receive it yet.

This system is still a public/commercial duopoly inasmuch as it is only the public channels which are financed through licence fee revenues and only the commercial channels which are financed through advertising (and a little bit of sponsorship). The existence of a strong commercial sector exerts an ever greater effect upon the BBC to justify the licence fee with popular programming, and to keep control of its own costs. Although advertising is still not allowed on the BBC channels, the Corporation operates commercially in other ways – selling its own wares in the global marketplace, merchandising tie-in products, forming deals with other broadcasters, etc.

The regulation of the BBC is as a State corporation, though one operating at arm's length from government under the control of a Board of Governors. The regulation of the commercial sector involved formalised, overt 'public-service' principles until the Broadcasting Act of 1990 introduced the ITC, which was intended to make regulation much lighter. Debates around franchise conditions keep alive the issue of public-service principles in relation to the commercial broadcasters.

As for satellite/cable transmission – this is all in private hands, though State licences must be granted. A large amount of satellite broadcasting falls within the media empire of Rupert Murdoch (the Sky channels): 'At September 1996 the cable and satellite programme channels listed by the ITC number 82 licensable programme services, with one third non-operational and 130 non-domestic satellite services' (Swales 1997: 27).

Any given viewer with a satellite dish or with cable access can consume within the global Anglophone TV marketplace (via CNN, MTV, Superchannel, Discovery and one or two other 'international' channels). It is also possible to be a European consumer by watching EuroNews or Eurosport, in their English-language versions, or European Business News (also in English).

A different kind of consumption is possible, too, for those with the linguistic capabilities to benefit – thanks to the large geospatial 'footprints' of the satellite channels, British viewers can watch programmes made for other national markets within Europe. To exercise this power it is necessary to opt for DBS technology rather than cable. Cable operators (who have local monopolies) control output from satellite to homes and exercise considerable 'rationing' of foreign-language channels. Cable and satellite technology has been slower to take off in Britain than elsewhere in Europe, though it is growing and will continue to do so on current projections. Only 6.5 million homes have been 'passed by' by cable as of 1996 and many of these don't choose to subscribe. For the satellite dish owner, foreign-language channels tend to be free-to-air, while more popular English-language satellite channels (such as Murdoch's Sky channels) are scrambled, requiring consumers to pay for decoding equipment. Regulation comes under the auspices of the ITC for services uplinked from the UK, but no public-service principles apply apart from those to do with constraints on advertising and 'watershed' restrictions separating family viewing from 'adult' viewing. The ITC regards itself as bound by the EU directive, *Television Without Frontiers*, but, unlike France, Britain has imposed no quota requirements for European-made production.

### German television broadcasting

A regular television programme service in Germany began in the mid-1930s and continued through the war to 1944. After the war, services were suspended nationally, and subsequently underwent separate development in the East and the West. East Germany favoured a centralised model, with its headquarters in East Berlin. West Germany adopted a federal approach, with control given to the federal states, the Länder.

The first postwar television was within the former British zone of occupation. Subsequently, the Länder of West Germany introduced services, though it was not until 1953 that they began to coordinate to produce a single, national channel. This channel still exists and is known as the First Channel, or alternatively as ARD (Allgemeine Rundfunkanstalten Deutschlands). A second public channel, ZDF (Zweites Deutsches Fernsehen), began in 1963 and is federally controlled in the same way as ARD.

The East German service (Deutsche Fernsehfunk) was dissolved in 1992 following unification. This resulted in some reorganisation of the existing third programme services in West Germany. Some of these services now cover parts of East as well as West Germany. The main result is that there is a regional service, or third programme, in every part of the country, East and West. The programming of these services varies from region to region (with 'spillover' at the boundaries) though they too are public channels as regards their ownership and control. Unlike the British public channels, ARD and ZDF accept commercial advertising. Regulation is determined by State Treaties between the Länder, but there is a national institution (the Broadcasting Council), which has equivalent functions to those of the BBC's Board of Governors in important respects, though with more directly political representation.

Broadcasting by privately owned companies came much later in Germany than in Britain, and indeed coincided with the development and takeoff of satellite and cable broadcasting in the 1980s:

> Constitutionally barred from acting directly in the sphere of broadcasting, the new Kohl government [in 1982] used its control of the Federal Post Office to initiate a massive countrywide programme of cable-laying that not only gave the Federal Republic in a very short time the biggest cable network in Europe, but also – as the government had intended – destroyed the argument of the opponents of commercialisation that there were not enough channels available. At the same time, the coming of satellite television confronted SPD-led Länder with services that offered no respect to whatever laws that might apply within their own geographical boundaries. And so, in 1984 commercial television finally arrived in Germany in the shape of RTL-Plus and Sat 1, the two channels that have remained the market leaders despite the establishment since then of numerous competitors.
>
> (Sandford 1997: 50–1)

A State Treaty of 1987 has established the legality of this dual system at the highest constitutional level. As a result of this history, in which the controlling role of the Länder in broadcasting affairs is crucial, Germans do not share the British sense of a dichotomy between terrestrial services (for the majority) and satellite/cable services (for the few). In 1997, professionally compiled audience figures published in one of the leading German TV magazines, *Hör Zu*, showed RTL in the lead with an average annual audience share of 16.8 per cent, followed by ARD (14.8 per cent), ZDF (13.4 per cent), SAT 1 (13.3 per cent) and Pro 7 (9.9 per cent) (*Hor Zu*, January 1998, p. 100). Third programmes also attract reasonably high audience figures in their regions of up to 10 per cent.

Together these channels account for the vast majority of the viewing in Germany.

Thanks to satellite it is possible for Germans to enjoy regional programming made for regions other than their own. The channel mdr is a notable example of this. Mdr is a thriving regional third programme targeting the former East German Länder of Saxony, Saxon-Anhalt and Thuringia. Yet it attracts audiences not only in its own region, but in the whole former East German territory as well as nationwide. If this is one kind of 'overspill' viewing, the other kind which has been common in Germany is the kind which allows Germans in certain regions to view German-language programming made for Austrians and Swiss-Germans. Sandford estimated that many German households could receive six or more German-language programmes as early as the 1970s (1997: 54).

The same viewers can, of course, experience overspill viewing in a vast number of other European and non-European languages (see Meinhof 1998, in press). A knowledge of the English language gives access to the 'international' channels already mentioned. As in Britain, Eurosport and EuroNews are available in German-language versions, as is the French–German public-service channel ARTE. Other German-language channels include Kabel 1, RTL2, Super RTL, tm3, vox, viva tv, viva 2, n.tv, 3 SAT (for Austrians and Swiss-German speakers as well as Germans), der Kinderkanal, DSF and, in an encrypted format, Premiere. MTV Europe, which recently split into three different regional networks – Northern, Central and Southern – now transmits up to four hours a day of tailored programming in German, targeting German, Austrian and Swiss viewers. The German media entrepreneurs of equivalent status to Rupert Murdoch are Bertelsmann, Springer and Kirch.

As in Britain, although the (economic) future of commercial broadcasting looks bright, the public-service broadcasters have managed to maintain a very strong position in a commercialising and deregulating environment.

# Part I

# The semiotics of time in the third age of broadcasting

Strong claims have been made about the role of the broadcast media in the social construction of time. Scannell (1988), for example, talks of 'The unobtrusive ways in which broadcasting sustains the lives and routines, from one day to the next, year in and year out, of whole populations ...' (Scannell 1988: 15).

Scannell here talks about *broadcasting*, not about television, and it is important for his argument (which is an historical one) that radio is included along with television. This is an 'effects' argument, but not, in the first instance, an argument about either ideological effects or behavioural effects of the kind familiar in positivist social science research. The perspective is a phenomenological one, and the primary emphasis is upon the nature of modern social life – how it is created and maintained, the kinds of communities it can sustain, the ontological security of individuals within the social order. The taken-for-granted intelligibility of the world, sustained in part by the routines and rituals of broadcast output, has a temporal dimension. At its simplest level, the broadcast media permit us to know *when* we are as well as *where* we are. Our television viewing, as well as our radio listening, can, if we allow them to, confirm us in our knowledge of: clock time, time of day (morning/daytime/teatime /prime-time/late/early), part of week (weekday/weekend), season and calendar date.

These claims are very convincing in relation to the broadcast media of the first and second age of broadcasting. But it is not yet clear whether or how they will apply in the third age – the age of multi-channel television. Television until the mid-1990s has had a form of appeal grounded in qualities of 'immediacy' and of 'flow' – qualities which depend upon a particular, familiar, relationship to the unfolding lives of the viewers. In the multi-channel world, however, this familiarity is at risk. For example, some of the new channels enhance immediacy, through a kind of permanent 'liveness'. Others undermine it, by replacing all live discourse with pre-recorded material. Given simultaneous availability of these channels, along with 'traditional' ones inserting pre-recorded material into a 'live' context, a possible experiential result of this is much less temporal coherence and 'groundedness' than heretofore. It is necessary to give analytical attention to what is happening on particular channels, particularly the ones which are new in the multi-channel environment, while not forgetting the importance of that environment itself and viewers' relations to it.

One emergent strand of programming on the new channels adopts a significantly different relation to *cyclicity* in the daily schedules. Cyclicity is the principle that particular programmes or segments recur on a regular, timed basis. This has always been an important part of schedule design. The most important cycles have been the daily, weekly and seasonal ones. This cyclicity has sometimes been recognised in the titles given to particular programme slots: 'the Wednesday play'; 'the nine o'clock news'. Cyclicity has also intersected with other kinds of schedule concerns, such as audience-building for prime-time programming. On some of the new channels, notably those which seek to combine liveness with 24-hour scheduling, cyclicity has become *hourly* – as well as daily and weekly. Twenty-four-hour news channels have adopted this format because it allows them, in principle, to refresh their agenda and renew their stories much more regularly than channels with fixed-point news programmes. The result in practice is considerable repetition, but on the understanding that the stories reported, the facts provided, are as immediate/recent as the best efforts of the broadcasters can manage. The principle of renewal comes as close as is currently possible to satisfying the impatience of the assumed viewer, who wants *only* the main news stories of the day, and wants them *now*.

Chapter 2 is concerned with the nature of 'liveness' in the multi-channel environment. The principal case study in that chapter makes further use of the Sky News/n.tv material discussed in Chapter 1 to explore one aspect of liveness, under the heading of 'the textual construction of immediacy'. Twenty-four-hour news channels sell themselves, in large part, on their ability to bring viewers the news 'as it happens'. For some critics, the principal risk here is the sacrifice of sense which occurs when 'being at the scene' is valued above the investigative work required *behind* the scene in order to establish for viewers what it might be a scene *of* (see MacGregor 1997). Our perspective is somewhat different. What we are interested in is 'eventhood' as a textual construction. One important property of 'eventhood' is *timeliness*. Events have their 'moments', i.e. they can be understood in terms of 'before', 'during' and 'after'. It is the 24-hour news channels which are best placed to capture 'the moment' of events they are interested in, can anticipate and have the resources to cover. What they actually do is to *construct* a 'before', 'during' and 'after', so that any bulletin can be understood in terms of that construction. All reportage does this, but only 24-hour broadcasting exposes the process so clearly, through its unremitting commitment to news delivery.

We are able to show, for a single story, that the news-event-as-it-happens is indeed a textual construction: anticipated 'beforehand' with future tense constructions, reported synchronously in the present tense, and announced retrospectively in the past tense. The indeterminacy of real life becomes determined textually. To watch any *one* bulletin would be to occupy a secure temporal place in relation to the reported event. But analysis across the unfolding hourly cycle of bulletins uncovers the real elusiveness of the event's 'moment'. The cross-cultural analysis of Sky News and n.tv offers further confirmation of this elusiveness, since the two channels offer significantly different determinations of that moment. From a linguistic point of view, these practices are of considerable interest. Speakers (presenters and correspondents) employ the kinds of time-coding formulae that linguists refer to as temporal deixis – expressions like 'now', 'then', 'soon', which take the moment of utterance as a 'zero point' and relate other events to that moment. Twenty-four-hour news, with its constantly moving zero point, exerts some pressure upon the conventional meaning of such terms, as we will demonstrate below.

Chapter 3 is concerned with the claim that *synchronicity* (of production, transmission and reception) is the basis of the relationship between broadcasters and their audiences (see, for example, Feuer 1993). This has been a commonplace characterisation of that relationship through the first and second age of broadcasting. However, it is vulnerable from two directions. It is vulnerable in the first instance from the large quantity of repeat programming which now occupies the schedules, since that programming is used with scant regard for temporal appropriateness. Scheduled programming of the 'old' sort, even if recorded, was made to fit its viewing slot, and flagged its temporal specificity. Such programming, when repeated, retains the flags – but their referentiality is undermined by the new viewing context. The synchronous relationship is vulnerable from another direction, too. Any 'natural' sign (a cough as a sign of a sore throat; the movement of tree limbs as a sign of high wind) can be appropriated in mimetic discourses – and many conventional signs have their basis in some such originally natural relationship. Liveness has its own natural signs. In the case of speech, for example, a degree of disfluency is regarded as a sign of liveness, the logic being that the demands of spontaneous composition give rise to the 'ums' and 'ahs' that would otherwise be edited out. When liveness becomes an aesthetic principle, rather than an ontological status, the requirement to look and sound live obviously requires the appropriation of just such conventionalising signs. It is a matter of degree, to be sure, but the passage of signs from natural to conventional status in this case may also mark a transition in the character and the quality of the trust which viewers are able to place in what they see and hear. At what point do we lose even the possibility of hearing live signs and inferring synchronicity?

# 1 Regularity and change in 24-hour news

Twenty-four-hour news channels have adopted the hourly cycle as the basis of their programming schedule. Just as the technology of picture transmission refreshes the screen image 30 times per second, so the institutional processes of news production refresh the news content once an hour. This is for the benefit of a viewer who cannot wait for the fixed-point bulletins on traditional channels. The metaphor is an apt one because in neither case does refreshment equal wholesale change. It allows for change, but it also allows for continuity, and anyone who has ever watched rolling news for any length of time will know just how repetitive the formula can be. But the impatient viewer need never notice this. She has switched off, and moved on, before the cycle starts again.

The refreshment strategy acts as a kind of guarantee that the reported news is always current, up-to-the-minute – as 'recent' as technology and institutional arrangements can make it. A static medium such as print journalism generates news as products, which can outlive their currency frame because of the material durability of the paper upon which they are printed. A dynamic medium does not have to confront the problem of the obsolete text. It has the converse problem: a report produced in real time 'expires' with the telling, even though its validity as a story about the world has not expired. In a dynamic medium it is repetition, not durability, which keeps news 'before the world' as long as programme editors wish it to be there.

There are moments when the recency of broadcast news, on traditional channels or on the new ones, turns into immediacy: a condensation to a single moment of happening, learning, and telling/showing. When this happens it has the potential to create the phenomenon which MacGregor (1997) refers to as 'global video howl round', turning the line from actors through broadcasters to viewers into a loop, with scarcely any passage of time:

> During the democracy riots in Thailand in 1992, events on the streets of Bangkok were reported by an international team consisting of the BBC's Hong Kong bureau led by reporter Brian Barron, his staff crew, a crew from the Australian Broadcasting Company and two local Thai crews. Material shot in the streets was edited locally and sent by satellite back to London

where it was transmitted by the BBC domestically and by World Service television which could be received in Bangkok. Within 20 minutes of this transmission, VHS copies of the reports were in the streets in the hands of the demonstrators. Television news, shot, edited and transmitted using new communications technologies, had created a global video howl round, a late 20th century hall of mirrors, with news itself entering the equation of events, and not for the first time.

(MacGregor 1997: 3)

Recency, immediacy, currency – these are the most salient characteristics of 24-hour news, and it is the cyclical formula which is the key strategy for producing these characteristics. The context within which this formula operates is the context of the 'liveness' of broadcast discourse.

## Television and temporal order

Broadcast discourse is 'live' in the sense that it is grounded in a 'live' communicative exchange between broadcasters and audience, even when it is delivering recorded programmes. By virtue of that property, it can be regarded as *temporally embedded* – not just in the sense that all discourse is embedded in the time and place of its origin, but also in the sense that it makes a textual feature of its contemporaneity. Viewers and broadcasters share a time frame, and understand that this is the case. Broadcasting thus plays its part in maintaining the social institution of the (Western) calendar, and marks out the world's passage towards the Millennium and beyond. The constancy of broadcasting output (one aspect of its 'flow') means that each unique moment in the world has an exactly corresponding moment in broadcasting time, *on every channel*. (Of course this is, still, an exaggeration: most channels cover part of the 24-hour day-cycle, not the whole cycle. But it is virtually true, since for most channels in Western broadcasting systems the 'default mode' is the broadcasting mode, and the 'down time' is regarded as the exception.) The unique time of broadcasting is occupied time – something is always happening, be it transmission of recorded or of live material. And audiences have had to conform their behaviour to the schedules of the broadcasters as they choose to fill the air waves. To catch a programme, by watching or recording the broadcasts, their own unique times had to be aligned with those of the broadcasters.

Some TV shows may, explicitly and internally, 'textualise' their relation to clock/calendar time. Breakfast-time programming typically insists upon reminding its viewers of clock time. Its viewers are people whose morning routines require them to be 'ready' – for school, for work – by a particular time. Their TV viewing is construed as subordinate to the requirements of preparation for the day's activities. At other times of day such reminders are less common. Indeed, explicit announcements of temporal specificity will be undesirable in many cases – they may do real damage to the possibility of re-transmission, at a future date. But broadcasters cannot do much about the unwritten, implicit and unintended coding of time, noticed in repeats but unnoticed in contemporary shows: the hairstyles, clothing, demeanour, speech styles, production styles, etc. which mark a programme by its decade of production. Even costume dramas can come to feel 'dated' in this sense, and won't be re-broadcast on terrestrial channels after a certain cut-off point unless there is felt to be some particular merit in the production that warrants it a re-screening. The early 1980s production of *Jewel in the Crown* was undergoing such a re-broadcasting (in July 1997) on Channel 4 in Britain. 'Dated' programming, both contemporary and costumed, is one of the principal resources for several of the new channels, so that Granada Plus, for example, has brought us not only *The Pretenders* but also *Upstairs, Downstairs*, both 1970s, the former set in the 1970s and the latter set in the early decades of the twentieth century.

In the terrestrial era it was the predictability of programming, so far as scheduling goes, which was the key to the maintenance of the traditional world. For some scholars this predictability is a benign contribution to the character of twentieth-century life. Scannell, for example, equates regularity, consistency, persistence, with intelligibility, and intelligibility with the psychic comfort of 'ontological security' (see also Silverstone 1993, 1994) as well as social solidarity. But these judgements are not unproblematic. From a different perspective, the routines of (traditional) television broadcasting can be seen as *coercive*, and we should welcome, not regret, any signs that the future of television may involve less complicity with the time frames of the (national; normal and normative) working day/week/year.

Technological developments are under way which certainly have the potential to undermine this traditional relation. What began with the video is continuing with pay-per-view arrangements, and digital television, which will allow audiences to choose start times to suit themselves. And, although the age of digital television is not yet upon us, it may be that the nature of broadcast output and of viewers' relation to it, has already begun to weaken the reliability of the 'traditional' patterns.

On the one hand, the newer channels tend to be *more* predictable than the older ones. They rely more heavily on stripping (broadcasting the same programme at the same time each day, rather than each week), on adhering to published schedules, and on using only the hour and the half-hour for start times. But, although more predictable than terrestrial channels, it does so in a much more mechanical way. For the older channels 'time of day' meant, for example, 'teatime' rather than 4.00 p.m. On the other hand, the predictability of scheduling loses its constructive power in a world where frequent channel-changing is the norm – especially if (as seems to be increasingly the case) some of the available channels have little respect for 'time of day' in the older sense.

## Flow

The continuous nature of news programming on Sky News, CNN, n.tv (news television), etc., is a development which deserves to be examined in relation to the observation (originating with Williams 1974) that the nature of TV experience is best understood as an experience of 'flow' and not one of engagement with discrete texts.

> In all developed broadcasting systems the characteristic organisation, and therefore the characteristic experience, is one of sequence or flow. This phenomenon, of planned flow, is then perhaps the defining characteristic of broadcasting, simultaneously as a technology and as a cultural form. In all communications systems before broadcasting the essential items were discrete. A book or pamphlet was taken and read as a specific item. A meeting occurred at a particular date and place. A play was performed in a particular theatre at a set hour. The difference in broadcasting is not only that these events, or events resembling them, are available inside the home, by the operation of a switch. It is that the real programme that is offered is a sequence, or set of alternative sequences of these and other similar events, which are then available in a single dimension and in a single operation.
>
> (Williams 1974: 86–7)

'Flow' is made possible through the technological property of the continuity of the broadcast signal. It is related to the constancy of output that we discussed in the preceding section, and our analysis of Sky News and n.tv below attempts to show how the cyclicity of the production cycle delivers a particular kind of 'flow'. Here we will briefly indicate the intellectual context for our analysis.

Any emphasis on flow as *unstructured* broadcast experience is something that we need to resist. The structures are there, and they are important in the management of the flow. Then, the technology which makes continuity possible is no guarantee either that continuous programming will actually be provided. Television content is not always 'on tap' in the home like water, gas and electricity – though, as we have argued above, it is not unjustified in European countries to regard it as being on tap – especially in cable and satellite homes. But not all broadcasters have the resources to provide 24-hour programming, and some political regimes may regulate the amount of transmission time. In Britain the terrestrial BBC channels still close down during the 'small hours' of the morning. Nor can it be assumed that the viewer's televisual experience is affected more by the continuities across segments than by properties integral to discrete segments. Corner (in press) has argued that Williams based his account in part on his experience of watching *American* television, in America, and his account of that experience is one of culture shock. It is the account of an outsider and not of someone with an acculturated familiarity with discourse of this type. Nevertheless Williams was right to indicate the relevance of sequence in defining the communicative character of terrestrial-era broadcasting in the sense that when the signal is being used to deliver content, the delivery is characteristically constant (the days of the 'toddler's truce' are long gone[1]), and the structuring devices are part of the flow, not external interventions into it.

Jensen (1995) demonstrates how very much more willing viewers are to submit to channel-initiated content changes than to use the remote control to change the content for themselves. The attraction of the 'flow' idea for some scholars lies in the idea that, across the formally marked and explicit boundaries of television discourse, there are other kinds of continuities – thematic ones, perhaps with the potential for some kind of ideological effect upon viewers (see Jensen 1995) – though we would agree with Corner's scepticism regarding the idea of *unitary* meta-level of sense – the notion that, across the unfolding of diversity, television has a coherent single message to communicate.

Consider, too, the MTV debate. This music channel has been around since the early days of satellite broadcasting. Some researchers were quick to see it as the channel which came closest to realising what Williams had merely anticipated, after all, in seeing 'flow' as the essence of TV's communicative character. MTV's flow-like character was then appropriated to postmodernism – a radical break with structured programming, still trying to impose inappropriate forms upon a medium whose nature would only fulfil itself when such imposition was finally abandoned: 'Important tools of sense making like sequence and priority are constantly rejected on MTV ... MTV has no boundaries ... It delivers random flow at all times' (Tetzlaff 1986: 82).[2]

Subsequent commentators (Goodwin 1993) have indicated that MTV's difference from network programming is exaggerated in such arguments – doing damage to the argument linking that channel to postmodern sensibilities; and further that, although MTV eschewed formal structure to a large extent in its early days, it ceased to do so from about 1986 when it needed a strategy to deal with falling ratings:

> MTV's new traditionalism was displayed in its use of broadcast television formats, such as its Beatles cartoons (first aired on the networks) and *The Tube* (which came from Tyne-Tees television in Britain). And MTV increasingly came to rely on nonmusic programming (comedy, a game show, a phone-in show, a movie news/review magazine, interview programming), some of it derived directly from broadcast television (*Monty Python's Flying Circus; The Young Ones*).
>
> (Goodwin 1993: 47)

The debate about MTV indicates one way to understand what cable and satellite have done to the TV environment: they have intensified tendencies already apparent in the terrestrial medium. Our case study of 24-hour news channels makes this very apparent for one particular form of broadcast content – news – and one particular principle – recency/immediacy.

## The flow of news discourse

Little has been written as yet on the formal character of news discourse on these new channels. The most useful account to date is that of MacGregor (1997), who writes about the changing character of news itself brought about by new technologies, new working practices and new institutional arrangements. Other writings on CNN and 'global news' in more general terms include: Larsen (1992), Paterson (1997), Cohen *et al.* (1996), C. Barker (1997) and Gurevitch *et al.* (1991). Regarding CNN's coverage of the Gulf War, see Vincent (1992) and Morrison (1992). Any assessment of the textual character of rolling news is bound to notice two features: an increasing emphasis upon 'showing', alongside or even at the expense of 'telling'; and an intensification of the 'recency' principle, which has taken over from fixed-point news broadcasting. Both are aspects of 'liveness'. In the following, for example, it is really the power to show which is the focus of attention:

> Of contemporary news services, CNN particularly makes a fetish of live reporting. They even go so far as to choose their bureau locations strategically to provide rooftop offices with panoramic views. Thus viewers got live pictures of a T-72 tank backfiring in the streets of Moscow in August of 1991, an event which was then duly replayed and discussed. CNN had five reporters in Moscow for the storming of the White House, including one inside the Kremlin, and viewers could watch events unfold live. Reporting of this type is inevitably accompanied by an extensive rhetoric constantly reminding the viewer that they are indeed eyewitnesses viewing history being made.
>
> (MacGregor 1997: 184)

The power to show is not an invention of the rolling news channels, though they, especially CNN, make a virtue of their ability to prioritise showing. But there have been celebrated instances on terrestrial television, too. Recent examples of these include the footage of the 1992 earthquake in San Francisco, which was caught on film during the reporting of a football game; another was the moment when six prisoners who had occupied Strangeways Prison in Manchester for more than three weeks in 1990 allowed themselves to be lifted from the prison's roof at 6.15 p.m., during BBC 1's 6.00 p.m. evening news. In the latter case, as in many events, the occurrence was predicted, though not its exact timing. The BBC 1 news team, together with those of all the other major channels, was present outside Strangeways Prison. However, the normal production requirements for organising news events into stories were disrupted. Such exceptions to 'normal', post-event reportage are often marked by less well-crafted, even confused and grammatically incorrect texts accompanying raw footage.

The value of the shown, on traditional or rolling news channels, is disputed, even within the profession. MacGregor points out that cameras can only film what they are allowed access to, which may or may not be relevant to the story. In the absence of significant pictures, the 'live two-way' has become a standard news device: the studio anchor interviews the channel's own reporter live on screen by satellite link, even though the reporter may only know what she has learned from headquarters via that same satellite link. Pictures themselves encourage speculation in the absence of hard information. The pursuit of pictures is conducted at the expense of investigation and interviewing of sources.

The recency principle, although it interacts with the emphasis upon showing, is a distinct characteristic. Shown news is maximally 'recent', because it is immediate, live. But 'telling' can itself be more or less recent, and it is this which matters for the overall structure of rolling news. The challenge for TV news (as well as for radio news) is to accommodate real-world 'eventing' (emergent, linear) to textual form, essentially cyclical, and to do so in a way which is maximally recent. The recency principle is the principle that reportage should be as close as possible in time to the moment of occurrence. In Britain, both ITN and BBC 1 news are cyclical. Their cycles break the day into parts: they provide news before the working day, in the middle of it, at the end of it, and during the evening. Newsworthy events get scooped up by one or other of these news 'slots' and are repeated in the following ones just until their novelty value is exhausted, or until there are no new developments. The key to the recency principle, in formal terms, is the interval between news programmes/bulletins, and thus the interval between opportunities to bring fresh stories and/or developments in running stories. On mixed-programming channels the interval between updates is variable. On BBC1 the shortest interval is two and a half hours – between 6.30 p.m., when the early evening news finishes, and 9.00 p.m., when the prime-time news begins. After the end of the 9.00 p.m. news, at 9.30 p.m. there is an interval of eight and a half hours until 6.00 a.m. the following morning.

The hourly cycle on Sky News and n.tv reduces the interval to one which is uniform, and short – one hour only. Both of these components have the potential to affect the viewer's sense of time. The uniformity of the one-hour cycle pushes viewing experience in the direction of greater abstraction, greater removal from quotidian routine. Counting in 60-minute blocks is more formal than counting in day-parts: breakfast-time, daytime, early evening, prime-time, late. And, although Sky News and n.tv still invoke something like these day-parts in the construction of their schedules, this is much less apparent to the viewer than the rhythm of the hourly cycle. It is the shortness of that cycle which gives added intensity to the update function of news broadcasting.

The 24-hour news channels hold out the promise not of recency merely, but of *immediacy*: the news 'as it happens'. In both cases, terrestrial and satellite, the approach adopted for accommodating the linear to the cyclical is the same. The universal conventions of storytelling provide the basis, adapted to the technological and phenomenological requirements of television. Storytelling is inherently a 'past tense' discourse: the 'historic present' tense is understood as a metaphor employed to convey immediacy. It does not and is not meant to undermine the understanding that the events described are in the past. It is therefore an appropriate modality for the delivery of broadcast news within the requirements of cyclicity, since the rationale of cyclicity is strict predetermination of when the 'telling' shall occur.

The more that broadcast storytelling orients itself to near-synchronous real-world events, the more it requires a discourse that positions the storytellers and their audience *in medias res*. No clear dividing line can be drawn between what 'has happened' and what is or may be going to happen.

In practice, therefore, immediacy/recency are compromised, not only by the highly structured nature of the viewing schedule, but also through the relative stasis of real-world events and processes. The result is a high degree of repetition: a strong persistence of content from one hour to the next.

## Modularity and meaning on Sky News and n.tv

The analysis which follows is offered by way of illustration for these general observations, and there is an emphasis upon description, for the benefit of readers who are not familiar with this kind of output. Our procedure was as follows. We decided in advance to record continuously all of the output broadcast on Wednesday 27 March 1996 on two news channels: the British Sky News and the German equivalent n.tv, from morning through till after midnight. This produced about 12 tapes, six from each channel. The continuous programming recorded and analysed here does not, of course, correspond to any viewer's experience. Even the hardiest news watchers will not commit themselves to 24 hours of continuous news broadcast. Our concern here is what Jensen (1995) describes as 'channel flow', rather than 'viewer flow'.

The nature of the flow on rolling news channels is a product of highly structured scheduling. Channel flow on Sky News, and on n.tv, is entirely cyclical; there are hourly, daily and weekly cycles, but it is the hourly ones which give these channels their distinctive character. Even at this hourly level, the 'lowest' level in the hierarchy of cycles, there are combinatory rules which are very restrictive. The patterning could be described as modular: each hour's production is based upon combinations of a finite number of component types. For Sky News the list comprises:

- Headlines
- News reports
- Commercial breaks
- Transition markers
- Weather forecasts
- Channel identity sequences
- Other components

Each of these components can be more finely specified: for example, commercial breaks are composed of trailers for other programmes (mostly on other Sky channels) and spot advertisements. It is the slots for 'other components' which form the basis of the daily and weekly cycles. The 7.30–8.00 p.m. slot, for example, is always devoted to sports coverage and recurs on a daily basis; while other slots, such as an interview with a medical journalist, recur in a weekly cycle. The week is also 'shaped' by the distinctiveness of weekend programming. The programming on this channel is thus *highly* predictable as regards its form.

A standard weekday news hour will look like this (minor variations are here ignored). It begins, on the hour, with three headlines. Each of those three headlines is then followed up with a report; there will be two or three other reports following that before the first commercial break. The commercial break is announced by the presenters, who indicate what stories will be dealt with after the interval. From headline to break is no more than 20 minutes. The commercial break itself will commence with a trailer for another show, probably on a different Sky channel, followed by anything between one and five spot advertisements. What happens after this point varies more according to features of the particular cycle. Depending upon the time of day, it might be a collection of sports reports; it might be a further collection of general news items; or it might be a collection of financial news reports. It will terminate with another commercial break, either on the half-hour, to make room for a half-hour slot before the next cycle begins, or at around 40 minutes into the cycle, providing a tripartite structure.

The flow of n.tv is as predictable as that of Sky News, though length and mix of components are different. N.tv is obviously less well resourced than Sky News, so the time that is devoted to general news reporting, especially 'on-site' reporting with original footage, is less than that on Sky News. Instead, n.tv has long regular slots dedicated to business news, a thematic emphasis further strengthened by a strip-tape referred to as 'ticker' – a terminology borrowed from the telegraph tapes – which runs continuously on the bottom of the screen showing current values from the stock exchange, exchange rates and other financial information. Only during advert breaks does the 'ticker-tape' stop running. There is also a different range of 'other components'. Notable here are the regular health programmes. N.tv includes health news segments, health magazine segments, and even a health-related weather forecast entitled *Bio-Wetter*. Presumably, because of organisational difficulties rather than intent, n.tv's cyclical pattern is not quite as reliable as that of Sky News. Occasionally the news block will begin a minute or two before or after the designated slot-time. However, apart from such details, cyclicity – and thus predictability of form – are essential structural features of both news channels.

Here is a full description of one hour's broadcasting between 11.00 a.m. and 12.00 noon on Sky News, 27 March 1996. The first 20 minutes follows the structure specified above, with three headlines preceding five discrete reports, culminating in a commercial break, which is composed of one trailer and three spot advertisements. This break is followed by sports news, then another commercial break of the same structure as the first. Back in the studio, the presenters reprise the original headlines, do an 'update' on one of the stories reported earlier, and then hand over to the business news presenter for her report. Her slot – comprising more than one story – occupies 18 minutes: she hands back to the main presenters, who instigate another commercial break by announcing what topics will follow it. The third commercial break, of identical structure to the previous ones, is followed by two fresh stories. This is effectively the end of the news: before the 60 minutes is up there is time for:

- the weather report
- a commercial break announcement
- a commercial break
- a channel identification sequence.

An hour earlier, at 10.00 a.m., Sky News took editorial responsibility only for the first half-hour of the cycle. The second half-hour was given over to a US current affairs show, ABC *Nightline*, broadcast the previous day to its US viewers. This re-broadcasting of American news programmes for a European audience is common, and gives rise to one effect which has the potential to be mildly disconcerting. The address of the show's presenter is very clearly to an American audience, even at the point where he announces the commercial break. Yet when we, Europeans, move into the commercial break, what we get is the familiar diet of European commercials. Unlike the programme, these *are* meant for us. Commercials within American fiction programming do not cause us any disquiet, presumably because we are more accustomed to it, and because the commercial break is not announced in the same way in drama series. It is the news context which unsettles us; though not to the point of confusion, and to no lasting effect.

Sports news and business news account for varying amounts of distinctive coverage in different cycles during the broadcasting day. One notable difference between the 24-hour channels and news on the terrestrial channels (with the exception of breakfast television) is that the screen image includes a digital clock overlaying the screen image, without obscuring it. Television's time-check function is taken very seriously on these channels.

## Form and content

If predictability of form is one of the key features of 24-hour news, the other is preservation of content. News stories do not 'come and go' within a single hour's reportage, but persist through many cycles. Of course the form, as described above, allows for variation of content. The 'slots' provided for headlines, stories, story-trailers, are constant: the material which fills those slots is in principle variable. The material that fills the commercial breaks is also subject to change. The Sky News day runs for 24 hours from 6.00 a.m. Within the news day, there is every opportunity to introduce new stories, to drop old ones, to vary the sequence so as to express different priority orderings. Such changes do happen, but from one hour to the next there are as many familiar topics as there are new ones, and a particular story can survive through many cycles.

On Sky News, 27 March 1996 the five main stories at 11.00 a.m. were as follows:

1   The trial of Rabin's assassin
2   The British beef crisis
3   The US presidential campaign
4   The US/Russian space expedition and the comet story
5   The flooding of the Glen Canyon Dam in Colorado.

In the news cycle commencing at 12.00 noon, stories 1, 2 and 4 are retained, and new ones are added on:

6   Plans for new school examinations
7   Gulf War syndrome
8   A cluster of very short items on Cambodia, the Jaguar firm, and Nicholas Scott's conviction on a drink/driving charge.

The 12.00 noon cycle devotes quite a large subsection to sport and another to business news, but it comes back to story 3, the US presidential campaign, before the hour is over. At 1.00 p.m., the number of main stories (those reported before the first commercial break) is double what it was at 12.00 noon – the break occurs closer to the half-hour point than in the earlier cycles. Stories 1, 2 and 4 feature in the sequence, as they had done twice before. Stories 6 and 7 are also included. The US presidential campaign item has been lost, as has the dam story. The new stories are:

 9   Electronic heart surgery
10   The salvage of the *Sea Empress* tanker
11   The commune siege in Montana.

The Nicholas Scott story (part of story 8 at 12.00 noon) is made more prominent than it was at midday. And so it continues. There is one story – that on the British beef crisis – which persisted through all 14 of the cycles recorded on 27 March. No doubt, it was in the cycles preceding and following our recordings, too. We have more to say about the reporting of this story in Chapter 2.

The German channel equally retained the British beef crisis through all the cycles. Indeed, if one restricted news analysis to those key stories which make the headlines in each cycle, there is strong overlap between both channels. Of the five main stories at 11.00 a.m. on Sky, four were headlined in the corresponding German cycle at 12.00 noon. Somewhat ironically, the only difference was that, instead of reporting the flooding of the Canyon Dam, story 5 on Sky News, n.tv ran another 'British' story. It reported a gaffe by the British Queen on tour in Poland, where in an important speech she mistakenly omitted a reference to the suffering of the Polish Jews under the Nazi regime. This thematic overlap in the key stories only changes when, at 6.30 p.m. in Germany, reporting restrictions imposed by the police on a family being held hostage in Rheinland-Pfalz is lifted. From then on, this important German news item starts to run adjacent to the beef crisis story on n.tv, continuing through the night until the middle of the following day (28 March), several hours after the hostages had finally been released.

## Assessment

Throughout this analysis we have emphasised the predictability of form and the persistence of content, in relation to the importance of recency in the discourse of the rolling news channels. News is 'now', and 'now' is, as it has to be, elastic enough to allow one story many passes through the delivery cycle before its newsworthiness expires. At the same time, the hourly cycle allows for coverage of particular stories that changes just enough from one hour to the next to 'track' the real-world processes that constitute the news event. Twenty-four-hour news channels can be regarded as providing a particular textual 'model' or metaphor for understanding the nature of 'eventing' in the real world. They have some things in common with soap operas, for, like the soaps, they code the processes of life as stories which give texture to reality in their concurrent, over-lapping dynamics. Thanks to the overlap, there is no closure in the discourse of rolling news. In other ways they are different from soaps: they tell more than they show, and they use repetition as a device which codes for currency, while running order codes for salience. The interesting characteristics of this discourse turn out to be characteristics of form which allow inferences to be made about the corresponding reality, not as a stock of propositional information, but as process.

# 2 Timeliness: textual form and the beef crisis story

This is the only chapter in the present volume which focuses upon a single story – though not upon a single text, since we examine the chosen story as a series of 'texts' (individual news segments) through a whole day's broadcasting on two channels. The analysis here is designed to show how, when immediacy is valued, news discourse can help to construct that immediacy notwithstanding some real indeterminacy in the real world which is the object of the reportage.

The case study which follows therefore is one of the stories – the most prominent one – which was recorded as part of our corpus from 27 March 1996 (see Chapter 1). It is an episode in the British 'beef crisis' which became a 'world story' about European politics as well as about food, risk and health. The story is a useful one for our purposes because of the way the relevant, reportable events (various meetings and speakings in Brussels) unfolded during the course of the day, in relation to the devices used by the news channels for keeping pace with those events, as well as honouring all of the other news stories which they tasked themselves to cover. The case study as a whole teaches us something about the elusiveness of 'events' as well as the routinisation of reportage in this new form, and throws up a few telling differences between the British and the German version of events.

The chapter concludes with a discussion of the linguistics of 'liveness' with special reference to linguistic deixis, where we seek to show that the relentless liveness of rolling news puts some pressure upon the conventional meaning of temporal deictic forms.

## Where's the beef? – the story according to Sky

On 27 March 1996, in 15 separate but continuous news cycles, from 10.00 a.m. to 1.00 a.m. on the 28th, the lead story on Sky News was a story about British beef – with one exception, at 11.00 a.m.[1] The prominence of this story is not surprising. 27 March fell during the period of the BSE scare, and this story had dominated the British mass media for over a week. The principal development which occupied journalists on 27 March was the introduction of a ban on the sale of British beef overseas – a European ban instigated by the European Commission in Brussels.

A quick way to look at some of the linguistic consequences of being caught between linearity and cyclicity is to look at all the on-the-hour 'headline' versions of the beef crisis story from 10.00 a.m. on the Wednesday to 12.00 midnight. These are the Sky News headlines. Our concern here will be to pinpoint the extent to which these headlines capture the present as a moment caught between the immediate past and various levels of futurity.

- 1 10.00 a.m. Beef back down: government set to announce mass slaughter
- 2 11.00 a.m. The British beef scare: Brussels is about to make a final decision
- 3 12.00 noon No beef health fears, say ministers: public confidence is the worry now
- 4 1.00 p.m. British beef crisis: decisions from Brussels but none yet from Westminster
- 5 2.00 p.m. 'We shall not be moved': European Commission ban on British beef stays
- 6 3.00 p.m. The ban remains. Europe confirms a worldwide embargo on British beef
- 7 4.00 p.m. Brussels slams a worldwide ban on British beef
- 8 5.00 p.m. Europe again says no to British beef: a cull is looking more and more likely
- 9 6.00 p.m. Worldwide ban on British beef. a cull's looking more and more likely
- 10 8.00 p.m. Jobs at risk as beef industry awaits decision on cattle cull
- 11 9.00 p.m. Brussels wields the axe on British beef: the ban is upheld
- 12 10.00 p.m. John Major vows to fight the EU's worldwide ban on beef
- 13 11.00 p.m. John Major says he'll fight the world ban on British beef
- 14 12.00 midnight   Major vows to fight Europe's world ban on British beef.

There are only 14 headlines here, not 15, because the 7.00 p.m. cycle is launched without headlines. Notice first of all that the preferred tense in headlines which have a finite verb at all is the present tense, 'back down', 'say', 'stays', 'remains', 'confirms', 'slams', 'says', 'awaits', 'wields the axe', 'is upheld', 'vows', 'says'. Headlinese commonly does prefer a present tense to convey immediacy, and little significance can be attached to this as a distinguishing feature of a 24-hour news channel.

On the other hand, grammatical tense notwithstanding, there is a strong orientation towards future developments, which finds linguistic expression via such phrasings as: 'is set to' in headline 1; '[is] about to' in headline 2; '[is] looking...likely' in headline 8 and 9; 'vows to fight ... says he'll fight' in headlines 12, 13 and 14. All of this is more or less explicitly about future intentions: at the same time, of course, the nature of the story itself concerns an event that controls the future. For an unspecified amount of future time, there will be no overseas market for British beef, starting now.

Different futures are at issue, but one of those projected futures refers to an event due to take place within the course of the Wednesday's events, and which has definitely become a 'past' event in the reports constructed for the after-noon's broadcasting. The issue, then, is this: when does the ban 'happen' – and how do we know? To answer these questions it is first necessary to describe the general characteristics of the beef story as rendered by each of the channels.

As the day's lead story, all versions of the beef story on 27 March on Sky are quite long, occupying anything up to six minutes' screen time. This timing does not include the 'headline' versions, and there are 'reprise' headlines as well as anticipatory ones within each cycle. The significance of the story is such that it leaks into other parts of the day's reportage. In some cycles there are follow-up, 'live' reports (of which, more below); there is a discussion of Creutzfeld-Jakob Disease (CJD) in the weekly health interview with a medical journalist. There is some US material on the Bovine Spongiform Encepalopathy (BSE) scare; and some discussion in the 'business report' section of the economic and financial effects of the scare. The most 'beefy' cycle is the one commencing at 12.00 noon. Beef is the lead story at noon, for six minutes. It is 'headlined' again at 12.29 p.m., it features in the business report at 12.41, and is the subject of a three-minute live interview with a spokesman for the National Farmers Union at 12.45. At 12.53, a medical journalist discusses CJD with the news anchor, Kay Burley. In all, the beef crisis topic accounts for about 11 minutes of this 60-minute cycle.

These lead stories are composed of different kinds of inputs, all familiar enough from terrestrial news programming. The principal choices are: introduc-tions, linking statements and summaries from studio presenters; live footage with commentary (not used for the 14 main 'beef' stories); live interviews with sources; live discussions with Sky journalists; film reports with journalistic commentary; film inserts without journalistic commentary. The presenters change throughout the day, and all seven of them take a turn at introducing the beef story at some point. Interviews are live exchanges between presenters and sources. Typically these happen in the second, more open half of each hour's broadcasting. The chosen interviewees include an incinerator owner, a union official, a medical journalist and an economist. Discussions take place between presenters and Sky's other reporters and correspondents. In the beef story the principal discussants are Aernout van Lynden, the Europe correspondent, and Adam Boulton, the political editor. Each of these two is produced more than once to add their own perspective on events. Boulton contributes during the 10.00 a.m. cycle, the 12.00 noon cycle and the 7.00 p.m. cycle; van Lynden during the 11.00 a.m., 1.00, 3.00 and 4.00 p.m. cycles.

The majority of screen time is occupied by filmed reports, and six named reporters contribute films for the beef story. Altogether, there are 22 distinct film reports from these six reporters during the 14 hours of recording, though this number exaggerates the amount of variation in the film input. For example, four of the 22 reports are attributed to Anna Botting. Yet, the purport of these four reports is very similar in each case – to discuss how a culling policy would be implemented. Botting's four films are each different from one another, but they share a considerable amount of both visual and verbal content, such as black-and-white archive footage of film from the foot-and-mouth epidemic of the 1960s. The 'same' Botting film is not always what it seems. On more than one occasion she retapes the voice-over in order to change a small detail. At 5.00 p.m., she tells us that Australia introduced a slaughter policy 10 years ago; later versions of this film put this 20 years ago. Aernout van Lynden provides two different film reports, but these are much more different from one another: van Lynden has the advantage of being in an area of reportage where the 'tellables' do change during the course of the day. His morning report includes a brief contribution from Neil Kinnock, one of Britain's EU Commissioners, walking into the European Commission meeting before the vote is taken. Van Lynden's afternoon report has shots of the EU Agriculture Commissioner, Franz Fischler, addressing the European Parliament in Brussels.

After 7.00 p.m. the bulk of the material from which the lead stories are composed can no longer be said to be new. The 7.00 p.m. cycle introduces the news that the Dutch government had ordered the slaughter of all British calves in the Netherlands. At 10.00 p.m. there is another new angle, mentioned by the presenter in her opening introduction. However, there is no new film or other new text to support this, and so it gets lost in the full report:

> Good evening. Britain was in more trouble over beef tonight, facing fines of eight point one million pounds for the misuse of funds from the Euro budget. Most of the penalty is for inadequate control of the public storage of beef.

There is one other type of input to mention which is used much more sparingly: the embedded film clip. These film clips are unlike film reports in that they are not accompanied by journalistic commentary. Instead, they are embedded within some other kind of input. One such clip of Stephen Dorrell at the Select Committee meeting in London during the morning is embedded within a 'reprise headline' at 10.36 a.m. (approximately). Another sound-bite clip of Michael Heseltine is embedded within a discussion between Martin Stanford (presenter) and Adam Boulton (political editor) at 10.03 a.m. (approximately).

## The story according to n.tv

The n.tv reporting is much less varied than that of Sky News. The channel's low production values mean more repetition of identical reports, fewer films, and fewer interviews. Key components of the 10.00 a.m. news cycle are the introduction in the studio, followed by a voiced-over report featuring the following footage:

- the House of Commons with John Major speaking
- a herd of cows, with a farmer running alongside them
- a picture of an abattoir with cow carcasses being pushed along, and
- a butcher's shop with meat product.

At 11.00 a.m. the report comprises the House of Commons footage, followed by the butcher's shop scene and an additional film sequence, which is of cows in the marketplace. The item concludes with a report from the US Senate. It is this collection of elements which is retained through subsequent cycles until 3.30 p.m. when, in the discourse of the channel, the beef ban becomes official. Although the German reporting of the beef story is much less varied than that of Sky News, it nevertheless shares the tendency of Sky to let the story 'leak' into other aspects of the day's reportage. In this case, surprisingly enough, it is in the sports coverage where the beef story makes an appearance. During the sports coverage there is a story concerning a soccer game between Germany and Denmark about to take place in the UK. Having discussed the players and other sports-related topics, the camera shifts from the football training ground to a kitchen, where the cook who is to accompany the German players to the UK reassures the viewers that his players will not need to eat 'BSE-infected meat in England'. To avoid such a risk, the cook tells us that there will be a *Fleischluftbrücke*, a 'meat air bridge' from Germany to the UK. This item is repeated several times in the morning cycles of n.tv.

## Capturing the moment: British and German histories compared

There is an interesting set of differences between the British and the German versions of events as captured in the news cycles of these two channels. It hinges, in part, upon the problem of when to announce the beef ban. Both channels spend the early cycles anticipating the ban, and later ones reporting it. But between 12.00 noon Brussels time (11.00 a.m. in London) and 3.30 p.m. there is a zone of indeterminacy which allows scope for different versions.

In the British version, a key moment for the reporting of this story comes at 11.27 a.m. London time, when, after some headlines, the presenter introduces a live two-way from Brussels with Aernout van Lynden, the Europe correspondent. The live spot has evidently been pre-scheduled, and as Burley and van Lynden talk the reason for this becomes apparent. He had given London reason to expect that, close to this time, an announcement – a news event – would have taken place:

> OK we can return now to the news that the European Union has been meeting in Brussels to rubber stamp the ban on British beef exports, joining us from there is our correspondent Aernout van Linden, Aernout, good day to you.
>
> Good morning Kay.
>
> Any announcement yet?
>
> No. We had been expecting the Commission to come out of its daily briefing at noon local time with a statement as to what the Commission had decided. Instead, we got a Commission spokesman saying that they had only begun discussing the whole issue of BSE and a worldwide ban on

British beef exports 20 minutes earlier. All sorts of other questions had passed for review before that and that the Commission was still meeting, it was still being discussed, and that no announcement should be expected before the Agricultural Commissioner goes before the European Parliament at 3.00 local time this afternoon that's two o'clock in London.

The initial pretext for van Lynden's slot is rendered invalid by the failure of the Commission to announce a ban at 12.00 noon (11.00 a.m. London time). The live two-way goes ahead anyway, and van Lynden uses it to replace the earlier expectation with a newer one. He goes on to develop a general discussion of the crisis with Burley.

The interesting thing to notice next is that the Sky headline at 12.00 noon evades the question of the ban. It concentrates upon a different aspect of the story: the attitude of British government ministers. Then, at 1.00 p.m., there is a headline which treats the ban as *confirmed*. At 11.30 a.m., van Lynden could not report the ban as he had wished, but the 1.00 p.m. headline is: 'British beef crisis: decisions from Brussels but none yet from Westminster'. (This is not the interpretation projected in the main text, where the ban is still talked about as a future event – something that everyone is waiting for.) At 2.00 p.m., the headline is more emphatic still: ' "We shall not be moved": European Commission ban on British beef stays'.

The point is this. The ban was an opportunity for a bit of media management. The European Commissioners sought to impose their own definition of events upon the day's activities. Their especial desire was to ensure some coverage from within the European Parliament. The citizens of Europe are thought to be indifferent to, ignorant about or contemptuous of this particular social institution, and the spin doctors saw an opportunity to redress these misprisions. The plan was successful, inasmuch as it did result in some footage of Franz Fischler addressing the Parliament. This went out on Sky – not live, but close to its point of occurrence – at 3.00 p.m.

This is the nearest thing to an 'event' that Sky can manage throughout the whole day's coverage. The footage is not live, but it is too close to the original event to have been incorporated into a film report, and thus appears more raw than the usual reportage. The ban has been voted on and agreed and 'now' is being communicated to the European Parliament. This is what the footage shows. The European Agriculture Commissioner, Franz Fischler, is speaking from the floor at the European Parliament session in Brussels. Wearing what the German report later will call his 'programmatic tie' – a colourful tie with pictures of cows – he is announcing to the Parliament that the Commission has confirmed the worldwide ban on British beef exports. The 'rawness' of this footage comes across in the fact that, instead of a summarising voice-over (provided in the later report at 4.00 p.m. London time), the verbal track provides simultaneous English interpretation, in a female voice, of Franz Fischler's German:

It is an extremely serious case, the European citizens are justifiably very anxious and we have to put health considerations first. We have a crisis of confidence, consumers have lost faith in the safety of meat, beef in particular, and EU citizens are challenging the credibility of scientific knowledge too now. Citizens are beginning to doubt politicians, they are not convinced that the measures have been taken, so now the measures must be taken even if financial, there are financial and economic implications. We have to restore confidence. We have to restabilise our markets and that should be our paramount concern at this moment.

But this is not the whole story. The media management techniques of the Brussels spin doctors required the journalists there to accept a definition of the situation from them – a definition in which the ban became a reality only at the point it was announced to the European Parliament. But this is a 'ceremonial' moment, and a different definition of the situation prevailed – one where the ban became a reality at the moment the decision was taken by the 40 or so Commissioners in the earlier part of the day. For a while, between these two possibilities, ambivalence prevailed. The emphatic 2.00 p.m. headline precedes the Parliament announcement, though it follows a statement made by 'a Commission source' to the journalists, announced as a newsflash by Kay Burley at 1.10 p.m. London time (2.10 p.m. in Brussels). The waiting journalists, van Lynden among them, were not at 11.30 a.m. in a position to confirm that the Commissioners had taken their vote, for the Commissioners were still behind closed doors. The press pack had been waiting until those doors opened – ready to treat the ban as a reality from the point that it was announced *to them*. That announcement materialises just after 1.00 p.m. (2.00 p.m. in Brussels). By the time the full news cycle is ready to recommence at 2.00 p.m. the absence of the Parliamentary announcement is not an obstacle preventing the presentation of the ban as a reality, on the basis of the Commissioners' vote and the source's confirmation of that to the press pack. It is perhaps of interest too that the confident 2.00 p.m. version is worded in the headline as 'ban on British beef stays'. Just as the broadcasters get the confirmation they wanted, they cool down on its significance. The ban had been in place all along. The events in Brussels are acts of *confirmation*.

In the n.tv version of events, the morning story is significantly different from the British account. It is constructed less in terms of build-up to the Brussels ban, and more in terms of a ratcheting up of the pain, as more and more countries decide to put a stop to the import of British beef. At 9.00 a.m.[2] German time the studio presenter reports:

Inzwischen hat auch Norwegen ein Einfuhrverbot für britisches Rindfleisch erlassen. Es folgt damit Schweden, Finnland und den meisten EU Ländern. (In the meantime Norway, too, has declared an import ban on British beef. With this, it follows Sweden, Finland and most of the EU countries).

This is again repeated at 10.00 a.m. At 11.00 a.m., the newscaster updates us on this as follows:

> Immer mehr Länder schließen sich dem Boykott gegen britisches Rindfleisch an. Nun hat auch Japan ein Exportverbot für britische and nordirsiche Rindfleischerzeugnisse erlassen.
> (More and more countries join the boycott against British beef. Now, Japan too has declared an import ban for British and Northern Irish beef products.)

By 1 p.m. we hear

> Immer mehr Länder schließen sich dem Boykott gegen britisches Rindfleisch an. Nach Singapur and Japan hat Thailand als drittes asiatisches Land ein Importverbot für britische und nordirsiche Rindfleischprodukte erlassen.
> (More and more countries join the boycott against British beef. After Singapore and Japan, a third Asian country, Thailand has declared an import ban on British and Northern Irish beef products.)

This listing of countries is only abandoned at the 3.30 p.m. newsclip (2.30 p.m. London time). This is when the German channel decides that the European Union has indeed banned British beef. This is more than one hour after the 1.10 p.m. (2.10 p.m.) 'newsflash' on Sky's report. At 1.00, 2.00 and 3.00 p.m., n.tv tells its viewers that the ban is still in the future. Its device for communicating this message is an interchange between the studio presenter and the correspondent in Brussels. Their dialogue, live no doubt at 1.00 p.m. but not at 2.00 or 3.00 p.m., goes as follows:

> Zur Zeit tagt die EU-Kommission. Martina Koch in Brüssel: Kommt der Exportstop jetzt oder kommt er nicht?
> Film report: Martina Koch in Brüssel: Ja er wird schon kommen, die Frage ist nur noch wann.
> (Verbatim, deliberately non-idiomatic translation: Currently the EU Commission is in session. Martina Koch in Brussels. Will the export ban come, or will it not?
> Martina Koch in Brussels: Yes, it will come, the only question is when.)

The recycling of this dialogue has the effect of making the referential meaning of 'zur Zeit' (currently, at present, now) stretch across two-hourly cycles. It is phenomena of this sort – the import of deictic forms – which must now come under the microscope.

### Forms of deixis in rolling news

An important element in the construction of 'liveness' is the use of 'live speech'. To be heard as live speech, broadcast talk should possess some of the same features as talk produced in the 'canonical situation of utterance' – i.e. face-to-face speech communication, without technological assistance, constrained by basic conditions of audibility within clearly delimited spatio-temporal boundaries. While recognising that what can appear 'live' may not be so, and vice versa, we can nevertheless indicate the properties of live speech as an ideal-type: it would possess interactivity, a degree of disfluency compatible with its being 'fresh talk' (Goffman 1981) and a range of deictic forms ('here', 'there', 'now', 'you') which anchor the speech in a here-and-now speech situation shared with the interlocutor(s).

Following Marriott (1996, 1997), in the present section we want to make some comments upon the use of systems of spatial and temporal deixis in broadcasting discourse – with specific attention to the discourse of the rolling news channels. First, some clarification of terminology:

> By deixis is meant the location and identification of persons, objects, events, processes and activities being talked about or referred to, in relation to the spatiotemporal context created and sustained by the act of the utterance and the participation in it, typically, of a single speaker and at least one addressee.
>
> (Lyons 1977: 637)

In linguistics, expressions of time and space are often differentiated as deictic or non-deictic according to their dependency on, or independency of, the context of the utterance (Fillmore 1975; Lyons 1977; Levinson 1983). So, while 'London' and 'July' are non-deictic codings of person, place and time, respectively, 'there' and 'then' are deictic codings which take their reference from the context. Non-deictic expressions of time and space, such as the names of places (Birmingham) or times and dates (12 July 1997), may be culture-specific, especially when one considers more exotic languages than those we are concerned with here (see Geertz 1960). But these are of no particular significance in the context of round-the-clock news reporting. Obviously, the great spatial distances across which satellite television channels can now be received can create different time zones between the utterance of the studio reporter and the reception of the audiences around the world. But this does not affect the language with which the utterance is encoded. When we are told, or shown, that a particular news programme is being transmitted at 1.30 p.m. on 25 January 1999 from London or at 2.30 p.m. from Berlin, we understand from our knowledge of the world and its time zones how this relates to our time as recipients of that information. Or we can readily find out if we are not sure. Such non-deictic expressions of time and place fulfil the same function in television reporting as they do in unmediated encounters: they can locate an utterance in temporal and geographical space.

But things are different when the encoding makes use of deictic forms. Although mediated talk which purports to be 'live' makes use of deictic forms as if it were in a canonical speech situation (with some accommodation to the spatial separation, which we discuss in Chapter 6), the meanings of those forms are put under considerable stress by the discourses of round-the-clock news media and their cyclical repetitive structures. Indeed, 'pure' time and space deixis (Levinson 1983: 74), especially the linguistic means of referring to the spatiotemporal zero point – the here-and-now (Lyons 1977: 638) is put under even more pressure by the discourses of satellite television than is commonly recognised in the already extensive literature on temporal relations in media discourse.

In an important series of lectures on deixis, Fillmore (1975), distinguishes between three types of accounting for time: the time of the speech act itself; the time to which the speech act refers, and, in the case of mediated communication, the time of the reception of the utterance. Fillmore distinguishes these as 'coding time', 'reference time' and 'decoding time' (Fillmore 1975: 9ff., 52–4; Lyons 1977: section 15.4; Levinson 1983: 73–9). Where coding and reception time are identical, as in face-to-face encounters, we can speak (with Lyons) of deictic simultaneity. Asynchronous relations, such as in pre-recorded programmes, depend for their deictic reference point on privileging either the coding time or the reception time (Lyons 1977: 685; Levinson 1983: 73). However, the situation on our news channels is more complex than that. One part of television broadcasting is indeed devoted to material which is truly synchronous (genuine live transmissions). Other material is clearly marked as time-shifted sequences in the discourse (Marriott 1995 discusses the 'action replays' of sports commentary in these terms), or is used by the viewers in a time-shifted way. However, there is another time relation, a pretended synchronicity, which occurs on the news channels (or at least on n.tv) which involves the use of recycled segments not marked as time-shifted. These cases of 'virtual' rather than 'real' liveness, in the context of news reporting, are the ones which create tensions in the way we would otherwise conceptualise the deictic references.

Temporal deictic expressions – 'within the next few years', 'at this very moment in time' – shift from being respectively similar to their conventional usage and meanings, to being dissimilar, on a scale which depends on how much further or closer they attempt to encode the spatiotemporal zero point. A repeat insert in an hourly news cycle retains its conventional deictic reference point so long as all the temporal references go 'outside' the period during which the repeat occurs. 'In six weeks' has the same meaning at 1.00 p.m. as it has at 3.00 p.m., and likewise for 'within the next few days', 'this evening' or 'within the next few hours'. These can be mapped on to the (approximately) same time axis, despite the elapse of two hours. But what happens with temporal references which operate *within* the two-hour frame of reference (or whatever the cycle of repetition determines)? The use of such 'narrower' deictic adverbials as 'now', 'at this moment', 'in this hour' would seem to constrain repetition. And yet segments using these phrases are indeed repeated. Most recycled segments within news transmissions comprise a plethora of precisely these deictic features which bind the virtual live segment to the 'real' live ones, including the talk of the presenter. During 27 March 1996, when we recorded all news transmissions on Sky News and on n.tv, a large proportion of time adverbials were of this latter kind. As an example of this, a segment already mentioned above, consider the following 'live from Brussels' segment on n.tv, which went out not only at 1.00 p.m., but also at 2.00 and 3.00 p.m:

> Zur Zeit tagt die EU-Kommission. Martina Koch in Brüssel: Kommt der Exportstop jetzt oder kommt er nicht?
> Film report: Martina Koch in Brüssel: Ja er wird schon kommen, die Frage ist nur noch wann.
> (Verbatim, deliberately non-idiomatic translation: Currently the EU Commission is in session. Martina Koch in Brussels: Will the export ban come, or will it not?
> Martina Koch in Brussels: Yes, it will come; the only question is when.)

The 'now' in these repeats is not a 'now' of coding time, since coding time can only occur once and the segments are repeated. Nor is it a 'now' of reception time; reception time lies 'outwith' the segment and is announced via the icon-sized clock in the corner of the screen – it is anchored to viewing time. Nor are these virtual live sequences marked in any way as having some other reference time. For the speaking reporter, they are motivated forms, genuine 'live' references. For him or her they retain their own deixis within the segment. They are thus different from the 'action replay' examples discussed by Marriott (1995), which are clearly marked by linguistic and semiotic means as 'not-now' sequences embedded in a 'now' genre of live sports reporting. The viewers of virtual live segments embedded in genuine live reporting are not made aware of these temporal disjunctures within the report – though we do not suspect any particularly manipulative purposes behind these editorial decisions. There is an unspoken understanding that the repeated showing and viewing of virtual live sequences is acceptable so long as the real-life events to which these segments refer have not substantially altered so as to make an update necessary. But since the studio reports often give an update on the event, from the studio as part of the hourly cycle, this stretching of a 'virtual' now across a linear sequence of time passing creates different discourses which are open for analysis and cross-cultural comparisons. When to replace a virtual live sequence by a genuine live one may be influenced by different resources (n.tv may not have enough money to update its film clips as regularly as Sky), or caused by different editorial judgements, but the result can be substantive differences in the event as shown.

# 3 Liveness as synchronicity and liveness as aesthetic

Television and radio in broadcasting's first and second age have been understood as 'live' media. The concept of liveness is one which claims a particular kind of relation between broadcasting and the external world – a relation of synchronicity between the time of production/transmission and that of reception. This is a question of ontology, not of textual form; however, material produced under conditions of synchronicity does give rise to certain characteristic textual features – some of which we have discussed under the heading 'Forms of deixis in rolling news' in the previous chapter. But there is more to the textualisation of liveness than its deictic characteristics. There are visual as well as verbal forms to consider – a range of features which can be imitated in asynchronous production and can thus form the basis of an *aesthetic* of liveness. The material in this chapter is concerned with both of these phenomena – one of which is to do with the 'outward' relations of texts to their context, and the other which concerns textuality itself. Our purpose in both cases is to foreground aspects of the new broadcasting environment which undermine synchronicity. The argument will be that synchronicity is undermined not just when viewers are exposed to a diet of programming which clearly belongs to times different from the one which they inhabit, but also, and perhaps more profoundly, when natural signs of liveness turn into arbitrary, conventional ones.

## Synchronicity

'Liveness' was an intrinsic part of the earliest television broadcasting, before the development of video technology and when the use of film as a source of broadcast material was also limited both through regulation and for technological reasons. 'Liveness' can be a slippery notion, but it has one meaning which is clear and precise enough, when it refers to the synchronicity between the time of production/transmission and the time of reception. It is this synchronicity which was present in most of the early television broadcasts, and which is now largely lost – most transmitted material is pre-recorded. But television and liveness have still been linked, throughout the second era of broadcasting, from 1950 to the present. Whether that link can still been sustained in the third era is an important question.

*Transmission* and reception are of necessity synchronous events. Across time zones, the nominal time may be different (6.00 p.m. in London is 7.00 p.m. in Brussels) but the experiential time is the same. Satellite links are now in principle possible from anywhere on earth to anywhere on earth, so any combination of nominal times is possible, within the parameters of the global system. Thus, if we concentrate only upon transmission, 'liveness' is the basis of the communicative relationship between broadcasters and audiences.

However, this is not what is usually meant by liveness. The conditions of transmission are not at all apparent to the viewer (until there is a breakdown of some sort); the interest in liveness is an interest not in transmission but in *production* – in particular, with a form of broadcasting in which production and transmission are conflated. Although recorded material now dominates the schedules, television has reserved a special place for liveness in two ways. First, it has retained a custom in 'presented' programmes, of giving, on air, the moment of transmission a privileged status as the true, shared, 'now'. 'Call us now ...' always means at transmission time, never recording time. This does not apply to fictional texts, which construct their own internal, 'representational' time frames connected to the present in terms of period congruence rather than temporal deixis, while costume drama relies upon period *incongruence*.

Second, broadcast television has continued to insert live programming into the schedules and to draw attention to such liveness as a selling point. This allows live sports broadcasts, for example, to produce the pleasure of shared uncertainty leading to ultimate closure, without fictional contrivance or concealment. Liveness is a virtue for other events, too, notably large civic occasions such as royal weddings and international concerts. It is not hard to see why such liveness is valued: the TV experience is to act as a surrogate for actual presence and participation. There is every likelihood that, resources permitting, coverage of 'occasions' will continue into the third age of broadcasting. But with greater choice of channels it may be that audience size for such events will diminish in comparison with the golden age of channel scarcity.

On a more mundane level there are certainly signs that respect for synchronicity is not what it used to be. Here is one such sign. Certain kinds of non-fiction programmes – originally made for, and transmitted on, terrestrial channels – are now going out as repeats on the new channels such as UK Living and UK Style. These programmes are interesting because they were never 'live' in the strict sense, even on first transmission, and they are recent enough to pass as current material on recycling. Often these are programmes originally made for daytime television. One such programme is *Style Challenge*. This is a 'makeover' show – members of the public undergo hair, beauty and fashion treatment from professionals and emerge at the end of 30 minutes with a new image. *Style Challenge*, in April 1998, occupied a regular, daily slot at 9.30 p.m. But the greeting from presenter to audience is not 'good evening'; it is 'good morning' – a small but significant speech-act infelicity. It is significant in the sense that an infelicitous greeting, because it is a framing device, proposes a 'bad faith' reading for the whole show.

Sceptics will want to argue that infelicities of this kind are not new to broad-casting, that they have been a normalised part of the experience since the schedulers discovered the usefulness of repeats. There is some truth in this. But, with the coming of the multi-channel environment and the increasing reliance upon repeats to fill the schedules, it is quite possible that 'bad faith' of this kind will become typical of the relationship between broadcasters and their audiences. Whether such a judgemental term as 'bad faith' will be an appropriate descrip-tion of that relationship is a separate issue.

### Synchronicity and celebration

A parallel argument can be made in relation to the higher levels of temporal framing. The grounding of TV discourse in synchronicity provides a further dimension to the congruence between broadcasting time and reception time. It allows TV and its viewers to share the celebration of seasonal festivals, and other recurring events such as sports fixtures and elections. Terrestrial broad-casting honours these cyclical events, and does so in a way which ties broadcasters and audience within a national context.

> Nothing so well illustrates the noiseless manner in which the BBC became perhaps *the* central agent of the national culture as the calendrical role of broadcasting; this cyclical reproduction, year in year out, of an orderly and regular progression of festivities, rituals and celebrations – major and minor, civil and sacred – that marked the unfolding of the broadcast year.
>
> The cornerstone of this calendar was the religious year: the weekly observances of the Sabbath through church services and a programme schedule markedly more austere than on other days; the great landmarks of Easter, Pentecost and Christmas; the feastdays of the patron saints of England, Scotland and Wales which occasioned special programmes from the appropriate 'region' … Bank holidays were celebrated in festive mood while the solemn days of national remembrance were marked by religious services and special feature programmes. Sport of course developed its own calendar very quickly. The winter season had its weekly observances of football, rugby and steeplechasing, climaxing in the Boat Race, the Grand National and the Cup Final. Summer brought in cricket and flat racing, the test matches, Derby Day, Royal Ascot and Wimbledon.
>
> (Scannell 1988: 18)

Scannell also argues that terrestrial broadcasting began to create ceremonials of its own, to replace those which had lost their resonance as a result of industrial-isation and secularisation.

How much of this can be maintained in the new era, now that the multicul-turalism of society is so much harder to ignore, when there is so much more choice in the use of leisure time, when national loyalties are on the wane, when 'public' culture has become unfashionable? In Britain, so far, it seems that the newer channels are much less interested in national ceremonial than the traditional ones, with the important exception of sports fixtures (though the most 'hyped' sports fixtures tend to be the international ones).[1] This lack of interest in cyclical events goes further. It allows the broadcasters to retransmit material which 'offends' the nation's sense of position in the cycle. The original production of British soap operas arranges things so that Christmas in the world of *Brookside*, *EastEnders* and *Coronation Street* coincides with Christmas in the world of the viewers. But what happens when those series are rerun on satellite channels? These 'classic' soaps are making a considerable contribution to the schedules of the new channels: *Brookside* on UK Living, *Coronation Street* on Granada Plus, and *EastEnders* on UK Gold. But the temporal parallelism with 'real life' is lost. Christmas episodes of these series are broadcast in March, or July, or September, indifferently, on the satellite channels. They are 'out of time' in more ways than one – they don't belong to the present, and their seasons don't correspond with ours.

The important consequence of broadcasting as a cultural form for Scannell is not just its production of intelligibility for the individual, but the production and reproduction of that intelligibility as a shared, collective resource. Synchronicity of production/transmission and reception (liveness) underwrites collective intelligibility in so far as time frames (past/present/future; then/ now /soon; before/after, etc.) are made to cohere with reference to that constantly moving synchronous moment. To abandon this principle of temporal coherence with reference to a 'now' which is guaranteed through the act of broadcasting ('really' live when it says it is, directly or by implication) would be to detach media culture from its grounding in a real-time (in both senses) conversation between broadcasters and audiences. Some of the tendencies in the satellite era point in that direction.

On a judgemental note, the impression given so far in this chapter is that the effect of the new broadcasting environment upon relations between broadcasters and their audiences is entirely one of destruction. But it may be a mistake to infer 'destruction' rather than 'deconstruction' from the increasing forms of mismatch between broadcasting time and viewing time. A positive view of this would point to the way it allows viewers greater insight into the constructed nature of the programmes they watch – contributing to more active forms of textual consumption on their part.

## Television and history

This leads in to a further consideration – the question of television and history in the new era. The different mixtures of documentary/fictional, dramatised /narrated representations of 'the past' ensure that only a fragmentary understanding of history is possible through television. But television has its own history, its own memories, celebrated from time to time in 'specials' of different types: the first episodes of long-running shows; early appearances of celebrities; what the BBC did for: the Coronation; the Royal Wedding; Churchill's funeral;

the 1966 World Cup. Scannell (1988) recognises the particular significance of the long-running soap operas in this context:

> It is a strange experience to watch the first ever episode of *Coronation Street*, recorded in grainy black and white back in 1960, and to follow this with an episode in colour from the recent past. There, twenty-five years ago, is Ken Barlow played by William Roache, then just turned twenty-one, an anxious grammar-school boy in his first year at college. Now here he is years later and with a chequered career and personal life behind him, an anxious middle-aged married man. Such an abrupt time lapse immediately makes visible the way in which actor and character (the two are inseparable) have aged over a quarter of a century. And this confirms the truth of the time of the tale as corresponding in all particulars with the movement of lifetime and its passing away.
>
> (Scannell 1988: 20)

We should remind ourselves, reading this, not only that Roache is the only actor from the original cast still participating in the show, but also that audiences are not much prone to anxieties about the characters who have moved on (they may have an interest in the fate of the actors, but that is another story). There are no mutual moral obligations between viewers and fictional characters, whatever their longevity and however much they seem to us like our own friends and families.

The coming of the satellite era has certainly made a difference to these 'lifetime' (or at least long-running – years rather than months) relationships. We have already noted that the satellite channels are allowing these series to be repeated. With hours and hours of programming 'in the can', the popular soaps obviously offer a large resource of extremely cheap programming with which to fill the new channels. Since this is 'old' material it must be boring; since it is not modern it must be untrue to itself as a 'real-life' series. Yet an entirely negative view of what 'old soap' means for television culture must be questioned. In this case, the multiplicity of channels may be adding layers to the semiotic environment rather than subtracting from it.

In any context, the 're-broadcasting' of material from the archives has the potential to add further levels of meaning, and the hindsight which soap watchers can bring to their viewing of past episodes is relevant here. For example, in Britain, UK Gold (an entertainment channel) is re-broadcasting *EastEnders* on a nightly basis on weekdays, thus speeding up the passage of time (the original broadcasts went out only three times a week). In June 1996, while we were working on the present chapter, the narrative had progressed to 1990. For aficionados, this was the week when Pauline's Auntie Nellie left hospital to be looked after in the Fowler household. Nellie says to Arthur: 'Try not to grow old.' His reply: 'I'll try not to.' Meanwhile, back in the 'real' *EastEnders* world, on BBC 1, the viewers of 1996 have been following the storyline dealing with Arthur's death. It is possible of course that, in 1990, behind-the-scenes schematic storylining had indeed anticipated Arthur's death. But this does not detract from the poignancy of the 'Arthur'/'Nellie' exchange as replayed in June 1996.

In place of temporal parallelism, the reruns of the soaps offer a different kind of pleasure – one in which nostalgia has a strong part to play. The memory frame is a relatively short one for *Brookside* and *EastEnders* (a few years only) since they have less in the bank than *Coronation Street* (*Corrie*, as it is familiarly known, has not gone right back to the beginning; only to the 1970s – the episodes are in colour, not black and white. Younger viewers can see such familiar characters as Gail, Ken, Alf, in their younger days; older viewers can remind themselves of what was 'going on' all those years ago.)

## Aesthetics

It has become common in TV analysis to find 'liveness' given a privileged position as the basis of the medium's essential communicative character and aesthetic. However, this interpretation has attracted some criticism. From an American perspective, Caldwell (1995) has challenged the emphasis upon liveness as realism, authenticity, directness. His own work draws attention to an alternative aesthetic; one in which, in different ways, elements of visual form are exploited and foregrounded, as in channels such as MTV but also particular shows, not necessarily on cable/satellite, such as *Hill Street Blues*. An aesthetic of liveness allows, even requires, a look and a sound which is simple and unpretentious. Ellis (1982) has compared film with cinema along these lines: where cinema can be visually artful, television cannot. It is this – traditional – view with which Caldwell takes issue.

A different view of how things are changing focuses upon the movement away from the canons of 'good television' to allow even *more* scope for 'liveness', valuing a rough, unfinished texture which does not seek to conceal its own artifice. In 'Zoo TV' and its derivatives, such as *TFI Friday* on Britain's Channel 4, it is not a case of *indifference* to whether or not the production conceals the production crew and avoids performance errors. The stance is not neutral – it is positive. There is pleasure for broadcasters and audiences in the 'rawness' of the transmitted text – an indication that this is not to be taken too seriously. There is humour, certainly, and also the possibility of a sense of collusion on the part of the audience with the broadcasters, redeeming television's power of enchantment for an audience with reason to be bored by 'mainstream' programming (see Lury 1997):

> Essentially, Zoo, on radio or TV, means that you can hear the people making the show sniggering in the background. That's only the starting point. Zoo also involves improvisation, irreverence, in-jokes, deep trivia and disposable news. It's also a clever conjuring trick. It's a way of going live and not going belly-up – mistakes are part of the fun.
>
> (McLellan, 1993: 50, quoted in Lury 1997: 15)

The textual appearance of 'liveness', or immediacy, in the era of the video recorder, available at both ends of the communicative axis, does not guarantee the corresponding ontological status, and it is certainly time to ask whether the meaning of textual liveness is stable, in the modern broadcasting environment. A lot of TV output is neither actually live nor constructed-as-live (most drama, for example). But a certain amount of output is still both textually and actually live; and a further proportion comprises what was 'recorded live' (i.e. before a studio audience, in a single take) and may even have been 'transmitted live' on a previous occasion.

In order to take a broader view, we now want to present a mini case study of the channel Live TV (or L!VE, as it still styles itself). Live TV also features in Chapter 5, because it has partially transformed itself into a local broadcaster. For the purposes of the present chapter, it is the earliest months of Live TV which are of interest.

In 1995, the Mirror Group, a newspaper publishing corporation, made its first venture into television broadcasting. Its channel, Live TV, was initially produced by Janet Street-Porter until she resigned out of conflict with Kelvin McKenzie, former editor of the *Sun*, brought in as Managing Director of Mirror TV. The style of McKenzie's channel, in 1997, is unapologetically tabloid television. It brings its viewers not only topless darts but, in the spirit of sexual equality, *Lunchbox Volleyball* as well. It has a soap opera which prides itself on the frequency of the snogging, regular horoscope and Tarot card-reading sessions, scenes from the latest catwalk shows every day, regular stand-up comedy slots, a lonely-hearts programme, news on the lives of celebrities, and regular news with non-verbal commentary from the News Bunny. The Whitsun Bank Holiday weekend in May 1996 made a special feature of its exclusive interview with James Hewitt, formerly a major in the British Army and ex-lover of the Princess of Wales. This interview was repeated every evening throughout the weekend. In 1997, material of this kind fills the schedules for half of the airtime. The other half, in certain British cities, is filled with programming made for a local audience – and we discuss this in Chapter 5.

So much for the Live TV of the present. The early days are more interesting in the present context, because of Street-Porter's firm commitment to the ethos of liveness. In a documentary completed and broadcast after her departure, and narrated by Robert Lindsay, Janet Street-Porter is filmed addressing prospective staff invited to Canary Wharf for interview about six months before the launch.

> It's a live channel, it's driven by live events and things that are happening. It's not a hard news channel, it's just events of the day, but at certain times of the day we're very live. For example between nine and one in the morning, three till seven in the afternoon and then nine till one in the evening we would have two outside broadcast units and live, things happening live in this space. So we could do interviews, talk shows, cookery, fashion, whatever you want to do in this space. Now we'll also be making features which will look like the live output and those will be

pre-recorded and dropped into our transmission. We haven't worked out all that stuff yet.

Later in the documentary she says to the reporter:

> It's not the *Daily Mirror* on television, we don't even have to begin to talk about what it is and it isn't, I've said it's live television. I've said it's not aimed at a particular class, it's not aimed at a particular age group. It's live, no one else is doing that at the moment. That's different enough.

As things turned out, the channel was never as live as the rhetoric promised. Technological problems caused difficulties for the live outside broadcasting, and Live TV found itself repetitively reusing, within different production cycles (daily and weekly) its own material, even if it was avoiding the use of other people's cast-offs. But Street-Porter did at least ensure that one of her goals was met – the desire for an overall channel 'look' was achieved and this 'look' was one designed to support the ethos of liveness. For example, the Live TV picture was planned to include an information strip at the bottom of the screen. The content of the information strip would change constantly. Constant change is not inherently a sign of 'liveness', but in the context of a channel dedicated to this principle, and promoting this view of itself at every opportunity, the frequency of the changes contributed to the sense of time passing, just as the changing numbers of a digital clock do. It is interesting to note that Live TV eschewed the onscreen clock, digital or otherwise, perhaps because such an overt reminder of the demands of external clock/calendar time in viewers' own lives is too much at odds with the principle of 'fun' to which Live TV was also dedicated. At the press conference, four weeks before the launch (quoted from the documentary):

Reporter:      Is there one particularly good reason why people should tune in to Live TV?

Street-Porter:      Well, in the evenings, terrestrial television doesn't cover openings and parties and play, theatre openings or premieres or anything like that. We've got a very simple ethos which is, if it's live, we are at it. So if there's one reason, it's 'You're at the parties you weren't invited to.'

The ethos of liveness led to the relentless pursuit of celebrities at the aforementioned parties and openings and premieres and exposed the channel's need to make a little go a very long way. Second-order celebrities would make jokes on screen about how often they had spoken into the Live TV microphones and smiled for its cameras. Celebrities, when 'doorstepped' on their way into venues, would give perfunctory, barely cooperative answers to exuberant questions from presenters: both participants would be seen to struggle with the conversation, and the focus of the talk was inevitably superficial in its orientation to 'the moment', the purpose which had brought both celebrity and presenter to the same spot. Even on Day One there were signs of making a virtue of necessity, as the documentary revealed. David Montgomery (Managing Director of the Mirror Group) comments to Street-Porter:

> TV has been sort of almost stripped of that raw energy in its traditional conventional sense, hasn't it, and in a way the viewers are being exposed for the first time to all the excitement and rawness, and that's the way I think it should be.

The heritage of 'Zoo TV' and youth television in general (see Lury 1997) is very apparent in this kind of comment. Montgomery is reacting to the 'behind the scenes' panic generated by all the flaws and near-misses in the first day's transmission. Onscreen presenters can't be quite serene in the context of this hysteria, but Montgomery approves – terms like 'energy', 'excitement', 'rawness' are all drawn from the lexicon of liveness.

We will conclude Part I by discussing another of Live TV's interesting experiments. If two of the characteristics of live speech are disfluency and deictic choices, a third is interactivity, or dialogue.[2] In the early days of Live TV there was an attempt to introduce this characteristic to one of the most traditionally monologic forms in broadcasting – the studio-based news bulletin (cf. Fairclough 1994 on the 'conversationalisation' of discourse modes in society).

Now there is already one style of TV news reporting to which the idea of 'conversationalisation' applies. It applies to US network news, where two presenters on occasion make comments to one another as their turns at talking alternate. It is this practice which is sometimes referred to as 'happy talk': it conveys a sense of a real social relationship, a successful one, between the two presenters.

Live TV's approach involves an element of this talk *about* the news between two onscreen performers. But there is more. Happy talkers on the US networks do not address the TV news *itself* to one another; they address it to the TV audience. The conception is, so to speak, that both participants are presenters, and hence they both already know the news, and it is only us, the viewers, who don't know it yet. What follows on pp. 59–61 is a transcription from one news bulletin in August 1995, aired as part of the daily show *Live with London* at that time (Table 1).

In Live TV's news-as-dialogue experiment (which has since been abandoned) there is an asymmetry in the roles of the two participants. One is the news presenter and the other is the host of the show (Simon London, in the programmes we looked at). The news presenter is knowledgeable about the news; the host is not. (The host has been too busy hosting to become acquainted with the day's events.) So the basic conception is that the presenter tells the news to the host, while the TV audience looks on and listens.

This item is presented from the working office space of the presenter, within the studio-cum-offices of the channel, rather than from a 'proper' news studio; it involves the host moving from his space within the studio to that of the presenter, and then *asking* to be told the news. This duly happens.

*Table 1* News as conversation on Live TV

| Verbal track | | | Visual track |
|---|---|---|---|
| 1 | SL | Hi there. Welcome back to Live with London. I just want to say, congratulations Frank Bruno! I always knew you could do it and I think you're a star | Medium Close Up [MCU SL] in studio corridor: picks up newspaper from off-screen desk and thwacks the front page in indexical gesture. Camera angle tilts slightly, then levels off. |
| 2 | | Let's go over and see the man who knows everything, and very little about everything, indeed, because it is, of course, Raffie! Back on the news desk. I can sit next to him and squeeze his buttocks like so. | Looks off camera left: walks left with camera tracking to desk: sits on desk, pinches R's bottom. |
| 3 | R | Hey. Oh. | Zoom to two-shot: camera oscillates gently as they both settle themselves on the desk. |
| 4 | SL | Hello | Interlocking gaze of performers alternates with gaze at news notes. |
| 5 | R | Nice to see you, too Simon | |
| 6 | SL | Yes | |
| 7 | R | How are you doing? | |
| 8 | SL | Very well thank you. And yourself? | |
| 9 | R | Not bad, nice and relaxed | |
| 10 | SL | Good. { I noticed | SL gaze into camera/audience |
| 11 | R | { Anyway. Over | |
| 12 | R | Into the top story, hey? | |
| 13 | SL | Yes please | |
| 14 | R | Boy George has cancelled a concert scheduled for tomorrow after his brother appeared in court charged with murdering his wife. His brother Gerald O'Dowd is accused of stabbing his wife Jill to death at their home in Hertfordshire. Boy George has issued a statement saying his family's been devastated by what's happened. Gerald appeared in court and was remanded in custody for a week. Boy George wasn't in court himself, but his elderly mother Edna was, and another brother of his, David | |
| 15 | SL | OK | |

| Verbal track | | | Visual track |
|---|---|---|---|
| 16 | R | Now the news, good news, for home owners. The biggest building society in Britain, the Halifax, has cut its interest rate to just under 8 per cent. This comes into effect immediately for new borrowers, and will take effect on October 1st for existing customers. Good news there for the housing market. | |
| 17 | SL | [nod] | |
| 18 | R | Elsewhere Britain's … rather the Ministry of Defence here has announced that it's going to review its ban on homosexuality in the army. This follows … | Zoom in on Rs face, excluding SL |
| 19 | SL | What's that, what's that, what's brought this on all of a sudden? | Back to two-shot |
| 20 | R | Well, it follows an unsuccessful attempt earlier this year to overturn the ruling which was thrown out in the High Court. The Ministry says it's going to appoint a team of experts to speak to servicemen and women here and abroad, and it's due to report back early next year. | |
| 21 | SL | I know we're not allowed to comment but I think, about time too. It's not exactly as if you're going to be in a war and go Oh, I quite like him. Or her. It's stupid, isn't it. | SL direct gaze at R with head lifted from normal position<br>Gaze to camera<br>Gaze off screen; raises arms in pretend gesture of holding rifle, then folds arms again |
| 22 | R | Well it's a bit out of step with other countries in Europe so | |
| 23 | SL | A bit out of step | |
| 24 | R | perhaps now's the time | |
| 25 | SL | Yes. Good. Next one please. | |
| 26 | R | Next story. You spoke about Frank Bruno. | |
| 27 | SL | Bruno! Bruno! | Gestures with both arms like a Bruno supporter at the fight |
| 28 | R | Well, all eyes are fixed on who he's going to fight next. It's highly likely that his next opponent's going to be Mike Tyson, and if it is then it's bound to be the biggest boxing match in history, grossing an estimated sixteen million pounds. Boxing promoter Frank Warren though says it's going to be at least another month before the next contender is announced | Zoom to close-up on R as before<br>Pull out to two-shot |

| Verbal track | Visual track |
|---|---|
| 29 SL OK Last story please, our Raff | |
| 30 R Last story. What's the most boring programme on TV? | |
| 31 SL Well, apart from. {Well, cos | |
| 32 R           {You were going to say, apart from yours! (*Laugh*) Because that's what I was going to say | |
| 33 SL it's not *Live with London* is it? It's not *Live with London* because everybody loves that. Um I don't know, what's the most boring programme on TV? | SL gaze at camera, thumbs-up sign |
| 34 R Well it's got to be party political broadcasts. | |
| 35 SL Yes, yeah. {Let's get rid of them | |
| 36 R           {Well now TV bosses | |
| 37 R Yes, exactly! TV bosses are saying they could soon pull the plug, because they're just so tedious. Interestingly enough this is being backed by MPs themselves. One MP, Tory Gerry Hayes has described them as dire, saying that at least they give viewers a warning when they're coming up, so that they can go and make a cuppa, go to the loo and do something more worthwhile. | SL arch gaze and exaggerated smile, leans in towards R and back |
| 38 SL OK thanks a lot for that Raffie (*continues in dialogue with R in moving between news segment and intro to next feature on sex in Disney cartoons*) | SL unfolds arms as he takes control back from R |

The presenter appears to ask permission to begin: 'Into the top story, hey?' (line 12) and the host grants it: 'Yes please' (line 13); but the 'please' indicates that it is he who is requesting and the presenter granting the request: the preceding question from R is needed in order to manage the timing of the discourse. As the segment progresses, there is licence for casual chat about the news in the interstices of particular items and at its ending, as here (line 21):

L: I know we're not allowed to comment but I think, about time too [to review the ban on homosexuals in the army]. It's not exactly as if you're going to be in a war and go 'Oh, I quite like him'. Or her. It's stupid, isn't it.

The meta-level remark, 'I know we're not allowed to comment', concerns the propriety of having opinions, not the interaction in which he and R are engaged.

This hybridisation of news presentation and chat is one where the conventions of the former still predominate. The 'conversationalisation' of the news here crucially depends upon the visual track, and the appearance of the host as an attentive listener for most of the time. London, the host, underscores his visual display of active listenership with vocal signs, including 'response tokens' at appropriate junctures, along with laughter and even physical actions where they seem relevant (lines 26–8):

R:   Next story. You spoke about Frank Bruno.
L:   Bruno! Bruno! (Gestures with both arms like a Bruno supporter at the fight)
R:   Well, all eyes are fixed on who he's going to fight next.

The newsreader is required to display a bodily orientation towards London, including gaze, when he is not looking at his notes. Since he does not have 'host' responsibilities towards the audience, he, unlike London, never seeks to engage the audience directly by gazing at the camera.

Both participants cooperate in the conversationalisation of news with their attempts to make the form interactive. R asks L: 'What's the most boring programme on TV?' There is a great deal of tolerance for such signs of informality as hesitation phenomena, performance errors, self-corrections, pauses, and turn overlaps. For a self-correction, see line 18:

R:   Elsewhere, Britain's … rather the Ministry of Defence here has announced that it's going to review its ban on homosexuality in the army.

For overlapping turns, see lines 33–7:

L:   I don't know, what's the most boring programme on TV?
R:   Well it's got to be party political broadcasts.
L:   Yes, yeah. {Let's get rid of them
R:              {Well now TV bosses
R:   Yes, exactly! TV bosses are saying they could soon pull the plug, because they're just so tedious.

The host admits he can't answer the presenter's initial question: 'What's the most boring programme on TV?' (line 30). So the presenter supplies the answer – and the host offers an agreement token, 'Yes, yeah'. This is enough for R, the presenter, who recommences his monologue. But L, the host, is not finished: he produces a statement which overlaps with what R is trying to say. R abandons his utterance, produces another one, agreeing with L's judgement on party broadcasts. Only then is he 'free' to recommence the abandoned monologue.

In spite of all this interactive work, the dominant note here is the spoken *monologue* of the presenter. His lengthy speaking turns are structured very much as they would be in any conventional news bulletin on radio or on TV, both at the paragraph level and in terms of sentence syntax. Thus, there is no attempt to render this as a real 'conversation' about news events. It remains a bulletin, coloured by aspects of chat (including London's comment on the army item, which he frames metalinguistically as ideologically unacceptable, while performing it as something which is generically acceptable, if not required). The presenter takes a little more responsibility than London to keep the discourse neutral, but even he allows himself a gently evaluative perspective on the army item, responding to London's own, the two of them establishing the terms of *their* evaluative convergence and inviting the viewers to share their liberalism.

This attempt, flawed as it is, to render the news 'conversational' is compatible with the story we are trying to tell about the vulnerability of 'liveness' as a rhetoric in an era when the traditional, natural signs of liveness are no longer trustworthy. Consider it in this way. 'The news' is traditionally live. The occupant of the studio, presenting the news, is assumed to be speaking at exactly the moment that the viewers are listening. But in the new era this *assumption* of synchronicity is no longer sufficient for a channel where 'liveness' is the *raison d'être*. Hence it is necessary to introduce further signs of liveness. Conversationality will serve as such a sign. Conversation possesses emergent properties. That is to say, conversation is constructed in real time, there is limited scope for pre-planning, and the form it ultimately takes is a consequence of moves made in ignorance of how they will be taken up and developed. This conversation possesses them 'for real', inasmuch as it is not the case that the entire conversation, as transcribed above, has been pre-scripted (though the monologic sections have). In this way, the dialogic features of the segment will *undermine* that characteristic of news presentation which has always compromised its liveness – the extent to which it is hearably a written idiom, pre-scripted and read aloud. In a longer time frame, however – as we have already suggested – those devices which are adopted by non-live material to signify liveness may become compromised by such self-conscious use – especially if there is a concurrent shift away from genuinely live programming, where the same devices functioned as natural signs.

# Part II

# The semiotics of space in the third age of broadcasting

The character of television is elusive. Its salient characteristics as a medium which is (audio)visual, electronic and 'mass' (Corner 1995) are clear enough, but the significance of these characteristics depends in part upon what it is compared with. Compared with the print media, one set of features and issues may be prioritised; compared with the cinema, other concerns seem more relevant; radio offers yet another set of comparators, as do face-to-face interaction, telephony or computer-mediated communication. Unarguably, television belongs among those forms of communication which transcend time and space, even if transcendence is a rather inflated term for a technical achievement which we now take for granted in this context. Television allows communication beyond the spatial and temporal limits of face-to-face interaction. Part I pursued this perspective in relation to the temporal relations of broadcasting, where the concern with 'liveness' has always been with the power of radio and television to couple spatial remoteness with temporal proximity. In Part II, concerned with the spatial relations of broadcasting, the spatial remoteness of 'speakers' from 'listeners' (viewers) is re-examined in relation to the new media environment. The focus here is upon the way that television helps to create socially significant contexts within which communication can take place. These places of communication are real places (Germany, Liverpool, the QVC studio), but they are also semiotic constructs whose televisual reality depends upon the rhetorical work, both visual and verbal, which 'real-ises' them for viewers.

Through the focus in Part II upon the construction of space, it can be positioned in relation to what has been termed 'the new cultural geography' (Morley and Robins 1995) and specifically with the contribution of television to the (re)configuration of the social world in the post-cold war era. The perspective of Part II is semiotic in the sense that, as with Chapter 3, it is concerned with textual forms (verbal and visual) which can be seen as constitutive of the social – in this case, with the construction of 'place' in televised discourse. It takes a wide view of the audiovisual construction of spatial relations, with particular reference to the presence of 'Europe' in the multi-channel world, to the localisation of television's frame of reference, and to spatial aspects of the social relations between broadcasters and their audiences.

Multi-channel TV broadcasting has become more spatially diverse than broadcasting in the terrestrial era. That is to say, there is a kind of diversity which consists in the coexistence of channels addressed to different audiences, geographically conceived. Channels for national audiences still occupy pride of place, but they are supplemented now by channels for supra-national (European) audiences and channels for sub-national (local) audiences, as well as channels for transverse, trans-national audiences. It is in terms of this geographical logic that we have constructed Chapter 4. Rather than emphasising the general experience of television which possesses this particular form of diversity, we have chosen in the first instance to concentrate upon specific channels which do not adopt the traditional, national address.

It is Chapter 4 which is specifically concerned with 'European' television. Critics such as Schlesinger (1993), Collins (1992, 1994) and Weymouth and Lamizet (1996) have expressed considerable scepticism, on cultural and economic grounds, about the prospects for television addressed to a European audience, as opposed to television for specific audiences within Europe. We share this scepticism, for all of the reasons given. Nevertheless, the existence of channels projected at 'Europeans', with European Union funding, is a reality. One of these channels is EuroNews. Chapter 4 provides a critical analysis of how EuroNews imagines and constructs 'Europeanness'. It reinforces through textual analysis precisely the point about the artificiality of the European cultural identity which other commentators have been at pains to argue in general terms – against the logic of the policy discourse originating within the committees of the EU. As in Chapter 2, this chapter includes some discussion of linguistic deixis; in this case, spatial deixis. Billig's (1995) discussion of 'banal nationalism' and its cultural significance sets great store by the unobtrusive presence of deictic terms which turn out to have the nation as their referent. Part of our argument concerns the impossibility of equivalent unobtrusive deixis to flag 'Europe'.

Shorter, less extensive case studies follow in Chapter 5, which focuses upon the sub-national and the trans-national in contemporary European broadcasting. These short case studies provide illustrations of the emerging possibilities, though we have no particular general argument to pursue with respect to this new 'narrowcasting', except to note that there is little glamour at this end of broadcasting, where audiences are small, and attractive for advertising purposes more to local traders than to the big investors, with the possible exception of TV addressed to travelling business executives in their hotel rooms. Both Britain and Germany are familiar with programming made within, and for, 'regions' of the country. But regions in this sense are large areas. In the case of Germany, with its decentralised tradition and immense cultural and linguistic differences between north and south, East and West, the third programmes have always addressed distinct regional cultural identities. Although quite a percentage of the programming is given over to repeats from the main first channel, ARD, there is substantial programming made for and by the regional broadcasters: region-specific live talk shows, folk-music programmes, news and documentaries in particular address a regionality which was not unsettled by the multi-channel environment. Third programmes still attract higher viewing figures than most of the smaller private channels. Paradoxically, most of these regional services can now be received nationwide as well as internationally via the Astra satellite. In the case of Britain, the national-regional components England/Wales/Scotland/Northern Ireland have comparable distinctiveness, but this is much less true for the so-called 'regions' *within* each of these countries. Intra-nationally, it is *city* identification which is more powerful. People identify with 'their' city (though in focusing upon Liverpool rather than any of Britain's other non-metropolitan centres we may have picked an extreme case), and it is useful to reflect, as we do in Chapter 5, upon the potential pleasures of city-level broadcasting, at a very early stage of its development in the European context.

The final chapter in Part II is less concerned with the specificity of the audience in respect of its social identity, and more concerned with relations between broadcasters and audiences. Our purpose in Chapter 6 is to offer some analyses which speak to two strands in recent television criticism. One of these two strands stresses the *sociability* of broadcasting, both radio and television (see Scannell 1996). In this argument, it is of the essence that television is thoroughly intelligible, thanks to its routinisation and to the kind of talk that broadcasters have trained themselves to produce. But this argument relies upon the patterns established in the era of *terrestrial* television. Our evidence shows, on the one hand, that these patterns are vulnerable in the new circumstances, yet on the other hand that there are particular channels in which the characteristics of 'sociable' television are actually *intensified*. Our case study for this purpose is the English-language shopping channel, QVC.

Another strand of critical argument in television studies takes much more account of the new developments, and argues that television today expresses or realises the depthless postmodern sensibility which expects of television nothing more than simulacra, visual excess and spatial/temporal dislocation. There are reasons for thinking that this argument is overstated, and thus Chapter 6 includes some discussion of the psychic and televisual conditions which might provoke experiences of 'dislocation'.

# 4 Constructing Europe

The purpose of the present chapter is to discuss the nature of 'Europe' as a tele-visually mediated place. The centrepiece of the chapter is a discussion and analysis of the semiotic and textual resources deployed by channels and programmes which seek to address, and construct, their viewers as 'Europeans', particularly EuroNews, a channel which derives much of its funding from the European Union.

The emphasis upon textual form and meaning here gives this study a focus which is complementary to that of scholars such as Schlesinger (1993, 1997). What textual analysis can do is to draw attention to the rhetorical *work* which goes into the construction of Europe in television, hence the emphasis we have given below to forms of spatial deixis. Spatial deictic forms such as 'here' and so forth are unremarkable when speaker and hearer have a shared location. TV broadcasting by tradition locates broadcasters and audiences within the same country, though at different points in that country. Something happens to such forms when the locatedness of the programmes and their viewers is not taken for granted but is an issue. But there is a wider context within which to situate this analysis. To understand that context it is necessary to review some of the current media-related research concerned with the 'new cultural geography' (Morley and Robins 1995).

## Satellite television and the new cultural geography

Researchers are keen to understand how communications technologies contribute to the new cultural geography, and in doing so have come up with the idea that satellite broadcasting and the Internet conspire with political and economic change in late modernity to 'reconfigure space'. This reconfiguration, however, is not only, or not so much, about the redrawing of spatial boundaries, substituting one set of dividing lines for another, but about new ways of constructing social relations in space. 'Space', here, has its most general sense, the sense in which it is the complement of 'time'. Reflections upon this theme lead to generalities such as the following:

Patterns of movement and flows of people, culture, goods and information mean that it is now not so much physical boundaries – the geographical distances, the seas or mountain ranges – that define a community or nation's 'natural limits'. Increasingly we must think in terms of communications and transport networks and of the symbolic boundaries of language and culture – the 'spaces of transmission' defined by satellite footprints or radio signals – as providing the crucial – and permeable – boundaries of our age.

(Morley and Robins 1995: 1)

There are some difficulties with this kind of perspective. The reference to the 'symbolic boundaries of language and culture' is significant here, for these were always the boundaries which mattered, even when it was the case that physical boundaries coincided with the symbolic ones. Furthermore, it is upon the political not the physical, or even the linguistic, map of the globe where boundaries appear most marked. The line between France and Spain disrespects the 'natural' boundary of the Pyrenees, running as it does right through the middle of that particular mountain range. Basque speakers are to be found on both sides. Boundaries, then, come into play in the political context when it becomes necessary to institutionalise and regulate the social groupings (see Cohen 1994 for an application of this idea to the 'frontiers of identity' which Britain finds it necessary to police – between the 'real' British and the immigrants, the English and the Celts, Europeans, etc.). 'Spaces' of course can be demarcated in different ways – politically, economically, culturally, linguistically, technologically – and the question of the 'fit' between the different demarcations is an important one to pursue, especially where there is reason to believe that new configurations at any one level have causal effects at other levels.

## The European TV experience

Received wisdom on TV worldwide positions the Western European experience as both like and unlike the North American experience. The Western European experience is like that of North America in that, postwar, TV very quickly obtained complete penetration of the market so that every home possessed its TV set, or sets. The difference between the two continents resides in the differences between the commercial model adopted in the United States as against the public-service or mixed commercial/public-service traditions of Western Europe. The other significant difference is the greater range of channels available in North America, on both sides of the US/Canada border. Because of 'overspill' from US transmitters, Canada shares the multi-channel experience of its southern neighbour, even though it has attempted within its own jurisdiction to follow a more 'European' approach in matters of policy. See Filion (1996) for discussion of the Canadian broadcasting experience.

The era of deregulation on both sides of the Atlantic opened up broadcasting to new kinds of corporate participants – Rupert Murdoch, Silvio Berlusconi,

Ted Turner, Leo Kirch. In Western Europe, this deregulation developed at the same time as the technology of satellite and broad-band cable delivery systems. The result, of course, has been the advent of multi-channel broadcasting in Europe (and no longer just the West of the continent), variously paid for (licence fee, advertising, sponsorship, subscription).

The multi-channel experience has, naturally, been available to Europeans crossing the Atlantic to visit the USA. Such an experience was important for Williams in formulating his early and influential notions of TV 'flow' (Williams 1974; see Chapter 1 above). More recently, Caughie (1990) has talked as a European about the pleasures and perils of watching US television.

The multi-channel experience, previously the privilege of North American viewers, is now available to Europeans, too – in principle. In practice the picture is rather different. Cable delivery systems are far from being generally available. DBS technology (Direct Broadcasting by Satellite, where homes receive satellite signals directly via their own dish and set-top decoder, particular channels being 'scrambled' to the non-subscriber) is available, but the uptake has, again, been highly variable (see Table 2).

In different European countries the range of new channels may be found to be smaller or larger according to linguistic considerations. Research indicates that where a choice is available viewers prefer programmes in their own language and grounded in cultural experience which they can relate to – and this is the case not only in Europe but worldwide (Parker 1995; Noam 1991; Ferguson 1992; Schlesinger 1993, 1997; Collins 1994; Weymouth and Lamizet 1996):

*Table 2* New technology in Western Europe circa 1995

| Country | Population (millions) | TV homes (millions) | VCR homes (millions) | Cable connection (millions) | Cable penetration (%) | Dish total (thousands) |
|---|---|---|---|---|---|---|
| Belgium | 10.1 | 4.1 | 2.1 | 3.7 | 91.6 | 15,000 |
| Denmark | 5.2 | 2.2 | 1.4 | 1.2 | 56.5 | 125,000 |
| France | 58.0 | 20.8 | 12.3 | 1.0 | 4.7 | 260,000 |
| Germany | 81.2 | 33.0 | 16.2 | 14.4 | 43.9 | 6,000,000 |
| Greece | 10.4 | 3.1 | 1.3 | nil | nil | 2,500 |
| Ireland | 3.6 | 1.0 | 0.61 | 0.44 | 41.6 | 60,000 |
| Italy | 57.2 | 20.3 | 9.1 | nil | nil | 110,000 |
| Luxembourg | 0.4 | 0.14 | n/a | 0.17 | 81.4 | 2,000 |
| Netherlands | 15.4 | 6.3 | 4.5 | 5.6 | 87.9 | 250,000 |
| Portugal | 9.9 | 3.1 | 1.9 | nil | nil | 110,000 |
| Spain | 39.2 | 11.6 | 6.3 | 1.2 | 10.3 | 180,000 |
| UK | 58.4 | 22.2 | 16.0 | 0.77 | 3.8 | 2,800,000 |

Source: Weymouth and Lamizet (1996: 25).

In principle, by beaming its signal down to individual home dish receivers, satellite-based television can bypass national governments and their restrictions, opening a cornucopia of programme alternatives to viewers. Yet to date the upsurge in viewership for international broadcasting – via satellite and cable – is, with few exceptions, at much lower levels than popularly imagined. Although satellites may make such broadcasts theoretically available on all contintents, the number of homes equipped to receive such signals isn't yet half of one per cent.

Moreover, in countries with competitive broadcasting, viewers, to a greater extent than once imagined, prefer to watch television produced and presented in their native language by people who look and act like them and reflect values similar to their own.

(Parker 1995: 2)

Parker is particularly concerned to challenge utopian media futurology for its unwarranted technological determinism and lack of attention to the political and economic factors which have shaped and will continue to shape the structure of the media industries, the character of their output and the nature of the viewing experience.

In short, a more cautious and realistic view of the future of international as well as pan-European broadcasting has now been accepted, both by the corporate 'players' who need to understand their markets for very straightforward economic reasons, and by academic analysts seeking to assess the balance of forces, economic, political and cultural which characterise the media environment and lock it into the rest of the social world. Research on inter- and trans-national broadcasting has now taken on a more focused character and several distinct areas of concern are emerging.

The trans-national possibilities of modern broadcasting have implications for media research in respect of both its political, 'public knowledge' agenda and its interest in popular culture. At the political level, the principal questions concern the character of the modern 'public sphere' (Habermas 1989/1962), formerly construed in national terms. At the cultural level, the questions concern the deconstruction of national 'communities' and the establishment of alternative groupings which cut across lines of national demarcation.

## The European public sphere

Within a political/legal framework, writers such as Venturelli (1993) and Price (1995) have wrestled with the familiar problem of determining 'public interest' in the struggle between market principles and state regulation. For Price it is the countries of Eastern/Central Europe – the 'transition societies' – for whom this problem is currently the most acute. A global media system can help to 'open up' closed regimes (Tiananmen Square is the oft-cited exemplar of this process at work), but it can also participate in the 'depoliticisation' of particular societies:

Deregulation, globalism and the lack of criticism of government may oddly coalesce: the emphasis on market forces can reduce the function of television and radio *as the press*, as a critic of the state. Heroic private networks and great public-service broadcasters have been praised (with a bit of golden-age romanticism) precisely because they can pose threats to a complacent status quo. Ironically, by subjecting these organisations to greater market forces, however, television programming develops a new form of neutrality; its managers become co-administrators of the global culture of consumption. Transformed, broadcasting no longer has the same politically subversive potential; if subversive, it is so in a new way, sapped of what was potentially its explicitly critical perspective. Globalisation becomes virtually synonymous with a tendency towards depoliticisation, part of an effort by the state to diminish the potency of the media to disturb the status quo.

(Price 1995: 17)

There is an obvious connection here between the political concern respecting 'depoliticisation' and the concern for cultural orders in the new 'global' society. The connection is consumerism: global media undermine politics not just because they undermine national coherence but because, in place of any distinctive public or national value system, they install a value system grounded in the desire to consume. Global TV means global entertainment, and distraction from politics except as spectacle.

It is not only within the realm of broadcasting that the displacement of politics by consumption has been a focus of cultural concern. If, traditionally, 'public space' has been the domain of the citizen, that tradition now seems to be at an end:

That much public space and interaction is dedicated to consumer practices and discourse becomes significant for the public sphere, since the role of citizen is displaced by that of the consumer; the cultural assumptions surrounding shopping malls, for example, do not make them prime settings for the public sphere.

(Dahlgren 1995: 20)

As far as communicative form is concerned, the literature here is concerned with specific genres of programming (news, current affairs, documentary) as well as with specific properties of meaning – rationality, truthfulness, partisanship (Dahlgren 1995).

## European culture and identities

Although this point of intersection between political and cultural issues is clear enough, the cultural critique of globalisation in the mass media is a distinctive one and one with a more diffuse range of concerns than the political agenda.

The principal questions here have to do with the limits of national difference and differentiation.

The resurgence of academic interest in nationhood (see Hutchinson and Smith 1996) has activated more general questions concerning the nature of human 'community' and in particular the difference between communities maintained through face-to-face interaction and those, such as 'nations', where co-membership has become an abstracted property. In Benedict Anderson's famous phrase, nations are 'imagined communities' – not because they are fictional or unreal, but because their reality depends upon the ongoing capacity of members to imagine their existence and thus the bonds which unite their co-members:

> An American will never meet, or even know the names of more than a handful of his fellow Americans. He has no idea of what they are up to at any one time. But he has complete confidence in their steady, anonymous, simultaneous activity.
>
> (Anderson 1991: 31)

The social and semiotic arrangements which these members daily experience must facilitate this imagination, must make it possible to 'live' a national life. National mass media productions form an important component in the construction of national imaginations: a point which is important for Billig (1995) in his analysis of the character of 'banal' nationalism.

If nations are imagined communities – what kind of 'communities' are those which transcend national boundaries? Does trans-national broadcasting foster anything which is community-like in its functioning and self-awareness? Does it have the more limited power to undermine the kinds of communities which have prior claim upon the imaginations of viewers and listeners?

These are the kinds of questions which are now attracting attention and discussion. Media researchers (e.g. Ferguson 1992; Schlesinger 1993, 1997; Dahlgren 1995) have a particular interest in the role of the mass media as it affects the future of nationalism and nation-state formations, but the issues are more general and have become important in general social theory (Giddens 1990; Featherstone 1990, 1992; Tomlinson 1991; Hannerz 1992; Robertson 1995).

Within Western Europe the advent of the multi-channel environment with inherent trans-national capabilities has encouraged three distinct lines of speculation with respect to the current and future television experience of European viewers. One line of reflection attends to the dislocating and fragmenting effects of the new media world: another attends to specific pan-European developments, and a third focuses upon the construction of 'taste publics' which cut across national divisions (prototypically the youth audience for MTV[1]): these 'transverse' formations of cultural consumption are both less and more than European in character. They are less than European in so far as it is only by virtue of a single shared interest that the group coheres at all – a fully voluntarist 'community' in its self-conception even if from a sociological perspective, common demographic factors exist and help to explain the taste choices. Such groups are also more than European inasmuch as their members are not confined to European countries. In this chapter we are principally concerned with the second of these concerns. Chapters 5 and 6 take up the other two lines of enquiry.

## European culture and community: a case study

At the level of pan-European developments it is the initiatives of the EU which have attracted attention (see, for example, Venturelli 1993; Collins 1994; Weymouth and Lamizet 1996). To imagine Europe as a nation-like entity is to imagine it with control over social institutions parallel to but larger than those of the component member-states – including mass-media institutions. But the world is not a fractal structure wherein smaller components replicate the forms of larger ones. The major policy document of EU telecommunications policy is the Television Without Frontiers directive (see Commission of the European Communities 1984) – essentially a text of the 'deregulation' era, notwithstanding its concessions to national (and public) interests. Within this policy discourse, the trans-national European broadcasting space already exists. It is not commensurate with geographical Europe, since not all European countries belong to the EU, nor is it commensurate with the footprint of any specific geostationary satellite. The existence of this space is underwritten by the constitutional powers of the EU itself, and critics of 'Europeanisation' at this level have objected that the policy discourse replaces a political conception of the nature of broadcasting with a purely economic conception.

In a more 'culturalist' perspective the defence of 'Europe' can take the form of the defence of *national* (French, German, Spanish, etc.) traditions in the face of perceived encroachments of the despised lowbrow global culture, linguistically Anglophone and culturally American. In this perspective, the UK is America's Trojan Horse – within Europe but linguistically affiliated to its enemy. The attempt to appropriate 'highbrow' culture as the creation and property of Europe, for example via the Franco-German co-sponsored Arts channel ARTE has a plausible prima facie rationale, especially when it concentrates upon concert, opera and ballet productions, forms with a history of transcultural success independent of broadcasting, at least within the West. But the idea that 'high culture' so understood is European, as distinct from Western, is untenable – and there is evidence not only of the channel's economic weakness (worthy but 'unpopular') but also of considerable tension between the co-sponsors (see Emanuel 1992, 1993, 1995).

The question of cultural 'Europeanisation', in current writing on this subject, is not followed through in respect of communicative form to any great extent. Instead, the issue is treated as one of medium (the existence of designated or *de facto* European satellite channels) or, to a lesser extent, of content. Thus Weymouth and Lamizet (1996) identify desirable kinds of media Europeanisation as: the extension of cultural knowledge; the creation of a common culture; and the coverage of issues of common concern. The extent to which these developments are likely to happen is admitted to be still a matter for speculation.

Thus, what is still missing in all of this is any attention to the forms of programming to be found on the new channels which are designated as 'European', and which attempt to *be* European in their mode of address and content. The analysis which follows is designed to open up discussion of 'European television' at that level.

How far can audiovisual media support or foster any kind of identity, national or transnational? Billig (1995) coins the term 'banal nationalism' to correlate the familiar and unobtrusive use of national symbols such as 'the unwaved flags on public buildings' with the equally unobtrusive everyday use of (relational)[2] linguistic deixis in the daily press, where the us and we, the here and now, the our space and this nation, act to reaffirm the listeners/readers in their national identity: 'nationalism is not confined to the florid language of blood-myth. Banal nationalism operates with prosaic, routine words, which take nations for granted, and which, in so doing, enhabit them' (Billig 1995: 93).

But what if the community that is appealed to is made up of the many nations, languages and cultures of the European Union or, wider still, of Europe itself?

Since the 1980s there have been various attempts to develop pan-European programming on the public-service model of terrestrial TV (see Schlesinger 1993). But the most deliberate, self-conscious and proactive attempt to create a European rather than a national identity through television can be seen in the forms and contents transmitted by EuroNews (EN), a channel launched in 1993 which is receivable by satellite dish or cable in 35 countries in Europe and its Mediterranean neighbours. EN's task to attract viewers is a difficult one. We have already mentioned that viewers' preferences lie firmly with their own national programmes in one of their national languages, notwithstanding the widespread distribution and consumption of dubbed or subtitled American entertainment programmes. How does EuroNews hope to counteract this tendency? Is there at least potentially an imagined community of Europeans to appeal to or to construct and, if so, how does EuroNews hope to foster this identity? And what is the nature of this construction, geographically, politically or culturally? In the first part of this chapter we reviewed some of the theoretical writing on the new cultural geography and the European public sphere; we will now investigate at the discursive level how one channel, in particular, imagines and constructs Europeanness.[3]

### Overcoming the language barrier

To start with, EN takes note of the preference viewers have for programmes in their own language, by transmitting in the five big languages of the EU: English, French, German, Italian, Spanish. Cable users, at present, do have their linguistic selection imposed on them by their regional cable company.[4] But satellite-dish users are able to choose freely one or all of the languages by tuning into the different sound frequencies.[5] The offer of linguistic choice signals the important fact that Europe is a multilingual community. Of course, only five languages are available, a restriction which runs counter to the EU's declared policy of supporting all national languages spoken in the Community, with special rights for its minority regional or ethnic languages such as Welsh or Catalan or Urdu. This restriction is presumably more to do with limited resources rather than any deliberate exclusion of the 'smaller' languages, but it does reinforce the sense of where the centre is as against the periphery, and thus the power differentials between large and small nations and linguistic communities. Still, being able to choose between at least five languages marks EN out against the other round-the-clock news channels such as CNN, Sky News, n.tv etc. which transmit trans-nationally, but only in their respective national languages.

The channel's multilingual policy influences the form and style of its programming in various ways. Since only the soundtrack can be tuned into different languages, the visuals, by definition, remain the same. This affects the relations between sound and image in the construction of the programmes, since the images have to be made to fit soundtracks in different languages, which in turn has consequences for the ways viewers are – or, should we say, are not – addressed.

Let us begin with the most obvious: EN has no anchor persons who introduce or lead through different sections of the programming. This would have created difficulties for the dubbing of the soundtrack, since decisions would have had to be made about which language to use for the speaker, with consequences for synchronising lip movements. Instead, we are shown a range of different screens/templates with a musical soundtrack and/or a voice-over. The particular genre or sub-genre of the programme, such as the weather forecast or the 'anniversary news' – sequences (with its template 'a year ago – vor einem Jahr – un anno fa', etc.) are either signalled in writing in all five languages or by a term specially coined in a form of 'Euro-Interlanguage' drawn from various Latin, Greek or Anglo-Germanic stems: for example *Economia* for business news, *Artissimo* and *Odéon* for two types of art magazines, *Sante* for a health magazine, *Ecologia* for an environmental magazine, *Mediterraneo* for a programme about the countries of the Mediterranean region, *Sesamo* for a programme about European mobility for workers and/or tourists, etc. Instead of the familiar image of anchor persons addressing individual viewers in seemingly personal face-to-face interaction in their own language, EN's multilingual template sequences unfold in a curiously empty, impersonal and abstract space.

Other features, too, underline this multilingual policy. Overall, the amount of written language on display is much higher than on any parallel news channel, even affecting the commercials. Many advertisements show slogans in English and German running across the top and the bottom of the screen. If the sound frequency of the channel is tuned into either French, Italian or Spanish, viewers will be exposed to three languages simultaneously. In contrast to this multilingual display on templates and ads, the names of countries and cities appear only in their native form and spelling – such as Firenze, Frankfurt, Praha, Wien, Italia, Deutschland, Österreich, Espagna, etc. This is not a contradiction: EN clearly expects viewers to tolerate, perhaps even to celebrate, the exposure to other languages while accepting the inevitability of viewers' preferences for their own .

The press review items are a good example of both of these tendencies in parallel. Against a background of newspapers running off a printing press, the original title graphics of major European newspapers are superimposed on the upper half of the screen and the original headline of the day on the lower half. The soundtrack summarises the item in the chosen language with music in the background. For example, the title of the newspaper *Journal de Genève* on 12 November 1996 is shown with its French headline, 'La vache folle revient sur le devant de la scène' while the soundtrack explains this in one of the five languages – here chosen in English:

> The *Journal de Genève* of Switzerland carries an article headed 'The mad cow returns to centre stage' and this coverage appears in numerous other newspapers. A study published in *Nature* confirms that the so-called mad cow disease can be transmitted to humans.

### Overcoming the national perspectives

#### Deixis revisited

This headline from the *Journal de Genève* is the only trans-national headline that EN shows from the national broadsheets in Europe on that day. The others confirm the obvious point that, in the absence of a truly international story, national concerns override European ones in the national press, with all deictic references pointing to the respective national spaces, just as Billig shows. Further examples quoted in the same press review show this very clearly:

- The Italian *Corriere della Sera*: 'Governo e sindaccati vicini alla rottura' (Government and trades unions close to break-up)
- The German *Frankfurter Allgemeine* 'Zehntausend Metallarbeiter protestieren gegen die Kürzung der Lohnfortzahlung' (Ten thousand metal workers protest against the cut of progressive wage increases)
- The German *Süddeutsche Zeitung*: 'DGB: Der heiße Herbst hat begonnen' (German Trade Union Council: the hot autumn has begun)
- The Spanish ABC: 'Los Recortes Presupuestarios situan a las Furezas Armadas al borde del colapso' (Budget cuts in defence spending are pushing the armed forces toward collapse)
- The French *Le Figaro*: 'Chirac célébre l'islam moderne' (Chirac welcomes the ideal of modern Islam)

In addressing their intended readership, the respective newspapers treat as self-evident that the 'government', the 'metal workers', the 'budget cuts' in the headlines above refer to the respective Italian, German, Spanish entities, just as national television news relies on being read that way. Transferred to EuroNews, these headlines need to be translated and attributed to particular nations by the voice-over (e.g. 'The German Conservative daily, the *Frankfurter Allgemeine* ...'), just as this would happen in any review of the international foreign press, where we look from the inside of our own nation to what the outside says. But the difference is that, for EN's interpellated audience, all these headlines from different national papers need to be constructed as internal ones – internal to the imagined space of Europe. In this way, the press review quoted above is not an international foreign press review at all.

There are, of course, other days when topics in large sections of the press do converge. On 2 May 1997, the day after Tony Blair became British Prime Minister, all the papers reviewed by EN led with the Labour Party's landslide victory in the British General Election. It is on such days where EN's own lead item is congruent with what is internationally considered a major event. But such occasions are less frequent than the divergence of reporting shown above. Convergence of topic in the national press or in the various national television news reporting does not in any way alter the deictic positioning of readers/viewers in their respective national spaces. Such convergence simply signals an assumed strong interest in an event of another state.

How, then, does EuroNews try to overcome this predisposition to view from a firmly grounded national point of view, and address its viewers instead as Europeans? The answer is – with difficulty. The press reviews quoted above are indicative here, since EN has to start from a not dissimilar national basis. Not possessing financial and journalistic resources to produce a great deal of its own reporting with its own news teams, EN's news reporting depends on lifting or adapting items from national public-service channels and overvoicing them with a different soundtrack. Most of EN's current affairs news, for example, consists of a collage of items which were originally produced for addressing a national audience, but which are now readdressed to an imagined European one. For example, an item lifted from the Italian channel Rai Uno may be followed by one from TVE (Spanish), followed by ARD (Germany), etc. The result is a succession of different national emphases in the context of an imaginary Europe where we would all share an interest in one another's concerns. Since the frame of reference of the various film reports usually originates from a national perspective, the soundtrack carries the burden of redirecting and resignifiying them as European, while the selection of items overall needs to suggest a European rather than a national space. Programming content and style thus become indicative of an utopian appeal to a joint political, economic, artistic culture of Europe – a Europe that by definition lacks a deictic centre, since no single entity can be referred to in the unselfconscious identity-confirming style of relational deixis identified by Billig (1995). This throws into relief the very tensions it attempts to overcome.

*Editing out*

Redirecting national stories to an imagined European addressee not only requires that all implicit national references (the government, the Prime Minister, etc.) must be explicitly located by discursive means (the government of such and such a country, etc.). Equally affected is the selection of information which the voice-over soundtrack relays over the original. News items, as is commonly known – be it for television or the press – are structured to fit in with the world knowledge, the interests, values and assumptions of an assumed target audience, and will include colourful details which depend on this shared knowledge. Since EN broadens the target audience from the national to the European, decisions need to be made about the editing in of particular pieces of information to contextualise them for the viewer, or about editing out information which is not considered relevant for the wider audience or would take too long to contextualise. This is, of course, not normally transparent to the viewer, since the voice-over either replaces the original sound completely or is spoken over it to make the original incomprehensible. In the latter case, we occasionally get moments where the voice-over pauses and we return for a few seconds to the original. This allows us brief glimpses of such editorial manoeuvres. One typical example on 12 November 1996 comes from a report originating from Finnish TV on the first entry to the European Parliament of new MEP, Marjo Matikainen-Kallström. To a Finnish viewer, she is best known as a famous cross-country skier, but this is not a piece of information which EuroNews feels it needs to relay to its viewers and they don't. They therefore omit to dub that part of her interview where in one such pause in the voice-over she is heard to say (in Finnish): 'I hope that I will still find time to ski'.[6] Though insignificant on its own, it is precisely the editing out of such local, mutually shared, often more personal detail which makes much of EN's reporting seem rather flat and colourless.

*Flagging Europe*

Instead of the subtle confirmation of national identity by the discursive means of relational deixis, EN needs to fervently wave its European flag. Unsurprisingly, the word 'Europe' itself becomes a high-frequency noun.

Below are examples from some of the previews for programme types on EN which hardly need further explication. We have highlighted the relevant phrases through italics:

- Preview for morning news bulletins
  Monday to Friday from six to nine. The latest news on *EuroNews*
  Every 15 minutes. All you need to know on the *top European* and international stories of the news, business and finance or sport and a look at the weather throughout the continent. Every morning from six to nine, all the news in 15 minutes.

- Preview for news bulletins in general
  If it matters, *if it's European*, if you need to know; it's on EuroNews, every day in every news bulletin. EuroNews.
- Preview for *Europa* magazine
  Das vereinte *Europa* im Aufbau? Was tut sich in Brüssel oder Straßburg? Welche Konsequenzen hat das für den Bürger? *Europa* macht die *europäische* Union für Sie transparent.
  (The construction of a united *Europe*? What's going on in Brussels or Strasbourg? What are the consequences for its citizens? *Europa* makes the *EU* transparent for you.)
- Preview for programme *Perspectives*
  What's making people talk *across Europe*. The big story in Spain, the headlines in Belgium or Italy. Every week *Perspectives* takes a look around the continent with reports of national news from national TV channels. Get a new perspective on what's making headlines *in Europe*. Watch EuroNews every Wednesday and Thursday (final shot of logos of different European national channels).
- Preview for *Euro Zoom*
  Every week *Euro Zoom* turns the television cameras of *Europe* on the world's hottest stories; the future for *Europe*, social conflict, war or terrorism; how does Italian TV see politics in Belgium; how does France cover strikes in Spain. Every week, for a *European* focus on an international news: *Euro Zoom*.
- Preview for *Economia*
  On EuroNews *Economia* means business. For the events shaping *Europe's* economies, investment trends, the currency and stock markets, watch *Economia*. *Economia*, each weekday on EuroNews.
- Preview for *Style*
  Slip into *Style* on EuroNews, street cred in London, haute couture à Paris. The look, the lines, the label. The latest in fashion and design from the creational capitals in the world. Get hip. Watch *Style* every week on EuroNews.

The references to Europe and its nations in these previews are not without paradox. The status of the word wavers ambivalently and fuzzily between a collective or a single-referent noun. On the one hand, there are, indeed, different perspectives and different foci – headlines in different countries, London or Paris, etc. Here Europe is a collective noun for different nations; but at the same time there is a unified European focus, there are people who talk across Europe, there are European news, and a European continent which includes the British Isles rather than referring to that part of Europe which is across the Channel – as is common in British usage. But, whereas the centre of Europe is European Union territory, there is also a periphery which EN takes note of by regularly transmitting magazines from the fringe. Again, the previews give an indication of how we are to construct the European space in relation to its neighbours.

- Preview for *Mediterraneo* (Sunday 8.15 p.m.)
  Every week EuroNews builds a bridge across the Mediterranean sea. From Algeciras to Istanbul, from Tripoli to Trieste, politics, art, religion, history, different worlds with much in common. Every week the people of the *mare nostre* meet on *Mediterraneo*.
- Preview for *90 Degrees East*
  Watch *90 Degrees East* for a closer look at the changing face of Eastern Europe. Each week feature stories from Europe's new democracies on *90 Degrees East*: the faces as well as the facts.
- Preview for *Alpe Adria*
  Explore the region from the Adriatic to the Alps via the Danube on *Alpe Adria*, a shared heritage from Slovenia to Austria, Hungary to Northern Italy – each week on EuroNews.

These previews are accompanied by visuals which are indicative of the type of items we are to expect. Interestingly a previous set of sequences for those three magazine programmes showed for *90 Degrees East* scenes of political struggle and violence and, for *Alpe Adria* and *Mediterraneo*, serene landscapes and beautiful buildings. The visuals for *Mediterraneo* and *90 Degrees East* have since been replaced by others which are less blatant in the stereotyping of the beautiful South versus the warring East. By the time of printing it is to be assumed that further changes will have been made.

## Constructing culture out of cultures

Let us now turn to the programming of EN to see how EN hopes to succeed in its project of constructing a joint European political, economic and artistic culture. Most of the examples come from the reporting of one typical day, 12 November 1996, when we videotaped the whole day's programme, though the points made are valid for the channel's programming in general.

### CONSTRUCTING A JOINT POLITICAL CULTURE

Unsurprisingly, given its close relationship to the European Union and the financial support it receives from it, EN places a great deal of emphasis on European institutions such as the European Parliament and the European Court. New Euro MPs may be interviewed on their experience of entering the Parliament for the first time; the working of sub-committees, parliamentary procedures and decisions are shown, spokespersons are interviewed, etc. Rulings in the European Court tend to get covered as long as they are treated as significant by one of the member countries, even if such an item is treated as entirely irrelevant by the other nations' media. For example, on 12 November 1996, the European Court rejected a British complaint against a piece of European health legislation (the 48-hour working week directive). This ruling was reported live and in great detail on BBC, ITV and Sky News. The German round-the-clock news channel *n.tv*, on the other hand, did not even mention this event, nor did the French channel TV5. EN, by contrast, treated it as a lead item, showing the same footage as the BBC, including the response from the British Prime Minister of that time, John Major, to this ruling.

## CONSTRUCTING A JOINT HISTORY

Items are shown which often stress a common past or a shared heritage. On 12 November, this included an arousing report from a reunion of Spanish Civil War veterans in Barcelona, accompanied by documentary footage from the 1930s. The voice-over celebrated their struggle as the victory of democracy – i.e. the modern, enlightened European values – against the dark European past of Fascism of Franco's Spain, Hitler's Germany and Mussolini's Italy. The documentary black-and-white footage from the fighting against general and future dictator Franco in this item made an intriguing contrast to the 1950s footage shown in another item on the same day, which was lifted from TVE for the *Media* magazine, of the 40th anniversary of its founding as the first Spanish television channel. Here, Franco the statesman is shown to receive foreign visitors, politicians and diplomats from Europe as well as US President Eisenhower, a poignant reminder of how Europe accommodated to Franco's long regime.

## CONSTRUCTING A JOINT COMMUNICATION CULTURE

The magazine programme *Media* regularly reports on what happens in the different European media industries. Apart from the quoted report about TVE's anniversary, there were items on the founding of a new Gaelic channel. Occasionally there are reports about non-European issues provided though by one of the European television channels. On 12 November, this included a report about how mentally disturbed patients were allowed to make their own films in Brazil.

## CONSTRUCTING THE EUROPEAN WORKPLACE

EN reports regularly such obvious business news as the values of shares, currencies, gold, etc. Whereas national channels give preference to showing the comparative values to their own national currencies, EN has three anchor points for its currency lists, the US dollar, the Deutschmark and, of course, the ECU. The ordering of the templates clearly separate 'first-, second- and third-division' leagues of currencies. The first template in each of the three comparative sequences shows the relations between the US dollar, the Deutschmark or the ECU in relation to the ECU, Deutschmark, dollar and Japanese yen. The second template in each series shows the currencies of the UK, France, Italy and Spain against the three anchor currencies, and the third template shows the rest: Belgium, Denmark, Greece, Ireland, Finland, Netherlands, Austria, Portugal, Switzerland and Sweden. For the European financial market, the deictic centres are thus as much global (inclusion of the US dollar and the yen) as they are European (Deutschmark and ECU).

More interesting than these currency figures are the many comparative statistics which are regularly shown, especially on the magazine programme *Label Europe*.

Below is an extract from 12 November 1996, which shows how EuroNews tries to construct the nation-states of Europe as regions of the larger unit of a continent or a Union:

> And now for this week's summary of the employment situation in Europe compiled by EuroNews and Eurostat. The most recent statistics show over the summer an increase in unemployment amongst women in Finland and a fall in Denmark and Sweden. These findings also reflect the overall tendencies in each country. The more one heads towards the south of the continent the higher the unemployment rate is amongst women. But even in the North there are equally surprising contrasts. In the United Kingdom women are less affected by unemployment than men, whereas in Belgium it is very much the opposite. A further contrast can be seen in the south of the Union, where in Portugal women are more affected by unemployment, but only moderately as in Germany, while in Spain the inequality is quite blatant.

An item which combines both comparison of employment in European countries and the advantage of European mobility can be seen in the following item about a Spanish doctor working as a trainee surgeon in a Luton hospital (UK).

*Dr Jon Mikel Echevarrieta*
*[dubbed into English]:*        I had a friend who'd been in the UK for five years learning how to become a surgeon. So when I decided I wanted to become a surgeon, I called him and he told me what I had to do. Then I came here.

*Voice-over:*        Jon's case shows that there is scope for exchanges between Europeans. Countries like Germany or Spain turn out more doctors than they need, while the UK doesn't have enough. So here's a portrait of a Spanish doctor who crossed the channel.

This film was originally made in Spanish, but included sequences of his speaking to patients and nurses in English. When played back on the English soundtrack, we hear bits of the Spanish soundtrack dubbed from the original English exchanges, but now voiced-over in English – an electronic version of a multiple vocal palimpsest.

But not only surgeons profit from European mobility. EN tracks down any number of situations where Europe can be celebrated for the advantages it bestows on its citizens. The (popular) art magazine *Odéon* of that day shows a sequence 'filming in progress' with the British pop duo the Pet Shop Boys, who give the interviewer all they could possibly have hoped for in Euro-celebration, though this celebration of Stansted Airport as an emblem of the new Britain in Europe sounds somewhat tongue-in-cheek.

| | |
|---|---|
| *Voice-over:* | Filming in Progress in London for the Pet Shop Boys' new album *Single Bilingual*. Still integrating the Latin influences they picked up from their South-American tour, the Boys are now looking to Europe. (Videoclip/original sound) |
| *Pet Shop Boys:* | Well, the song, which is called *Single Bilingual*, is sort of a funny song about the British Euro businessman travelling to Europe; he loves all the perks and is showing off and so we thought of Stansted Airport – you see, an airport is mentioned in the song; and it's got that kind of modern British look. I think it's rather a beautiful building, really, and it's just got the right kind of modern European feel for the song.<br><br>Well, we always try to write songs that are about what's happening around us, whether it's our personal lives or, you know, public life, life in general, and it's a big issue in Britain, isn't it, Europe, and we like actually the fact that Britain is part of Europe and that we're Europeans, and you know in my life, things have changed so much, and really you feel nowadays that we are part of Europe, and so I thought it would be nice to have a song where the lyrics kind of dealt with that in an amusing kind of way. |
| *Voice-over:* | So there's an airport business dance sequence in the clip. Who said business can't be fun? |

Other typical concerns of EN are comparative programmes about advertising regulations (here about the different European laws about advertising cigarettes and alcohol), about the labelling of household products, etc. These are items independently produced by EuroNews, often with the support of European Commissions such as the Directorate General for Consumer Policy of the European Commission.

CONSTRUCTING THE EUROPEAN CONSUMER

Apart from informative programmes directed at a European consumer with an interest in safety or wider ecological concerns, EN also has its own TV market with telesales of products to be ordered by phone or fax. These ads copy the styles of the Shopping Channel rather than that of the more glossy commercials known from other commercial television channels. The objects for sale are usually gadgets which get described and shown in action in great detail and for several minutes – such as machines for training stomach muscles or special slimming stockings, ladders that fold in amazing directions, silver-cleaning equipment that works in seconds or a special stick for removing unwanted fibres from furniture or clothing. Often the origin of these ads is American rather than European, a fact which is more obvious to the listeners of the English soundtrack who get their version spoken with an American accent rather than voiced over in one of the other languages. We will have more to say about the language of such ads in our discussion of the Shopping Channel. Important for us here is the way that potential shoppers are invited to locate their 'tele-shop'. At the end of each commercial, national flags are displayed, sometimes with an additional name or abbreviation of the respective country. Buyers are asked to find their local – which here means national – phone/fax number by locating their respective national flag. This use of a national flag is quite different from the function which Billig ascribes to national flags in his book – namely that of subconsciously confirming national identity in everyday life (Billig 1995). Here their function is similar to an area code, a purely indexical guide to the nearest shop.

## Constructing a joint artistic culture

Of all the programming on EN, those that deal with art seem least self-conscious in their insistence on Europeanness. When EN simply lists major exhibitions and events in Europe, as in *Agenda* and *Affiches*, this is easily accommodated as the kind of information travel agencies supply for the Eurotourist. When EN reports from major artistic events anywhere in Europe, as in *Artissimo* – the arts, especially music (popular or classical), opera, ballet and the visual arts travel easily and can be assured of their respective Europe-wide audience segments. When *Odéon* transmits the Spice Girls' newest song, the shared interest can be taken for granted, since they will have hit the top of the charts in most European countries anyway, though even here the self-conscious Euro-construction of EN is never far away, as was shown in the interview with the Pet Shop Boys. And items such as the report on *Artissimo* of a Poetry Festival in London's Covent Garden hardly received notice anywhere in the British media.

But where art is concerned – high art or popular culture – EN's Europe seems less of an artificial construct than in all the other features it carries. Here EN can draw on a shared interest among different taste publics which pre-exist the deliberate construction of Europe through EU regulations and policy making, though they are undoubtedly strengthened by the greater accessibility of artistic events through mass tourism and the media. This development will be touched upon in Chapter 5, concerned with 'narrowcasting' – local audiences and taste segments. The European arts channel ARTE will be considered more extensively in Part III, which is concerned with the 'quality' issue.

# 5 Narrowcasting

One speculation about the future of television is that the metaphor of 'broadcasting' will become an inappropriate one. There will be less programming constructed for the general, national audience. With more available channels, TV broadcasting will become more specialised and the need for programmes accessible and enjoyable across wide differences of social background will become less of a constraint. Social background here covers class, ethnicity, gender, taste, interest, educational level, intellectual level and geographical location. Viewed positively, this development would point towards a TV distribution system more like that of printed periodicals. Viewers won't have to waste time on things that don't interest them or which take them out of their depth. Viewed negatively, it points towards a culture where television's contribution to the social cohesion of the national community is reduced by comparison with the past.

So-called 'narrowcasting' has already arrived, in the sense that there now exist channels dedicated to particular types of programming – sports channels, arts channels, comedy channels, news channels – as well as channels designed to reach a local population rather than the country as a whole. To be sure, such programming still constitutes mass communication in the sense that it goes out to large and anonymous viewing audiences. And television as such is still diverse – the diversity previously seen as the responsibility of a single channel can now be spread across a range of channels. The mixed programming channels themselves show no sign of disappearing, notwithstanding current anxieties about 'dumbing down'.

A further aspect of this diversity is the specifically spatial aspect. Channels with geographically distinctive remits coexist in the multi-channel environment. That environment includes not only EuroNews, with its supra-national audience, and the traditional channels like BBC 1 and ARD with their national audiences, but also channels with a local, sub-national audience such as mdr, Liverpool Live and Channel One, as well as trans-national niche audiences like ARTE (see Chapter 8). To describe the range in these terms is to underline the extent to which the range confirms a highly stable cultural geography. The hierarchical structure is simple and easily understood: Europe – nations – localities. The middle level of the hierarchy remains the dominant level. On the face of things, the transverse programming is the nearest thing to a disruptive element within this mixture.

But this is not the whole story. The stability of the geography as described depends upon homology between the audience-as-constructed and the actual audience. The relationship begins to be confounded by channels which are received by audiences *other than* the ones for which they are intended. In the present chapter we have tried to address this phenomenon by providing two case studies. The first looks at two local channels broadcasting in Liverpool from the point of view of the canonical, Liverpudlian audience. The second looks at mdr (= 'Mitteldeutscher Rundfunk'), a channel which also has an audience outside of the region in East Germany to which it belongs. One subcategory of 'narrowcasting' takes us into discussion of 'transverse audiences': audiences which may well be European in spread, or even global, but which are narrow in the sense that they are defined by cultural interests or tastes. The other significant subcategory is that of the local audience. In relation to the latter we have some points to make about the character of local programming, using the new cable channels in Liverpool (Liverpool Live and Channel One) as a stimulus for our observations. But we also want to talk about the more extraordinary phenomenon of the German channel mdr which projects a sub-national, 'regional' culture to a very much wider audience via satellite.

## TV's local audiences

As in the previous chapter, it is appropriate to begin with some remarks about the similarities and differences between Europe and the US with respect to 'local' programming. Our own interest within this book is with television broadcasting rather than with radio, and for reasons of space it will be necessary, from here on, to ignore the nature of regional/local radio broadcasting in Europe. The situation of radio is importantly different from that of TV.

'Local' in this context is a term which, along with 'regional', requires some clarification. It can mean *city-level*: Price (1995) talks about 'the geographical community' (see below). It can also mean *sub-national* communication, though 'regional' is perhaps a better term here. Regions will typically be much larger than cities. The difference is important, since, while it is possible to 'image' cities as communities (however tendentiously), the task is very much harder for 'regions'. Regions may have cultural coherence, but they need not: their existence is determined by geographical/technological factors as much as by political/cultural ones. In Britain, 'Granada' is the name of a commercial broadcaster within the Independent Television Network, the franchise-holder for its particular region. However, there is no 'region' of Britain which knows itself as Granada-land: the territory stretches from the England/Scotland borders down to Chester and Crewe in the upper-middle of the country on the west side of the Pennine mountain range. Notoriously, it takes in not one, but two, key cities of the region, less than sixty kilometres apart. These are Liverpool and Manchester, and each of these would like to be the singular centre of a region rather than sharing that privilege. In practice, Manchester rather than Liverpool is more central to Granada's operations, much to the chagrin of the latter.

In Germany, with its strong federalist tradition, the situation is different again. Here, the public-service third programmes deliberately target the population of their respective federal states by producing a range of specifically regional programmes, often using speakers whose accents and intonation mark them clearly as natives to the region. We will have more to say about this at the end of this chapter, when we take a closer look at one such channel's programming (mdr), which was newly created to serve three regions of the former GDR. Since the national first programme, the ARD, is itself composed of the different broadcasting institutions of these federal states and controlled by a broadcasting council made up of political and other representatives from these states, the influence of regional flavour is stronger in the national media as well.

In the US the origin of broadcasting was local in the narrower sense, though it quickly became regional (state-level) and national. Local broadcast stations continue to exist, 'as perhaps the most decentralised model of broadcasting in any country' (Price 1995: 214).

> The idea of the 'local' has, historically, been the antithesis of the national in US broadcasting law. Congress and the FCC long emphasised the opportunity for local broadcasters to programme differently from the networks, to strive for diversity and local voices. Licences were and are issued on a community-wide basis; elements of the community spirit were to be reflected in station operations. An emphasis on local ownership, on determining local needs, on the integration of ownership and management – all of these were designed to reinforce a vision of American life and imagination in which the geographical community had dignity.
>
> (Price 1995: 215)

Price is writing about the legal arrangements which regulate US broadcasting and about the philosophies which determine these arrangements. The point he is actually making here is that there is a discrepancy between the ideal and the actual: economic and other pressures have created a media environment in which, up to the present, the national is very much more significant than the local.

In the European context the term 'regional' has a meaning within the phrase 'a Europe of the regions' in which it *can* mean 'national': the point being to recognise and respect (but without taking sides in controversial cases) the existence of 'small nations', both those like Luxembourg which exist as states on the political map and others – such as Wales, the Basque country and Catalonia – whose cultural/ethnic/geographical distinctiveness is recognised, whose nationhood is, to a greater or lesser degree, a matter of dispute, but who certainly fall short of statehood under the present political dispensations. The autonomy of broadcasting within regions of this kind is just one of the foci of political struggle. Perhaps the general moral of this story is that 'local' and 'regional' are both contrastive terms: with the focus upon 'Europe', the BBC itself becomes a local broadcaster, while, within a global perspective, a 'region' is not sub-national at all, but refers to clusters of nations which can be reached by singular satellite systems – Europe being one such 'cluster' and North America another.

United States viewers have always had access to local TV channels in the narrow (city) sense. But this is a new experience in the European context and even now it is the exception rather than the rule. As of summer 1996, two channels available to Telewest subscribers in the northwest franchise region are 'Liverpool' cable channels. In fact, both are actually national channels 'customised' at local level, and in both cases the locally originated content forms only a proportion of the schedule. It is possible that these two channels will be merged into a single one (Hall 1996).

## The new local television

There is much talk within cultural studies of the so-called 'global–local nexus' wherein global commercial operations have a lot to gain by investing in particular localities and contributing to the renaissance of local economies and cultures, while, at the same time, local cultures are discovering and asserting themselves 'from below' in resistance to national structures. To the extent that this thesis assumes the weakness of existing national formations it must be treated with some scepticism. Nor is the resurgence of localism necessarily a development to be welcomed:

> It may well be that, in some cases, the new global context is recreating sense of place and sense of community in very positive ways, giving rise to an energetic cosmopolitanism in certain localities. In others, however, local fragmentation may inspire a nostalgic, introverted and parochial sense of local attachment and identity.
>
> (Morley and Robins 1995: 118)

In any event, there is little research within this tradition which specifically addresses itself to television's contribution to localism in this sense, for good or for bad. It is the cable-only services which permit television to 'go local', in Europe, though the extent to which this is happening varies considerably. Conversely, it is satellite technology which enables regional programmes such as the third programmes in Germany or national channels to go 'global', thus potentially supporting an expatriate (national or international) audience. The expatriate work-force in the EU such as – for example – the Turkish communities in Germany and elsewhere have several Turkish channels available on the Eutelsat satellite.

In Liverpool, city-wide cabling has taken place and the vast majority of homes can be connected to the Telewest-operated cable network, for phone or for television services, or both. There is a connection fee and a monthly TV subscription as low as £19.00 for a 'basic' package, and as high as £36.00 with premium services (in 1997). The 40–50 channels which can be received in this way are predominantly satellite and terrestrial channels. Only a few are cable-only. Liverpool's first cable franchise was granted in 1983, though the operator (Cable North West at that point; now operating in the name of its parent company, Telewest Communications) was not in a position to operate the franchise until 1990, and the wiring of the city continued for some time after that date. The latest development was in 1996, which saw the commencement of not one but two 'local' cable channels: Channel One and Liverpool Live. It is the extent and character of the localism on these channels which will be the subject of the next section.

### The channels

#### Channel One

The best way to explore the communicative dynamics of any of these new channels is to watch it for an extended period of time (a period of several hours) with the video recorder in operation. Preliminary thoughts about the communicative form and content of the broadcasting can then be developed into a tighter analysis, and any generalisations emerging from this analysis can be tested through much shorter periods of exposure to the channel on other days and at other times of the day. This was the procedure we adopted on 9 April 1997, from 2.05 p.m. until 7.15 p.m., while checking the channel's printed schedule for that day in the listings magazine, *Cable Guide*. First, some observations about the schedule.

On air, the channel presents itself as a 24-hour broadcaster. The listings, however, present a schedule which runs from 6.00 a.m. until 12.00 midnight. If Channel One is transmitting in the small hours, it is likely to be more of the same. The 18 scheduled hours are divided up into half-hour broadcasting slots, 36 in all. Of these 36, half comprise local programming, and these start on the hour all day long. The remaining 18 slots are filled by named 'programmes', non-local in origin and syndicated through the regionally differentiated versions of Channel One. The material here is mostly magazine-type shows and documentaries. There is nine hours' worth of material here, but it is not nine different hours' worth: taking account of repetitions, there is probably about four and a half hours of fresh material (though some of this was recycled from the previous day and some was to be recycled on the following day).

What of the nine hours of airtime for local programming? This consists of news, sport, weather and traffic – the formula is the standard one. Its 'localness' is compromised by the inclusion of 'arts' and other items which are non-local both in origin and in focus: on 9 April we repeatedly saw an item about an American dancer performing in London, and another about the release of the film *The People vs Larry Flynt*. The news on Channel One purveys a largely mainstream notion of what constitutes the Liverpool community: its vox pop sequences are recorded 'downtown' in the shopping centre and in Albert Dock.

The stories covered include follow-ups from 'national' stories after the national press has moved on to other things. On 9 April it was still running stories concerned with the postponement of the Grand National steeplechase on 5 April, following an IRA bomb hoax. Crime and courtroom stories are heavily featured: the running stories on 9 April included five out of about 15 with crime/court-room associations, and two of these had a sex-and-violence theme. The news values then tend towards the tabloid, yet they remain *news* values: true tabloid TV (journalism in the service of pure entertainment) is to be found on the other 'Liverpool' channel, Liverpool Live.

Beyond this content level of analysis it is worthwhile making a few further comments regarding Channel One's localism, for there are other dimensions to this, other ways in which a sense of locality is constructed. One is visual and two are verbal.

- The representation as media images of places and people known also from 'real life'.
- The verbal characterisation of Liverpool-ness and of Liverpool people's distinctiveness.
- The framing of city celebrities – the great and the good as well as the merely famous – as distinct from more familiar national celebrities.

All of these devices are employed by Channel One, and all can be illustrated with material from the recordings made on 9 April. First, the visualisation.

The visualisation of place is the stock-in-trade of Channel One, unsurprisingly, and ranges from those locations which are known publicly and nationally to 'signify' Liverpool – the Pier Head buildings, the cathedrals – to others which will only have the resonance of unmediated familiarity to a minority. One of the 9 April items, as it happens, came from the Senate Room of the University of Liverpool, very well-known to one of the present authors but not to the majority of Liverpool citizens.

Is there still any enchantment to be derived from seeing, 'on the box', places and people known to us from 'real life'? Is it the role of local television, within the new media environment, to offer that kind of pleasure? The scope for an enchantment effect is probably much less than it used to be in Western countries, although this is different in countries less used to home-produced programming. Viewers in Kasakhstan shown on ARTE's *Soap Around the World*, for example, stressed the significance of seeing:

> How our Alma-Ata, our Kasakhstan, is shown on TV; normally we are used to watching Santa Barbara, America or Brazil – here you're looking directly at our Alma-Ata, and you say 'I know these places' or 'I've been here myself'.

For Liverpool residents, however, who live in what must be the most-represented city in all of Britain, with the possible exception of London, the witnessing of familiar locations is scarcely a new experience. Local radio in particular has accustomed us to the scaling-down of the broadcast media's geographical frame of reference. Hearing and seeing oneself and one's acquaintances on TV may still generate excitement, though this excitement is likely to be milder if the appearance is on Channel One than if it is on national television.

The verbal characterisation of Liverpool-ness is of interest because it is not something that can be done 'officially', as it were, within the remit of the channel. It is rather a case of finding occasions to produce Liverpool-talk – and it is better if that talk is produced by interview subjects, including non-Liverpudlians, than for it to come from the presenters themselves. Thus on 9 April one item consists of an interview with Rod and Marty from the old-established band Lindisfarne, in town as part of their national tour. One section of that conversation runs as follows (slightly edited for fluency):

P:  Now you're from up there in Tyneside. Did you ever get a bit jealous of what was happening down here with the Mersey Beat, down here in Liverpool?

R:  I think everybody did for a while.

M:  Everybody did, yes.

P:  Did you ever think 'Oh God we could have this up there.' Did you ever try and emulate that?

R:  Yes, I think we probably did in a lot of ways.

M:  In fact, that happened as well.

R:  Yes, a lot of Newcastle bands were inspired, a lot of bands all over the world were inspired by that. I mean, you know Liverpool obviously has got pride of place in inspiring people to take up instruments and play a bit of rock and roll.

P:  Why do you think, your personal opinion, that Liverpool spawned so many talented musical acts?

R:  Oh, I think it's well recognised, because it's a part, you know, there was a lot of throughput you know of music from the States and things like that, and the sort of unaffectedness of the people which I think, dare I say, is something that we share on Tyneside.

M:  Similar approach.

R:  Similar approach to life, aye.

The performance requirement for the band members here is to respond to the presenter's invitation to engage in Liverpool-talk. They respond admirably, and with appropriate caution when the suggestion arises that 'unaffectedness' might not be a unique Merseyside characteristic.

As for the attention paid to local celebrities, a brief example will suffice. All day on 9 April, Channel One reports the birth of a baby boy, second son of one David Alton. Alton was a Merseyside MP, a Liberal Democrat, who did not stand for re-election in the General Election of May 1997. Here is what the channel said about this event:

Retiring MP David Alton is a father again only minutes after quitting politics. Mr Alton's wife Lizzie gave birth to son James shortly after the dissolution of Parliament. Liverpool's Lord Major Frank Dorren, a close family friend, will be godfather to the baby boy. The Altons' elder son was born within an hour of Margaret Thatcher's resignation.

Brief as it is, using only a single still photograph of Alton by way of visual illustration, the item recalls this lower-order celebrity to our minds by making a news story from the 'timeliness' of events in his personal life. The dissolution of Parliament and Margaret Thatcher's resignation are national, public events, while Margaret Thatcher is a *much* better known national and international figure. These events, and this name, are needed to enhance the newsworthiness of the story sufficiently to bring it into the realm of the tellable. The circumstantial details of the birth have permitted the channel to carry the story, thereby adding to the Liverpool viewer's stock of personal information about one of its own.

## Liverpool Live

Liverpool Live, like Channel One, is a local version of a national channel, and uses the same basic structure, with alternate half-hours of locally originated and non-locally originated programming. The national version of Live preceded the local version and was launched in 1994. It is sometimes mocked as the channel which is more talked about than watched (see Chapter 3).

> The fact is that no one really knows who watches Live TV. The target is to get 1pc of total television viewing in the 1.5 homes [i.e. one per cent of the 1.5 million homes] that pay to take cable TV. Official figures are due out later this year but, until then, the evidence remains anecdotal. But that's usually good enough for Kelvin. Live TV's psychic gets 6,000 calls a week and its Norwegian weather forecaster receives 750 fan letters a week...
>
> 'The conversation about Live TV is inversely proportional to its audience size,' comments Roger Luard, head of media group Flextech. He adds that the much-derided channel has actually secured key and very valuable 10-year distribution rights with Britain's cable companies. This effectively means it gets paid 25p for every cable subscriber, regardless of how many people actually tune in.
>
> (Gresser 1996)

Its notoriety derives from its introduction of such features as the News Bunny, topless darts and the national weather report spoken in Norwegian with English subtitles. Its managing director is Kelvin MacKenzie, former editor of the *Sun* tabloid newspaper, whose project is to give Live the television equivalent of the tabloid image, which the *Sun* developed under his editorship and which it continues to perpetrate. A well-publicised row between MacKenzie and Janet

Street-Porter, who ran the channel in its early days, led to the latter's departure within a few months of the launch and a change of tack for the channel. The localisation of Live took place in 1996 but there is still space to broadcast the nationally distinctive features – the News Bunny and so on.

Live is no more 'local' than Channel One in quantitative terms, but the local sections do make more effort to position themselves within local knowledges, using names and nicknames that (sections of) Liverpool people could be expected to be familiar with, with unexplained references to 'The Reds' (Liverpool FC) and the dockers' strike – a long-running unofficial industrial dispute on Merseyside. At the same time, detailed knowledge of storylines on the nationally screened soap opera *Brookside*, set in Liverpool, is also presumed, but such knowledge is not likely to be restricted to local residents.

The local presenters have a higher profile than their counterparts on Channel One and the studio presenters also undertake location reports, which allows for a more 'personalised' relationship between presenter and audience. Interviews with local people (both celebrities and people with a tale to tell) are heavily used. The emphasis is upon the arts and popular culture, including sport, and this takes the cameras to public spaces of a rather different kind: to the pubs, clubs and performance venues, rather than to the council chambers and shopping precincts. One of the channel's 'localising' gimmicks is worth mentioning. It uses local people to read the weather and traffic reports for the day. These are not updated very often so there are many opportunities to see the same local people perform. On 11 April:

*Weather*
Two teenage girls on camera, one holding a Liverpool Live microphone:
Hello, I'm Roisin and this is Kate.
Hello.
And here's the weather on Liverpool Live. It's going to be another dry day so leave those hats at home (Kate displays hand-drawn picture of a top hat). Winds will be light to moderate so take that dog for a walk (Dog drawing, captioned WALKIES!) The temperature will reach a groovy 15 degrees Celsius (drawn picture of person in groovy clothes; then the handwritten figure 15°). And that's the weather from Liverpool Live, Channel Eighteen.
*Traffic*
Man on green motor scooter, wearing a crash helmet and holding a piece of paper from which he reads aloud:
Traffic report. Hi, my name is Tim and I'm here to bring you the latest traffic update. No problems on public transport. Allerton Road is down to one lane, so there are hold-ups on the way into the city. In Bootle there are roadworks causing diversions away from Stanley Road. And with the weekend approaching, you can expect to be busier on the city roads.

*mdr*

The third programmes in Germany use similar regional forms of address in those programmes made by and for the region. The level of independent programming differs from one third programme to the other, since all channels have the option of recycling programmes made for the national ARD. Most third programmes, for example, relay the national main news programme of the first channel, the Tagesschau, simply supplementing it by regional news similar to the BBC's and ITN's practice of transmitting regional news after its main news programme. One of the most popular third channels is mdr (= Mitteldeutscher Rundfunk), which produces more independent programmes than most of the others, including its own independent main news. Mdr was founded with head-quarters in Leipzig (Saxony) after unification brought about the collapse of the East German centralised radio and television system. Its brief is to serve the regions of Saxony, Saxony-Anhalt and Thuringia. The remaining former East German regions of Brandenburg were also given a new channel of their own (ORB – Ostdeutscher Rundfunk Brandenburg), the rest was merged with the existing former West German services of N3 (Norddeutscher Rundfunk) and SFB (Sender Freies Berlin). Mdr is received as a terrestrial channel in its regions, with some overspill into neighbouring areas, but in addition it uplinks like most of the other third German channels to the Astra satellite. This creates the paradoxical situation that a channel which addresses a local audience can actually be received everywhere in Germany and in other European countries within the Astra footprint. Any viewer in Britain with a satellite dish can thus find out what the weather will be like in Leipzig or Dresden, or hear about local events in Saxony; though, apart from expatriates from the area, it is unlikely that mdr will have a great appeal to such viewers. Mdr, like all other third programmes, shows repeats from ARD (for example, talk shows like *Boulevard-Bio* or *Sabine Christiansen*, soap operas such as *Marienhof*, as well as bought-in programmes). But its address to its viewers, and the majority of its programming, is distinctly regional, clearly appealing to an identity which geographically, historically and linguistically unites three former GDR regions and separates them to some extent from the other former GDR regions, but most distinctly from the Western Länder. The viewers in the regions reward this attempt at reconstituting a regional sense of pride by tuning in: mdr in 1997 achieved the highest viewing figure in its region for all third programmes. Table 3 extracts a typical mix of two consecutive days on mdr, with the days' viewing figures in per cent, including our annotations, which show whether these programmes were produced for and by the region as regional (r) or as repeats from the national (n) channels.

This list shows that the majority of mdr's programming is made by and for its region with audience figures regularly rising above 10 per cent (even as high as 16 per cent). Let us now look at the format of these programmes in more detail. Typically for regional and local programmes in general, many of mdr's programmes have an interactive component via phone- and fax-ins, walkabouts

*Table 3* Scheduling on mdr

| Time of day (p.m.) 14 January 1998 | Title | Viewer percentage | Annotation |
|---|---|---|---|
| 2.55 | Marienhof | 4.9 | n: repeat of soap |
| 3.20 | Verbotene Liebe | 6.6 | n: repeat of soap |
| 3.45 | Bei uns entdeckt | 1.6 | r: programme about regional specialities; here the chess museum in Altenburg |
| 4.00 | Hier ab vier | 8.2 | r: (Here from four) daily magazine programme from 4.00 to 6.00 p.m. with separate components |
| 4.30 | Rucksack | 12.3 | r: travelling in the region |
| 5.00 | Studio live | 9.3 | r: invited artists, often ex-GDR stars |
| 5.30 | MDR aktuell | 9.9 | r: national news, regionally produced |
| 5.43 | Vorsicht: Fettnäpfchen | 12.2 | r: (Careful: Faux Pas) a programme about dos and don'ts |
| 6.00 | Brisant | 12.2 | r: regional version of national magazine programme |
| 6.28 | MDR aktuell | 11.4 | r: national news |
| 6.30 | Telethek | 10.4 | r: family advice programme |
| 6.52 | Sandmännchen | 9.9 | r: (Little Sand-Man) popular children's programme, dating back to GDR times |
| 7.00 | MDR regional | 14.2 | r: regional news |
| 7.30 | MDR aktuell | 15.1 | r: national news |
| 7.50 | Tierisch, tierisch | 11.4 | r: programme about animal sanctuaries where viewers can phone in and offer new homes for the animals featured |
| 8.15 | MDR regional | 7.5 | r: regional news |
| 8.45 | Die MDR-Reportage | 6.5 | r: various topic |
| 9.15 | Donnerwetter! | 6.3 | n: unusual happenings in Germany |
| 9.45 | MDR aktuell | 8.1 | r: national news |
| 10.00 | Großstadtrevier | 8.1 | n: crime TV film, repeat |
| 10.48 | MDR-Spot | 7.3 | r: various topics |
| 10.50 | Musical event | 1.2 | n or r |
| 10.55 | Lindenstraße | 0.1 | n: repeat of ARD soap |

| Time of day (p.m.) 15 January 1998 | Title | Viewer percentage | Annotation |
|---|---|---|---|
| 2.30 | Tierisch, tierisch | 2.4 | r: repeat of animal programme from previous day |
| 2.55 | Marienhof | 1.9 | n: repeat of soap |
| 3.20 | Verbotene Liebe | 3.1 | n: repeat of soap |
| 3.45 | Ein Anruf genugt | 2.0 | r: (A Phone Call Suffices) phone-in 'Notes and queries'-type programme |
| 4.00 | Hier ab vier | 11.0 | r: see above |
| 4.30 | Hobbythek | 8.1 | special topic; here a programme on humour |
| 5.00 | Studio live | 8.9 | r: see above |
| 5.30 | MDR aktuell | 11.0 | r: see above |
| 5.43 | Unter Sex Augen | 10.3 | r: (Under Sex Eyes): advice programme about relationships |
| 5.48 | Schwimm WM | 10.4 | r: world swimming contest in Perth |
| 6.00 | Brisant | 10.8 | r: see above |
| 6.28 | MDR aktuell | 10.4 | r: see above |
| 6.30 | Telethek | 9.4 | r: see above |
| 6.52 | Sandmännchen | 6.9 | r: see above |
| 7.00 | MDR regional | 2.0 | r: see above |
| 7.30 | MDR aktuell | 11.7 | r: see above |
| 7.50 | Mein lieber Mann | 7.6 | r: magazine (Oh Dear!) |
| 8.15 | MDR hilft | 10.5 | r: (Mdr Helps) advice programme |
| 9.00 | Damals war's | 16.6 | r: (Those Were the Days) oldies show |
| 9.45 | MDR aktuell | 12.3 | r: see above |
| 10.00 | Artour | 3.9 | r: cultural programme |

Source: mdr home page quoting GfK TV Quick

of reporters, voting by phone, etc. Participants tend to be identified by the town or village they come from, with the exact location sometimes reinforced by the display of a regional map (e.g. in the phone-in programme Ein Anruf genügt = A Phone Call Suffices, similar to the Guardian's 'Notes and Queries'). The same emphasis on regional origin is stressed for those who form the subject of the reporting, be they an ordinary person such as the owner of an animal clinic, a famous swimmer, or a historical personality. These are referred to as coming from: a town 'ein Chemnitzer' (= a man from Chemnitz), 'ein Magdeburger' (a man from Magdeburg); the Land, 'eine Sächsin' (a woman from Saxony), 'ein Thüringer' (a man from Thuringia); or from the area covered by mdr 'aus unserem Sendebereich' – from our reception area). Although the majority of the moderators and interviewers speak standard German, some with a hypercorrect accent bordering on the stilted, viewer participants and interviewees are almost entirely made up of dialect speakers of Saxonian and Thuringian. Since, in nationwide opinion polls about dialect preference, Saxonian invariably gets named as the least desirable dialect and accent, the visibility of so many dialect speakers on TV clearly must have an identity-supporting function, counteracting the general awareness of the stigma attached to their dialect in the rest of Germany. For example, after one young Saxonian contender for the Miss and Mr German beauty contest from Saxony did not get into the top three, a disappointed supporter, himself a dialect speaker, blamed this in part on his dialect:

> Ich glaub der von Sachsen, der hat'n bisschen Nachteile, weil ja über den sächsischen Dialekt immer 'n bisschen gelächelt wird.
> (I think the one from Saxony, he was a bit disadvantaged, since people always laugh a bit about the Saxonian dialect.)

Mdr, then, right across its programming, favours a strong regional address with deliberately identity-enforcing forms and contents. Below are some of the key elements of this emphasis:

- folk traditions (for example, folk music, handicraft, local costumes and modern derivatives, local recipes and traditionally prepared health products)
- historical traditions (famous historical towns and cities, as well as undiscovered gems; famous personalities who lived and worked there, e.g. Goethe in Ilmenau, museums both well-known or quaint, such as the Chess museum in Altenburg)
- geographical highlights (e.g. walking and trekking in beautiful countryside)
- cultural/artistic events and personalities (e.g. an interview/phone-in featuring two jazz musicians, Uschi Brüning [Leipzig-born] and Ernst-Ludwig Petrowski, who used to be well-known [and occasionally banned] in the GDR but totally unknown in the West
- news (mdr produces its own version of the national news as well as its own regional news, which again stresses the regional origin of politicians and other subjects of the news)
- sports (in the week 10–16 January 1998, the World Contest in Swimming took place in Perth, Australia. Mdr sent its own reporters to this event, and reported regularly about the successes of the German swimmers, many of whom come from the mdr regions or were born in an mdr region, or at least from a former GDR region. This fact is spelled out by reporters and interviewers whenever feasible.)

Mdr thus embeds the everyday concerns of the contemporary regions of the three new Länder in a long historical cultural tradition marked by a sense of pride in the geographical and cultural achievements emanating from them. Although the emphasis of the channel is less on the more recent past and more on the present-day and the longer historical perspective, it does not avoid airing difficulties experienced during the GDR times, or the successes and difficulties experienced since unification. In one programme, entitled *Mein lieber Mann* (literally 'My Dear Man', but figuratively 'Oh Dear!'), a Swiss moderator visits various places in the mdr region. In the programme of 15 January 1998 he talks to a woman who has had huge success with her invention of a hand-knitted new design of a traditional cap (a 'Zipfelmütze', which doubles up as a scarf). The programme stresses that this was 'an idea that changed her life', and the focus is on the woman's initiative to retrain after having lost her job:

> After the 'Wende' (literally: the turn around) one wasn't needed any more; so I made myself familiar with handicraft.
> (Nach der Wende war man halt nicht mehr gefragt. Ich hab mich dann mit dem Kunsthandwerk vertraut gemacht.)

Particularly interesting is the passage below, transcribed from another daily programme, the magazine series *Hier ab vier* ('Here from Four'), also from 15 January 1998, where the moderator asks his studio guests, two jazz musicians – he a saxophone player, she a jazz singer (mentioned on p.99) – how they fared during GDR times. The ensuing narrative, jointly told by the husband-and-wife duo, unfolds in a well-tuned conversational style marked by joining rather than interruption (Coates 1996). It is at once a story of absurd state repression, coupled with an account of the pluckiness and spirit of survival of individuals during these times. Below is a brief extract from the exchange with the moderator:

| | |
|---|---|
| *Moderator (M):* | How was it during the GDR times. Could you play whatever you wanted? |
| *Uschi Bruning (UB):* | Oh no, not at all. There was this regulation 60 to 40 or vice versa. |
| *Ernst-Ludwig Petrowski (EP):* | There was this term VE. |
| M: | And what did this refer to? |
| EP: | These are not the letters for VEB [= Volkseigener Betrieb – the acronym for people-owned e.g. state-owned factories and businesses], but for 'verbotene Einfuhr' [= forbidden import], and this could even happen if you were within the permitted region of 60 per cent East . |
| UB: | yes, 60 per cent |
| EP: | and 40 per cent West, but also if you added something forbidden into the Western mixture. |

UB: then you got a 'Berufsverbot' [you were forbidden to work in your profession]

EP: Exactly

UB: all of that existed

M: now this would be really interesting. Could you play from the cold something that was forbidden then and something that wasn't – just a little bit of it to give us an idea of the difference, or does one not hear this difference?

EP: We wouldn't hear it any more. They interpreted into the music some degrading, decadent or peace-endangering topic and that could be {whichever way}

UB {in the texts or even when you were only playing}{the saxophone}

EP: {Decisive} was the origin of {the piece}

M: {I see}

UB: {and then}

EP: {I remember} we had this piece, the *March of the River Kwai*. We had teamed up with a legendary Saxonian band, called Eberhard Weise, they always had three to four trombones, quite a bit dominated by the trombones, and with this piece we had a lot of success; and together with it we were banned, so in a way we went under while playing the *March of the River Kwai*.[1]

This brief extract also demonstrates the assumed shared knowledge between viewers and speakers: a central piece of information, the '60 to 40' regulation, for example, is never fully explained, since it is taken for granted that the viewers will know that it refers to the regulation that all live bands or discotheques in the GDR had to play a minimum of 60 per cent home-grown music, with only 40 per cent allowed to come from the West. This experiential bonding and mutual knowledge with mdr viewers who lived through the same period is further reinforced by the programme's invitation to viewers to phone in and ask questions of the guests. Callers to the programme on that day again provide links to a shared past, in their case from a more nostalgic rather than critical viewpoint: they either know the couple personally from old times, or reminisce about past concerts they heard the couple give, enquire about records from the past, etc., or enlist some geographical bonding devices – they come from the same region, or want to know when the couple will give concerts in the region. The device of the phone-in acts here like in many of the other mdr-produced programmes, as a strong confirmation of a regionally shared identity.

In summary – the strong regional traditions in Germany and its devolved federal structure give rise to thriving third channels with a distinct regional identity, in ways unknown to British viewers. This is true for both East and West Germany. In the case of the new third channels in the newly founded Länder, especially mdr, the programming and the style of address points to a deliberate policy of supporting the identities of its viewers, sometimes with proselytising fervour. The fact that these public-service regional channels, with their mixed diet of infotainment programming, enjoy more support than most of the available private channels (with the exception of the two major terrestrial channels, RTL and SAT 1), is a powerful argument for the retention of the dual system in Germany. How they will fare when digital technology floods the market with its 200-plus channels remains to be seen. But, at present, regional programming is seen by German viewers in their different regions as an attractive component of their daily television consumption.

# 6 Spatial relations and sociability

It is a commonplace that television, like radio, is a 'domestic' medium; often in saying this the implicit or explicit point of comparison is the cinema. The domesticity of TV is of considerable interest in the field of television audience studies, where researchers have, for example, been concerned to examine the ways in which familial relations impinge upon viewing and the use of domestic technologies (see, for example, Morley 1986; Silverstone 1992, 1994; Gray 1987).

In the old broadcasting order, the great achievement of radio and television was completely to have inserted itself in the 'taken for granted' daily lives of its listeners and viewers.

> ...programme output, as a whole and in all its parts, has a deeply settled, ordered, orderly, known and familiar character. Without it being so, how could we find our way about in it – as we quite clearly can and do – in a quite untroubled way. That we can do so – that the character of output is *essentially* unproblematic – is what needs accounting for.
>
> (Scannell 1996: 7–8)

What viewers and listeners took – and take – for granted is not just the availability of broadcasting as such, but the character of that output both in respect of its content and of its form. Viewers know what to expect and we rely upon its continued availability – knowing when we can catch the news, knowing that the soap life of Alma Baldwin in *Coronation Street* is to be continued, knowing how to synchronise personal schedules in relation to those of 'the box', assessing disasters, natural, political or social, according to their consequences in the TV world. Scannell's assertions about the intelligibility of broadcasting can be taken as a starting point, though we shall later want to question these claims from the standpoint of viewers whose experience of television takes in a full range of the new TV channels as well as the familiar ones that Scannell is concerned with.

It is indeed 'normal' and ordinary for viewers (as well as listeners) to have access, on TV's terms, to the world beyond the living room. That world can be as remote as outer space (when we taped Sky News all day on 24 March 1996, as reported in Chapter 2, one of the updated stories was brought to our screens live from the MIR space station) or as close as another, similar living room (the BSE story we discuss in Chapter 2 included footage from the home of a CJD sufferer, and from that of her grandmother). The accessibility of these places within the living room is as mundane as it is miraculous. A spatial vector connects the remote and the proximate, though the process can be construed both centrifugally (taking the viewer out and away) or centripetally (bringing the pictures to the home).

For the viewer, then, there are many 'theres' but only one 'here'. Scannell (1996) talks about the 'doubling' of space (and time) via broadcasting, and this is accurate if we are thinking about TV (or radio) at a single, given moment of its output. But it is also necessary to remember the multiple and constant *changes* of location to be found within the TV viewing experiences. Considered from the perspective of face-to-face interaction and the ontological security this is meant to guarantee, the multiplicity of 'theres' is both normal and aberrant. It is normal to the extent that 'there' is *somewhere else*, Other, a place to be spoken about, in the third person. It is less normal when 'there' is the place spoken from. In respect of participants, the grammar of English and of German makes a three-way distinction between source, destination and object in the communicative exchange. I speak, You listen, we talk about Him (see discussion in Chapter 3 of linguistic deixis). But, in pronominalising place, our grammar fudges the distinction between destination and object. 'Here' is always the place of the speaker. It can be the place of the speaker alone, with both participants allowing for the reciprocity of perspectives, appropriately construing each other's 'heres' as 'theres'. Or it can be the place of both speaker and listener, the spatial equivalent of the inclusive 'we'. In the latter case, 'there' is 'elsewhere', remote from both speaker and listener. In the former case, 'there' can likewise be 'elsewhere'. But it can also be the place of the listener, the spatial equivalent, not of he/she/it, but of *you*.

In this context, it is interesting to note the shifts that have recently taken place in German usage as a result of unification. Before 1989, the words 'hüben' (over here), 'drüben' (over there), 'rüberkommen' (to come across) and 'rüber-genhen' (to go over there) clearly marked for Germans in either of the two states the position of home and of the other. With unification, these demarca-tions no longer make sense, since Germany is now home for all, and the GDR (one of the 'drüben') has ceased to exist as a separate state. There are, of course, new terms for referring to the former area ('die neuen Bundesländer' – the new federal states – for example), and in some cases these old deictic reference points are still used to express what still seem to be different lifestyles and stan-dards of living. This is particularly noticeable when the topics under discussion highlight perceived differences between the East and the West. In a talk show on 17 April 1998 (*Sabine Christiansen*, ARD), almost a decade after unification, several participants used all the former deictic terms in their discussion of the recent success in the East and lack of success in the West of the newly founded political party PDS. But overall, the whole system, once so clear, is now on the move. Liebscher (1997) shows clearly how the gradual awareness of the new deictic relations gives rise to confusing and contradictory references in the language of talk-show hosts and guests between 1989 and 1993.

When TV is content to let 'here' be the place of the speaker (i.e. its own enunciating place) it relies upon the viewer's spatial competence to sit at home and see herself addressed from 'there'. Normal lexical semantics prevail. But even here difficulties arise, potentially, from the constant shifts and relocations of TV's 'here'. The other difficulty for broadcasting is the problem of a spatial equivalent for inclusive 'we' – viewers and broadcasters *in the same place*. The practical/semiotic solution to these difficulties is *virtual co-spatiality* – which can, but need not, take material form as 'the studio'. The studio is not, of course a place which is 'really' shared by source and destination of message, but strenuous attempts are made through camera work and linguistic deixis to construct it 'as if' it were so shared. The importance of the studio to broadcast discourse is a recurring theme in media research (see Scannell 1988, 1996; Livingstone and Lunt 1994):

> The radio or television studio is a public place into which people come to take part in a wide variety of political, cultural, educative or entertaining programmes. In all events, to enter the studio is to cross a threshold, to enter a social environment that creates its own occasions with their particular situational proprieties, discursive and performative rules and conventions. To enter this place is to assume, for the duration, a role and identity appropriate to the particular communicative event that is being staged: thus, interviewers and interviewees in political news interviews display an orientation to the character of the event by sustaining the part they are called upon to play ... The design of the setting – whether for a political interview, a chat show or a game show – structures the communicative character of the event and orients all participants (including studio audiences) to the roles and performances they are expected to produce for absent viewers and listeners. In short, those in the studio are committed to the communicative situation and their part in it.
>
> (Scannell 1996: 140)

Within a perspective such as this, the communicative characteristics of most importance are those which concern television's mode of address. The speech and talk of broadcasters and other participants is accorded priority, ahead of either visual analysis or attention to written linguistic form. Yet we should not forget the importance of the visual dimension in coding 'mode of address' – the pioneering work here is that of Horton and Wohl (1956).

## Television's spatial relations in the era of satellite and cable channels

So far, so traditional, in televisual terms. What then, if anything, changes in the world of satellite and cable broadcasting? There are three general points we can make about spatial relations in the multi-channel environment. One concerns the waning of channel loyalty; one concerns the abandonment of vocalised continuity announcements; and one concerns the extent of studio-based production.

In a multi-channel world, channel changing is more common and channel loyalty is on the wane. By frequent channel changing, the viewer can override whatever devices the channel uses to offer the viewer a spatiotemporally grounded experience. Specifically, if, as has been suggested, continuity announcements function in 'traditional' television to locate viewers in a 'home base' before and after their journeys out to the wider world, then viewing strategies which avoid this material may lose that sense of grounding, to be 'set free' across locations which bear no particular relation either to one another or to a starting point.

Within channels, the abandonment of *vocalised* continuity announcements has become very common on terrestrial as well as satellite and cable channels. Channels which still make use of continuity material tend increasingly to favour graphic mode display. The loss of vocalisation is a small but significant loss of humanity, a depersonalisation of the discourse which has a concomitant de-spatialisation since, if no one is speaking, they do not need a space to speak from. This observation can be related to the point, often repeated by postmodernists, that culture in modernity has become a matter of surfaces. A screen which shows, with pictures and written text, a sequence of forthcoming programmes is significantly flatter, more 'depthless' than one in which a voice, even from an out-of-sight speaker, talks to viewers about what is to come. Some channels have recently reintroduced the studio announcer on camera, though often in significantly different forms from their 1950s and 1960s predecessors. In one such case, the announcer sits with headphones on, as if in a radio studio, she does not face the camera, or a co-present interlocutor, and her comments may consist of tongue-in-cheek commentary on programmes seen or to come. It would be an exaggeration to describe her role as a parody of the earlier continuity announcers (Suzie Blake offers such a parody in the Victoria Wood shows of the 1980s and early 1990s) – the stylistic coding is too subtle for that – but there is certainly something of an oblique, quotative relation to this convention.

There is a notable amount of studio-based production in the schedules of the late 1990s. Studio production here is different from set-based production, where set-based production refers to the use, in drama, of spaces constructed to represent particular kinds of social location. Studios are undisguised locations for the presentation of television, and studio-based production is cheaper than either set-based production or location-based production. This tendency thus speaks to the need in the new broadcasting order for quantities of low-cost programming to fill the schedules.

In order to go beyond these general points, it is necessary to focus upon particular channels to see how they fit within this context, and the particular forms they have developed in attempting to construct a social relationship with the audience.

## QVC: *spatial solipsis*

The multi-channel environment does not necessarily mean the end of mixed-programming channels, such as the UK's BBC 1 and ITV or Germany's ARD and ZDF. But it does mean the growth of dedicated channels, including some which can be seen as pandering (if that is not too pejorative a term) to the solipsistic viewer. A case in point is the European Shopping Channel, QVC (Quality, Value, Convenience). QVC is studio-based production, root and branch. The quality it has which is shared by no other channel that we have encountered is that it broadcasts all day, every day, from the *same* studio. This is a slight exaggeration (the studio has one space which is more kitchen-like for displaying kitchenware) the regular space, however, has the feeling of a living room. There are occasional taped 'location' segments, e.g. for demonstrating gardenware. Within that context, the talk-to-camera (to the viewer) is remorse-less, and strongly deictic, since items have to be described and demonstrated in great detail. The programme barely talks of things, people, processes outside of the studio; even less does it show things outside of the studio – though indi-vidual viewers do 'call in' and conduct telephone calls with programme hosts for the benefit of other viewers at home. And it is possible to watch this without interruption through its hourly 'programmes' or sections. If it is solipsistic to watch endless television and not to talk to other human beings, as Peter Sellers does in the film *Being There*, then to watch QVC is to take this solipsism to an extreme. It is to be hoped that no one watches QVC in this way. Before the cable era, no such possibility existed.

In the development of QVC we see a channel which has deliberately narrowed its spatial horizons, almost to vanishing point. It is not the only channel in the new configuration to have adopted this strategy. The same kind of concentration is to be found on the Parliament Channel, though here of course spatial constancy derives from the loyalty of the channel, not to a studio, but to a single location – Westminster Palace – and within the Palace to one of three 'sets': the Chamber of the House of Commons; the Chamber of the House of Lords; and the Select Committee room. (There may in reality be more than one Select Committee room, but in television terms they are equivalent and hence may be thought of as a single space.) Of these three, it is the first which gets the most coverage, unsurprisingly. Programming on the Parliament Channel is austere, minimal, respectful, formal. It is almost completely lacking in voices (oral or visual) from outside the diegesis of the proceedings: the inter-pretative work, such as it is, is managed via camera work. The *mise-en-scène* is 'given' by the nature of the location itself. The Parliament Channel can be seen as a realisation of the potential of television in one respect, envisaged at the beginning of the industry but never developed, owing to the shortage of frequencies until recent times. It speaks to the desire for completeness, for exhaustive coverage that misses nothing because the cameras remain in place, and transmitting, *all the time*. Of course, completeness is a chimera – it cannot be achieved. Yet, in Parliamentary debate, this desire found a pre-existing mode of discourse which was already in a sense 'camera-ready': fit to indulge the myth of exhaustive coverage, as well as being serious enough to be worthy of the camera's attentions upon this extraordinary basis.

QVC is available across Europe as one of the BSkyB satellite channels, but its target audience is evidently the population of the UK and Ireland. The presenters speak (southern) English and the principal telephone number for prospective purchasers is a UK 0800 number. As suggested above, it is a channel which perturbs the pattern of traditional TV broadcasting, which has encouraged viewers to expect images from a variety of locations across an extended period of viewing. These locations include fictional ones, real ones given fictional identities, and real ones with real identities (within both fictional and non-fictional diegeses). Locations also include *studios*: points of departure for ventures out into the wider world, and/or locations 'shared' by presenters and their audiences. But in the world of QVC the studio is (almost) all there is (see Richardson 1997 for a fuller analysis of QVC discourse). Thus, the channel's important characteristics for the purposes of the present analysis are those through which this shared space is constructed – all for the sake of its commercial project. These characteristics are, first, the audiovisual construction of the studio space, with particular attention to spatial deixis and demonstrative reference; second, the integration of topographical familiarity with interpersonal familiarity; and, third, the function of the telephone call between presenters and their customer-viewers.

## The audiovisual construction of studio space

As mentioned above, QVC's parasocial relations with its audience are sustained across a constant 24-hour broadcasting cycle, and these relations include an orientation towards the studio space within which the sales talk takes place. Use of a studio in which a shared space for viewer and presenter can be discursively constructed is not unique to QVC – far from it. Studio production goes right back to the origins of sound broadcasting. What is less common, or possibly unique, is the *constancy* of QVC's spatial arrangements, dictated in large measure by economic considerations, but not without potential consequences for the loyal viewer's experience. Spatial continuity is not absolute (i.e. it is not the case that all talk and action takes place within exactly the same three 'walls' from the same side). But there is a very small range of 'sets' between with the presentations alternate; within each hour of broadcasting the set remains the same; very few sequences take place away from these sets (some live, some prerecorded in the style of terrestrial channel commercials); the range of viewing angles is the same whatever set is selected, and this includes close-ups so tight as to exclude any sense of a three-dimensional background. Flat-colour backgrounds are very common in such shots, an effect achieved naturalistically by judicious prearrangement of the *mise en scène* rather than by technological manipulation.

*The visual semiotics of QVC space*

Within the context of the pro-filmic space – the 'actual' set/studio as discussed above – it is necessary to say something about the way this space is rendered for communicative purposes, and especially upon the mixture of two-dimensional and three-dimensional spatial properties which characterise it.

The screen image normally encountered when tuning in to QVC is the result of combining a two-dimensional graphic screen with a three-dimensional photographic screen. The former overlays and partially masks the latter, excluding about a third of the latter from view. Part of this mask is on the left-hand side of the full screen; part is along the bottom. The two-dimensional screen space is used for displaying channel, programme and product information, including the telephone number which prospective viewers are meant to call should they decide to make a purchase.

The photographic screen space is naturalistically three-dimensional, though the limits of vision are set by the 'walls' of the set and the camera positions. As already mentioned, close-up shots of the products, the objects of desire, are heavily used as part of this promotional discourse. These shots reduce the effect of spatial depth even further. Foreshortening effects are much reduced; backgrounds are simplified down to very basic properties of colour and form so they can no longer be 'read' as the objects they are, and appear to be in more distant shots (doors, walls, cloths, tables, display stands ...). Only effects of light and shade evoke three-dimensionality, along with (sometimes) camera movement (from tight to extreme close-up) or the rotation of the item on its 'platform'. At such moments all items are the same, spatially speaking, for whatever their actual size in centimetre and metres, they occupy the same screen area, and are displayed at the size of the viewer's monitor at home. There are no scalar points of reference such as human hands to help viewers construe the 'true' size of the displayed item. These display shots always occur at the same point in the presentation – right at the end, just before the talk moves on to the next item in the collection (though they can also occur, in a less marked way, at other points). During these marked display moments, the talk ceases and music takes its place in the foreground of the audio track.

There are other kinds of close-up shot, however, which do involve attempts at a visual discourse of size. This involves the use of the presenter's body and especially of her hands; where more precision is required, it will also involve the use of an old-fashioned wooden school ruler.

*The verbal semiotics of QVC space*

The verbal discourse which QVC presenters engage in only makes sense within the visual and contextual parameters discussed above. Below we have transcribed a representative extract from the show (Table 4), originally broadcast live on 15 April 1997 (slightly edited for fluency).

'We' in this discourse refers to the QVC team, a somewhat mystified usage,

*Table 4* Sales monologue on QVC

| | |
|---|---|
| Medium shot of Julia Roberts, presenter, in the studio. | Welcome to this hour of jewellery. We've got some really pretty jewellery to look at, including our Today's Special Value. It sold very well earlier on when I showed it you at two, so if you weren't watching at two, where were you? Do take advantage of the very special price. It's absolutely lovely this necklace. It looks very, very |
| Extreme close-up of JR's neck, displaying necklace. JR hands in shot from time to time. | luxurious. It's six-two-oh, one-six-seven, eighteen inches in length. It's a nice broad thickness and a really good weight. One or two people earlier on were looking at this and thinking 'that never weighs nine point one grammes'. Well it does weigh nine point one grammes. Basically, because you've got such a close link there. There are no holes, there's no gaps, it's just a strand of gold. And |
| Medium shot JR. | quite a thick strand of gold as well there, around the neckline. That's what gives it the weight. Also, I'm just moving my body round so you can see the lights as they dance along that bevelled |
| ECU display shot (a different bracelet of the same kind). | edge there. That's an edge that's sharp if you see what I mean, but not sharp to the touch, obviously. And that's why the light catches there and really sparkles and twinkles. I know that some of you were actually ordering when I was wearing this in the three hour |
| ECU JR neck. | that I did with Alison, lots of you were ringing in and asking what it was. So if you like the look of it then do give us a call now, it's a very, very good price. Normally we say red box price is about ten pounds per gramme of gold, so you'd be looking at about ninety- |
| ECU on the links of the display bracelet. | one pounds normally in a red box price. So how we've got this Italian made necklace for just seventy-one pounds ninety-seven. I wouldn't even dare go through it with our jewellery-buying department. But they've done it somehow. Maybe it's the quantity |
| ECU display shot. | they've bought, obviously when it's a Today's Special Value they have to buy more. So it could be something to do with the quantity they've ordered. But it is a very special necklace, something you can wear casually with a nice casual denim skirt, T-shirt even, a smartish T-shirt, or you could definitely wear it with a little off-the-shoulder number, or put it in the neckline of That Black Dress that you've got, it really is very, very versatile. Six-two-oh, one-six-seven. If you've always wanted a superplex necklace and you've seen the ones that are less well made and they're actually quite sharp among them, this not like that. I actually ran the sleeve of my jacket over this earlier, which is silk, and it didn't catch at all, it's completely smooth, it's beautiful. Very, very nicely made. Seventy-one pounds and ninety-seven pence, Today's Special Value price. Six-two-oh, one-six-seven. That's the close-up shot that shows you how smooth it is. Even *Lavers* isn't that smooth. Even *Lavers* is not that smooth, I promise you (*laughing*). Seventy-one pounds and ninety-seven pence is Today's Special Value |

unclear in its specificity. 'You' is sometimes singular: 'If you weren't watching at two, where were you;?' sometimes plural: 'I know that some of you were actually ordering when I was wearing this in the three hour'; sometimes ambiguous; and sometimes a kind of dummy subject: 'Basically, because you've got such a close link there'. The presenter can see what the viewer sees, thanks to a monitor in the studio, but out of the camera's line of vision. As in other TV productions, this studio monitor helps the presenter adjust her positioning, posture, gaze, etc. so as to be read in the appropriate way by the viewers; unlike most TV, however, the presenter actually talks about her own adaptive conduct: 'I'm just moving my body round so you can see the lights … ' The camera angle changes not at all, but the upper torso indeed is seen to move, and light reflects from different positions on the necklace as it does so. This is a demonstrative semiotics which is simultaneously visual (body movement) and verbal (linguistic self-description, with deictic reference to the here-and-now); more commonly such demonstrative semiotics involves the use of the *hands* to hold, touch and point, but the whole body can be recruited to the task, and this is one of the reasons why the presenter is wearing the necklace in the first place.

Notice also the references here to 'the red box price': a concept unique to the discourse of QVC, and in fact tied in with the features of the screen space that we described earlier. The graphic screen which partially masks the photographic one contains different types of product information: reference number, name, price and salient characteristics. The background colour on which this information is displayed is blue. Occasionally, a little more of the photographic screen is obscured by text on a *red* background: this is the 'red box', and what it displays is a third price: not the recommended retail price, not the QVC price, but the Special Value price, a 'discount' offer, applied to selected items within each hour. For this particular item, in the verbal text a fourth price is mentioned: not the recommended retail price, not the QVC price, but the price which QVC ought to set as its Special Value price on the principle that 'good value' gold should cost about ten pounds per gramme. And the actual Special Value price is lower even than that! Here we see the value of spatial properties of the visual image being used not just to anchor viewers' understanding in the immediate shared viewing experience, but to do so in a way that implicates viewers in an ongoing familiarity with the conventions of the channel and of its categories for regulating price and value. Constructing this familiarity with the channel is another requirement of the presentational task: it can also be seen in the way this presenter refers to previous events in the day's broadcasting, quite as if the viewer has watched it all, or else is in trouble for not watching: 'It sold very well earlier on when I showed it you at two, so if you weren't watching at two, where were you?' It can also be seen in the ways that presenters of different sections talk to, and talk about, one another: 'Even Lavers isn't that smooth' – a reference to Paul Lavers, who presented the previous hour and who would appear to be still within the studio environment, in off-screen space with the camera crew and the director, when Julia Roberts jokes about him.

### Dislocation and fragmentation

The importance attached to cultural fragmentation and dislocation is all the greater if the integrative function of TV in its 'earlier' mode of existence is stressed, as Scannell (1988) does, and also Peter Dahlgren in the following formulation:

> one of television's definitive features is its central position in our semiotic environment. This centrality can be understood in terms of quantity – the sheer volume of output is staggering – but also in terms of its cultural

legitimacy. Television functions as a purveyor of shared frames of reference: it serves as a producer/reproducer of implicit sociocultural common sense. This view, however, must confront the modifying fact of the large number of channels available, many of them specialised genre channels: in a situation where television is decentralising, the collective common sense may be on its way to becoming plural and fragmented, rather than unitary.

(Dahlgren 1995: 40)

A different kind of 'spin' is placed upon the experience of dislocation and fragmentation within postmodernist accounts of contemporary sensibilities and identities – one which is more celebratory of the new tendencies for their subversive potential. In this logic, if the unitary is repressive, the fragmenting must be liberatory.

In one form of postmodernism, the emphasis is on the nature and experience of the new spatiality produced by international communications and image networks. This is a global space of image, screen and surface, where real and imaginary orders become fused. The experience of this decentred hyperspace, this space of absolute proximity and instantaneity, may be one of disorientation, dislocation and fragmentation, or, alternatively, it is possible to 'make a virtue of the capacity to negotiate disorder', to accept disorientation and fragmentation as a state of authenticity.

(Rustin 1989: 121, from Morley and Robins 1995: 74)

Within this perspective, questions of communicative form become very important, as for instance in the debate regarding the communicative innovations of the MTV channel and their implications for postmodern youth sensibility (see Chapter 1).[1] The relevant kind of formal analysis here refers to moves across levels and planes of textual construction in the flow of output, as well as with unit-level analysis, with especial attention to the visual dimensions of meaning.

The formal features which are held to underpin the televisually mediated experience of 'dislocation' come under the headings of intertextuality (with an attitude), bricolage/eclecticism and unguided transitions between different and incommensurate viewing positions (see Collins 1992, whose analysis is concerned principally with the popular and critically acclaimed *Twin Peaks*). These textual properties are to be found at all levels (sequences, programmes and channels) as well as within the viewing experience of individuals equipped with remote control devices and VHS machines. Below, we give some attention to the kind of dislocation effect which has to do with spatial positioning. But it is appropriate initially to give some thought to the concept of dislocation itself in relation to the terms upon which television offers viewers an experience which makes sense. 'Dislocation', then, at the maximal level, suggests an experience in which there is no relation of sense between one component and another which follows it in time. If this is the experience we get when using the remote control device to move from one channel to another, chosen arbitrarily, then the dislocation effect is self-inflicted; furthermore, there is no principled difference between this order of 'dislocation' and the experience of shifting attention between any communicative frame and another, close enough to be in competition with it. There is nothing novel about the experience of shifting attention between a TV show and a conversation on an unrelated topic.

Dislocation does not become a characteristic feature of the new communicative order until such 'shifting' practices become the norm and outweigh in their extent and significance the practice of continuous viewing. Jensen's (1995) evidence suggests that, as yet, this is very far from being the case. An alternative approach would be to think of dislocation in relation to the principle of *connected sense* in TV viewing and to explore the extent to which that principle is now flouted in contexts where it has formerly operated – which is to say within the context of continuous viewing of a single channel. But here we must bear in mind the ways in which different kinds of 'discontinuity' have already been naturalised by TV viewers. Six-spot advertisements within a commercial break do not set out to make sequential or collective sense. They may permit thematic and formal connections to be made by their viewers, but *authorial* responsibility for such connections is denied. Before such discontinuities are naturalised, the possibility of dislocation effects exists: afterwards, viewers' knowledge of the medium allows them to recognise and respond to the boundary markers which constitute the structural devices of the medium. There are, of course, different cultural conventions for doing this. British television favours formal boundary markers at the end of each commercial break, just like the German public-service channels do. Most German commercial channels on the other hand mark the beginning of a commercial break with a formal device but, at the end, simply slide back to the interrupted programme with no further marking.

If dislocation effects are relative to a particular state of naturalised conventions for incorporating variety within a single programme or channel, and if those connections change, then presumably the forms and devices which realise dislocation also change.

The potential for producing non-sense takes place within an understanding of broadcasting and audiovisual conventions offering a number of options which can be used to restore lost coherence. Ultimately, it is the coherence of the world, not of the text, which must be protected, 'saved' by the viewers' sense-making practices. If the text fails to continue, it may indeed lack coherence for the viewer, but her world is still normal on the assumption that there has been a break in transmission. Bearing this in mind, it seems likely that individuals' ability to protect the phenomenological coherence of their world may prove to be rather robust, and that the destruction of ontological security through forms of programming with no respect for laws of object-constancy, reciprocity of perspectives, or sequential/causal event structures is very unlikely. In the first place, a vast quantity of programming does in fact respect coherence. The conventions of TV naturalism in drama productions, for example, are still very strong whether the setting is outer space (*Red Dwarf*), a modern leisure centre (*Brittas Empire*), or the England of 1818 (*Pride and Prejudice*). Dislocation effects within programmes are uncommon (*Twin Peaks* is a special case, not a typical one); dislocation effects between programmes (or between programmes and commercials/promotional texts, or between either of these and continuity sequences), are rendered ineffective through familiar boundary-maintaining devices; and dislocation effects which arise from the use of the remote-control device are outside the control of the broadcasters.

Having said all this, it must be acknowledged that the multi-channel environment does offer more scope for dislocation effects than the world of traditional TV broadcasting in Europe. It is a mistake to equate dislocation effects only with the production of absolute non-sense in the flow of programming. More specific, more localised kinds of disrupted expectations should be the focus of our attention. If location in space is a condition for coherence, what (if anything) on the new channels undercuts that condition? What follows is an anecdote, relevant to that question.

By tradition, the discourse between programme segments is understood to be live (even if it is not) and to emanate from the channel's 'home base' (even if there is no studio to be seen). Another emergent convention, related to this, is the convention that, while programmes may be out of time and out of place (i.e. repeated, after their original, ur-broadcast, and not in the original country which produced them), commercials are for us, here and now. Commercials are not live, and they are repeated (often), but they are about products, services and companies operating now, and available in the viewer's country. Any other assumption (e.g. that we Britons are watching commercials made for Australians, Germans, Brazilians) denies the sense of commercial discourse (Why advertise things that are not on sale to the people watching?) as well as the logic of commercial television (Why give airtime to advertisers with nothing to gain from reaching your audience?). In this sense, commercials play their part in binding the broadcaster/advertiser and the viewer into a shared time and place – a shared country and a shared year. The temporal horizons are fuzzier than the spatial ones.

So, what might be the effect of the public-service announcement/ commercial broadcast during 1997 to cable/satellite viewers by the organisation promoting the desirability of patenting new inventions? The facts are these.

This 'commercial' is broadcast during a regular commercial break – a British phase even on channels dedicated to US repeats. The 'Britishness' of the commercial break has been undermined on several channels, to this extent – that an American voice-over no longer seems unusual, and does not damage the assumption that the broadcast is still for the benefit of its current British viewers. The patent commercial uses an American voice-over. It is broadcast between the two halves of *Frasier*, a popular and fairly recent US sitcom. The advert's pitch is this: 'Be famous like Alexander Graham Bell, not forgotten like Elisha Grey' – two claimants for the title of the inventor of the telephone, only one of whom patented the invention (both Americans). And the commercial provides viewers with a telephone number to call – an 0800 number for which no charge is made to the caller in the UK.

This example could be put to the test of audience research, but the way we hear it there is a problem. Is it really incontrovertibly 'for us' in the way that all other commercials undoubtedly are? The location of the ad, during an episode of *Frasier*, the US accent, and the Americans it refers to, constitute a set of signals which *could* signify not-now, not-here television, like the programme itself. The 0800 telephone number, and the categorisation of the ad as part of the commercial break, ground it in British contemporaneity. In the end, these signals are the ones that matter, and the Britishness of the commercial is confirmed, at least for us. But, if viewers have to think about it to come to this conclusion, then something has happened that hasn't traditionally happened for British viewers: the question has been raised and has foregrounded the spatiotemporal status of commercials. This is no defamiliarisation *device*, but a (potential) moment of uncertainty which stands out in relief against the still more usual certainty which has traditionally prevailed.

# Part III

# Trash and quality

Much of the debate about the future of TV broadcasting is conducted in terms of fears and hopes for the future, with the present (or the recent past) as a yardstick by which to evaluate that future. 'Quality' is the key word here. For Part III we have extrapolated two tendencies in current programming to stand for two distinct projections, one pessimistic and one optimistic. The pessimistic projection sees ever more cheap programming of dubious quality. The optimistic projection sees an increase of choice and a continuing market for high-quality production.

But 'quality' is a notoriously under-defined term in relation to broadcast output (see Brunsdon 1990; Corner *et al.* 1993; Corner 1997). Fears for low-quality broadcasting in the future rely upon an economic argument: that the programming of the future will be worse than that of the past because less money will be spent on it (advertising revenue will be spread more thinly over the commercial channels; public-service channels will lose audiences and will be able to command less money from the public exchequer). But money is only part of the story. Debates about cultural value in contemporary European society are profoundly shaped by legacies of social-class hierarchy, as well as the special pleading of interested parties, including media entrepreneurs. As a result, it is not at all the case that there are known forms of programming which are accepted without dispute as 'good' or 'bad'. Celebratory discourses often invite us to consider previously overlooked merits in programmes normally regarded as banal or as pernicious. 'Popularity' can be used in approval of programmes without reference to specific textual characteristics; or as a phenomenon to be *explained* in terms of the pleasures of the texts. To explain something is not necessarily to approve it – explanations propose both negative and positive views of media power as well as negative and positive views of human susceptibilities. For a while it seemed (wrongly in our judgement) that all programming was 'good' provided that the audience was 'active'.

The existing confusions and cross-talk don't provide an easy context from which to construct accounts of TV quality that can be projected into the future. However, it is possible to draw a picture of the current cultural dispensation which seems plausible enough to provide a rationale for the two case studies in

Part III – one on US talk shows as broadcast in Europe, and one on the Franco-German culture channel called ARTE.

The legacy of social class in the cultural sphere is a taste hierarchy that is now widely seen as superseded, although it still makes itself felt in the late twentieth century. The products of that hierarchy at the upper level persist as artefacts and as performances, to the extent that they can still command support either through the marketplace or in other ways. The values of that hierarchy can still operate as a discourse for the evaluation of cultural production more generally, but only as one voice within a cacophony. The world of television is no longer, if it ever was, under the domination of that value system. Television's world is necessarily more relativistic, and on those terms it certainly makes room for the old 'high culture' as a well-defined but minority market. Yet this relativism is awkward: different-but-equal taste values intersect deeply with ethical ones, and these are much harder to relativise.

One possibility for the future is that 'niche marketing' will take the place of the kind of broadcasting intended for the mass national audience. Another possibility is that the desire to maximise audiences will become more desperate, and more programming appealing to the 'lowest common denominator' of popular taste will be made. This will also include extensive use of repeats. But even programmes which were innovative and challenging on first screening can become boring with repetition and fill the airtime at the expense of more contemporary innovative programming. Risk taking becomes an expensive luxury.

The usual context for discussion here relates either to the quality of broadcast journalism or, more commonly still, to TV drama. Fears for the moral well-being of children are especially important in these arguments. We do not intend to follow these familiar paths. Instead, we want to use the 'quality' context to discuss two phenomena in the new European broadcasting regime: American talk shows and the channel known as ARTE. The former is interesting as a type of programming from the 'debased' end of the scale; and the latter, as a channel dedicated to 'high culture' and its values.

In English-language broadcasting, US talk shows are now extensively used to fill airtime. These shows have been around in the United States for quite some time, attracting opprobrium there, but also viewing figures healthy enough to ensure their continuation. In Britain (and in Germany) they have inspired imitations which, holding back from some of those shows' excesses, fail to attract the same degree of calumny (*Vanessa*, *The Time*, *The Place* and *Kilroy* in the UK; *Vera am Mittag*, *Sonja*, *Bärbel Schäfer*, *Ilona Christen*, *Hans Meiser* and *Fliege* in Germany – all going out in the afternoon hours).[1] But English-language channels in Europe also re-broadcast US originals – *Sally Jessy Raphael*, *Rolonda*, *Ricki Lake*, *Geraldo* – and thus represent a potential 'cause for concern' in the European context. The nature of the anxiety can be compared with the anxiety provoked by pornographic broadcasting. This anxiety is well developed: pornography is undoubtedly one of the driving forces behind the growth of the market for satellite services. And pornographic broadcasting is a matter for national public policy. Satellite/cable pornography is only available on encrypted and subscription channels.

On the other hand (at the other extreme?), however, the 'niche-market' opportunities offered by the new channels may provide optimism for viewers whose tastes run to conventionally defined 'high culture'. English-speaking viewers have the Performance Channel as part of the basic multi-channel package (both on satellite and cable) without paying extra. Also available across from the continental mainland is the State-sponsored channel ARTE, a joint venture between the French and German governments, and an extension into satellite broadcasting of the public-service principles which have been the foundations of both of these national broadcasting systems. It is the discourse of the latter we wish to analyse in Chapter 8. These two case studies, then, of talk shows and of ARTE, will allow us to explore issues of 'quality' in television with particular reference to satellite and cable broadcasting in the early years of television's transformation.

If television in the future continues to offer both ARTE and an extensive supply of American talk shows, then it could be said that viewers of very different cultural preferences will find themselves catered for; a highly desirable outcome, which should certainly not leave us mourning for the golden age of channel scarcity. A less complacent view is that the scarcity of channels encouraged viewers to watch material that they would not necessarily have chosen for themselves. This exposure contributed not only to social cohesion, with very different people watching and talking about the same programmes, but also permitted television to fulfil its (public-service) obligations to inform and educate as well as to entertain.

In relation to this argument, it is not so much the existence of the talk shows and the culture channel which is the issue, but the extent to which programming of one kind or of the other kind monopolises the leisure time of the viewers. A viewer who fills her leisure time with *Jerry Springer* and *Sally Jessy Raphael* is likely to be a very different kind of consumer from the one whose channel of choice is ARTE. The problem for ARTE in the future will be in deciding whether it can treat its viewers as individuals who are as familiar with soap operas and talk shows as they are with the history of European civilisation.

# 7  Bad television?

The perspective in which modern culture is 'bad culture' can be traced back to the cultural pessimism of the Frankfurt School; and in Britain it is associated with the legacy of Matthew Arnold, F.R. Leavis and (of course) Richard Hoggart. The equation of television with 'bad culture' is almost as old as the medium itself. Postman (1985) offers a widely cited recent version. In academic circles, such cultural pessimism is now unfashionable, and writers such as Fiske (1987), Gripsrud (1995) and Ang (1985) have begun to develop ways of approaching the study of television which recognise and value the pleasures they offer to their audiences, and the contribution audiences make in appropriating television texts to their own ends.

A related development in scholarly work was the re-entry of the term 'quality' into the vocabulary of British academic discourse on the mass media in general and television in particular, at about the time when the government was exploring alternative ways of funding the BBC, as well as deregulating and reregulating commercial broadcasting. It became much more necessary than ever before for academics with an interest in the future of broadcasting to become involved in discussions of what was, and what was not, worth defending in the 'old' ways of doing things, and the extent to which there was a role for the State as well as the market in deciding what would be available on screen in the future. We have already mentioned the anxiety provoked by the expanded possibilities offered by cable and satellite delivery systems as to the diminution of 'quality' in the new era. Satellite TV is exposing European viewers to much more 'trash TV' than before. Talk shows, prima facie, fall into this category. But Performance and ARTE provide a television retreat from such trash for those whose tastes run to 'high culture'. The former is true to its name in serving as a 'relay' mechanism rather than as a medium in its own right for the transmission of cultural performances: opera, classical music, ballet, etc. The latter is located more in the world of 'arts discourse' around these (and other) tastes such as might be associated with 'arts' programmes on the terrestrial channels (*The Late Show* and the *South Bank Show* in Britain; *Kulturreport* and *Aspekte* in Germany), as well as the discourses of rationality and knowledge.

## Bad television: the problem of judgement

To discuss the new talk shows in relation to the quality issue is to invoke a perspective upon TV as 'bad culture' (see Corner 1995), either in general or with respect to particular genres or particular programmes. The focus therefore is upon what would count as 'trash', and why, in any broadcasting regime. 'Trash', here, is the obverse of quality, not because it is not-good (the sense in which, say, an episode of *Coronation Street* would be said to have less aesthetic quality, as drama, than a stage production of *Macbeth*), but because it is *bad* (the sense in which, hypothetically, pornography is bad because it helps develop woman-hating qualities in its viewers). 'Trash' is a judgemental term and one which must be justified, in moral/aesthetic terms – ultimately within a logic of effects. This does not preclude the ironic appropriation of the term 'trash' in work which seeks to rehabilitate/celebrate television productions which could be all unthinkingly dismissed as rubbish without sufficient thought for the plea-sures and satisfactions they offer to their viewers. There has been a recent attempt to re-evaluate the significance of televised wrestling in these terms (see Bachmair and Kress 1996). We concur with the view that scholarly research in this area requires a sociological perspective upon the nature of these pleasures and satisfactions. To that extent, we are in accord with Hunter and Kaye (1997):

> The most vibrant current research is committed to taking audiences and their pleasures seriously. Going beyond either castigating them for poor taste or worrying obsessively about the effects of popular culture, it asks instead what real, unruly, socially situated readers and viewers *do* with texts. Audiences are no longer envisaged as passive consumers, but as active producers of popular culture.
>
> (Hunter and Kaye 1997: 1)

And yet there is a problem with this perspective, one which we seek to avoid in the present volume. Hunter and Kaye are residually ambivalent regarding the problem of judgement. Thus, as they formulate it, although it is not OK to judge these audiences and their pleasures negatively, to castigate them for poor taste, it is OK to judge them positively, for being so 'active' in the production of popular culture. Beneath this ambivalence, we suggest, there is a confusion of *process* and *content*. The process of interpretation can be construed as active or passive. (In 'active audience' arguments, the activeness of interpretation is sometimes construed as *necessary*, intrinsic to the process, so that only a profound misunderstanding of what interpretation means could see viewers/ listeners/readers as 'passive'. Alternatively, 'active' interpretation is good/ positive/desirable, as against bad/negative/undesirable 'passive' interpretation. Sometimes it is unclear which of these two positions is being proposed.) The *result* of (active) interpretation is another matter. Taking this seriously, as Hunter and Kaye advocate, is important, and there is no reason in principle why seriousness should exclude evaluative/ethical considerations. Serious attention to audience pleasures must include a licence to judge them, for good or for ill, within value frameworks (feminist, neo-liberal, communitarian, Marxist, libertarian, etc.) explicit enough to allow for reasoned debate. In short, to follow this approach is to shift from the evaluation of *texts* (programmes) to the evaluation of *interpretations, responses, effects* and *uses*, rather than to abandon evaluation altogether.[1] This will still permit evaluation of the *textual strategies* of programmes as likely to provoke particular kinds of interpretation, response, etc. Evaluation can even take account of viewers' autonomy from textual determination. Gripsrud (1995) demonstrates what appears to be a full circle of movement from text to audience and back to text again, showing that the possibility of reading *Dynasty* 'subversively' became incorporated into the textual strategies of the programme itself.

Viewers' 'activeness' is to be valued, of course, if what we want to say is that viewers are not automatically and inevitably trapped within the ideological perspective of the texts they encounter. But to say that is to be positive about the *process* of interpretation, not about the *content*. The result of exercising interpretative creativity can be ideologically conservative/reactionary in substance as well as progressive/resistant. This was indeed what Martin Barker (1997) discovered with one of his informants in an audience research study concerned with the film *Judge Dredd*. The informant was a self-styled fascist:

> He *is* influenced by Judge Dredd, there is no reason to deny him this. And that influence does reinforce a tendency, which we may as well call 'fascist', towards believing in some total police state. But what shows in his discourse is a search for an ethical ideal which has found some cultural materials which, precisely because of their real textual characteristics, he can use as a resource. That is how real thinking goes .... Smith is poised between two different ideological accounts of the world: an authoritarian/ fascist approach; and a socialist rejoinder. Given his life circumstances, a settled choice might never be made – I can't know. But if ever I were to meet my respondent, my goal would be to argue with *him* about visions of a future world, not to cleanse him of some wayward media influence.
>
> (M. Barker 1997: 28–9)

This is not the place to enter into detailed argument with Barker regarding media effects in general. The relevance of Barker's perspective in the present context is the way that it underlines our own concern to separate the process of interpretation (very much 'active' in the case of this respondent – Barker constructs him, not the text, as the master in this communicative relationship) from the result (fascist) as well as Barker's opposition to those fascist values in his respondent rather than 'in the text'.

However, a critique of audiences and their values does not invalidate or render irrelevant the critique of texts (and it begs the question of how audiences came to hold those values in the first place). It should, and it does, make us circumspect in our claims about particular texts and their effects. Perhaps the fascist meanings of *Judge Dredd* are just too obvious for Barker to concern himself with. The same cannot be said in relation to the value discourse of the talk shows, which have generated public dispute as to the precise character of their ethics.

## Schedule and genre – characterising the new talk shows

In the US context the talk shows we are concerned with here are known as the 'daytime' talk shows, to distinguish them from the ones made for and broadcast during the evenings. The difference is important, since the latter are for the most part celebrity talk shows – *The Tonight Show, The Late Show* – whose hosts are also celebrities (Jay Leno, David Letterman) because of the profile of their shows in the schedules. Europe also has its share of celebrity talk shows – in Britain, the old 'armchair'/'sofa' format associated with Michael Parkinson, Michael Aspel, Terry Wogan, Des O'Connor has recently been supplemented (if not supplanted) by a newer 'desk' format copied from US models, in shows fronted by Jonathan Ross, Clive Anderson, among others. Breakfast and daytime TV has its own versions of the former model (e.g. *This Morning*). There are also spoof/parodic versions to be found in *The Alan Partridge Show* where the host and the celebrities are spurious (Partridge is 'really' the comedian Steve Coogan), as well as *The Mrs Merton Show*, where the host is spurious ('really' Caroline Aherne) but the guests are real. The earliest of these spoofs probably comes from *The Edna Everage Show* of the 1970s and 1980s, where the host was Barry Humphries in his well-known drag persona, the eponymous Edna (see Tolson 1996b). As for the desk format, a 'zoo TV' (see Chapter 1) version of this is associated with *TFI Friday*, a 'youth' programme hosted by Chris Evans, the former Radio One DJ.

The new talk shows must also be distinguished in the first instance from the 'political' public debate/audience discussion programmes, where the role of the audience is to debate contemporary political issues. The BBC has long had a regular slot for *Question Time*, where a panel of public figures, including politicians, discuss issues and answer questions from the studio audience.

Radio Four's long-running *Any Questions* is a model here, at least in the British case. Recent general election campaigns have made use of phone-in programmes based around audience questions to political candidates, and there has recently been a move towards 'specials' involving studio audience discussion such as Channel 4's debate on the future of the British monarchy, which proved highly controversial. Various experimental formats for exploring public issues have been attempted from time to time on all terrestrial channels.

However, the 'daytime talk shows' which are the concern of the present chapter do not fit into any of the categories identified so far. The most obvious point of difference is that, in principle, with the exception of the host, they involve no celebrities or public figures. The participants are *all* 'ordinary people', and it is from their experiences and their views that the programmes are constructed.

Within this genre, however, some discriminations are required. Livingstone and Lunt (1994) include within the scope of their analysis such American examples of the daytime genre as *Oprah* and *Donahue*. In the US context these shows are very long-running (though *Oprah* in particular has seen some changes of format and emphasis over the years). *Oprah* has been broadcast on terrestrial television in the UK, and *Donahue* is currently broadcasting on satellite channels. There are some comparable examples from the British context on terrestrial television, made with British presenters, with British participants, for the British audience. (The US talk shows by tradition are made for local audiences first, but then, if successful, are syndicated and distributed nationally.) The most familiar of these British shows are *Kilroy*, *The Time, The Place* (with John Stapleton), *Vanessa* (Feltz) and *Esther* (Rantzen). *Oprah*, *Donahue* and these British examples constitute a sub-genre of the daytime talk shows inasmuch as they are not perceived as 'exploitative' in the way of the sub-genre whose properties we shall shortly be discussing.

Our proposed division into two sub-genres, the 'exploitative' form and the 'non-exploitative' form is not an absolute or fixed one, in terms of either form or content, and we would wish to remain circumspect for the time being as to the applicability of that evaluation to either or both of the sub-genres concerned. But there are certain characteristics which provide the parameters for daytime talk shows. As far as content is concerned, there is a choice to be made as to whether the topics to be addressed may include public issues (such as the closing of mental institutions in favour of 'care in the community'), issues of private (usually sexual) morality (such as the morality of sleeping with the partner of a close relative), and more light-hearted issues (such as the difficulties of being married to a soccer fan whose enthusiasm for the sport is excessive). In general, the British shows we have identified cover topics in all three of these areas, as do *Oprah* and *Donahue*, while there are shows which only operate in the territory of personal morality.

Then, too, there are questions of *form*. The 'new' talk shows are more about argument (i.e. conflict, especially within families) than about debate. This difference is facilitated by the use of studio space. The new talk shows focus upon particular individuals whose 'case histories' illustrate the theme of the show: 'I married my rapist', for example. The 'case-history' participants are physically separated from the studio audience, facing the latter directly, with the host mediating between the two spaces. *Donahue* and *Oprah* also use this form of presentation, but the British talk shows do so much less. Instead, the studio participants are undifferentiated by the seating arrangements – all the participants have the right to talk during the broadcast and some will specifically be selected by the host to do so, while others will self-select. Some may decide not to contribute at all. Distinctions between experts, case histories and audience members, then, are blurred in these arrangements, a fact which contributes somewhat to the downplaying of expertise noted by Livingstone and Lunt (1994) in their analysis.

Now we can be more specific in defining the kind of talk show which seems to be giving rise to a 'moral panic' in the US and which may in time do the same in the European context. These are the US daytime talk shows, which focus on issues of personal morality, and which use a 'case-history' approach, separating their 'cases' from the audience physically in the deployment of studio space. Shows of this type available via English-language non-terrestrial channels in Europe include *Sally Jessy Raphael, Geraldo, Rolonda, Ricki Lake, Jenny Jones, Jerry Springer* and *Gabrielle*. The channels which use these shows are principally Granada Talk, Sky One and UK Living – though *Ricki Lake* broadcasts on Channel 4, a terrestrial, free-to-air channel. In Britain, it is almost possible to watch talk shows of this kind without interruption, from 9.00 a.m. until 6.00 p.m.

A note about data collection – for the purposes of this chapter, examples were collected of all the shows which fell into the category described above. Examples of other types of talk show were also collected so that comparative points could be checked, if necessary – such as the celebrity talk shows. There are some 'minor forms' of talk show (mentioned later in the chapter) which were uncovered in this process. The data collection took place between 1 and 8 May 1997, and on 14and 15 May. The shows taped were as follows:

- *Sally Jessy Raphael*    Newly weds who cheat
- *Donahue*    Older women and younger men
- *Geraldo*    My mom looks like Peg Bundy
- *Sally Jessy Raphael*    I want to say I'm sorry
- *Jenny Jones*    My mom had an affair with my man
- *Jerry Springer*    My man's no good
- *Ricki Lake*    Today I'm ready to confront your family and find out why they hate me
- *Jerry Springer*    Unusual love triangles
- *Oprah*    Today we're finding out what your house says about you
- *Donahue*    What makes a good marriage
- *Geraldo*    Who is the daddy?
- *Jenny Jones*    Inter-racial dating: when cultures clash: My family won't accept my inter-racial lover
- *Oprah*    Road rage tragedies
- *Ricki Lake*    I know you're taken but surprise! I want you anyway
- *Rolonda*    Prisoners of love (families and victims in Death Row cases)

Subsequent broadcasts were viewed, as time allowed, to ensure against the use of unrepresentative examples. The representativeness of the examples *actually* used was thus determined by our own judgement rather than through any formal procedure. However, since the nature of the formula behind these shows is so transparent, and the product so standardised, we are confident that our own examples give a good sense of what this discourse comprises and how it functions.

## The ethics of talk shows

There is a prima facie case to be made that the US talk shows are voyeuristic, and thus exploitative (we will refer from now on to the new talk shows, not strictly accurately, though they are new on European screens, but to avoid the offensive implication that the population of the United States is uniquely committed to values we will wish to criticise). Before we enter into any analysis we will consider the frameworks within which these talk shows have been judged.

The viewpoint in which television embodies 'bad culture' is one with a considerable history and which takes a variety of forms. Corner (1995) identifies five principal arguments of this kind. TV viewing:

- it wastes time, drawing viewers away from more worthwhile activities
- it invades and replaces authentic cultural activities
- it debases the tastes of its viewers
- it influences viewers' attitudes for the worse, and
- it impairs their cognitive skills.

Such criticisms can either be made of television in general, or focused more specifically on particular genres, series or programmes, even on particular themes. As far as the chat shows are concerned, the kind of criticism which is of most relevance is the kind which focuses upon taste-debasement. A prominent US critic may be quoted here:

> There are more than 20 nationally syndicated talk programmes on the air this fall, many of which can be seen here in the Washington area ... After watching a number of these shows, and learning more about the behavior of their hosts and producers, it is clear that talk is indeed cheap, and too often demeaning, exploitative, perverted, divisive, or, at best, amoral.
>
> Those are strong words, but it is difficult to exaggerate the willingness of some of these shows to parade any and every pathology and dysfunction into our living rooms.
>
> (Lieberman 1995)

Interestingly, this critique is not undiscriminating and exceptions are made within the genre. Senator Lieberman is jointly responsible with Senator Bennett for the US campaign against these shows. It was the latter who wrote this:

> It is important here to point out who we are not talking about. We are not talking about shows like *Oprah*, or *Regis* and *Kathie Lee*. The shows which are the object of our criticisms are not close calls, they go way over the line of decency. They are at the bottom of the television barrel.
>
> (Bennett 1995)

This critique has not gone unchallenged. There is a predictable libertarian strand of response which defends the talk shows largely on right-of-speech grounds as well as on the grounds of their popularity, in an anti-elitist spirit:

> When Sally Jessy Raphael said on *America Online* that 'I believe that it is more important to do the shows that the majority of the public asks for than to determine by myself what I want them to sees', she was demonstrating a greater respect for the masses than any of her critics can comprehend.
>
> (Doohan 1995)

A more thoughtful line of response to the senators was produced by Barbara Ehrenreich for *Time* magazine. Ehrenreich pointed out that the dominant discourse, ethically speaking, in these talk shows is precisely one of middle-class morality:

> As anyone who actually watches them knows, the talk shows are one of the most excruciatingly moralistic forums the culture has to offer. Disturbing and sometimes disgusting, yes, but their very business is to preach the middle-class virtues of responsibility, reason and self-control.
>
> (Ehrenreich 1995)

Ehrenreich certainly does not lend her support unequivocally to this dominant discourse. On the contrary, it is her purpose to draw attention to the use of particular kinds of people – victims, in her analysis, both of society and of television – to produce spectacle and entertainment:

> There is something morally repulsive about the talks, but it is not anything Bennett or his co-crusader Senator Joseph Lieberman has seen fit to mention. Watch for a few hours, and you get the claustrophobic sense of lives that have never seen the light of some external judgement, of people who have never before been listened to, and certainly never been taken seriously if they were. 'What kind of people would let themselves be humiliated like this?' is often asked, sniffily, by the shows' detractors. And the answer, for the most part, is people who are so needy – of social support, of education, of material resources and self-esteem – that they mistake being the center of attention for being actually loved and respected.
>
> (Ehrenreich 1995)

Another contributor to this debate in 1995, when the senatorial campaign began, was the feminist Camille Paglia (Paglia 1995). She, like Ehrenreich, was not afraid to foreground the social-class dimension.

> Daytime talk shows now resemble stunt wrestling, stockcar racing, or video games. Colorful confrontationalism and quick, bruising skirmishes are the rule. Psychologists (Dr Joyce Brothers was the beaming prototype) are carted out like priestly confessors to dispense bromides and give dramatic

closure, but they are relatively peripheral to the shows' fascinating panorama of contemporary sociology. Nowhere else do lower-middle-class and working-class citizens have such direct access to coast-to-coast communications. Every race and region is represented among talk show guests, with their rich backwoods accents or hip, mean-streets attitude.

(Paglia 1995)

The source of this is an ephemeral polemic on the World-Wide Web, rather than a fully developed academic argument. Nevertheless the contours of Paglia's position are clear enough, and suggest that she is not unhappy with the voyeurism of the format, justified because the people on display are so interesting. Her own position is far from amoral, since she gives Donahue credit for helping to inculcate a more generous popular attitude to gay sexuality. Finally, she singles out *Donahue* and *Oprah* as the best of the talk shows and discusses the 'artistic' decline of the form in recent times. In this selectivity, she belongs to a consensus which includes her adversaries, Bennett and Lieberman.

In the European context little of this debate has been heard. Largely this is because the type of show it is concerned with has not been seen on European TV stations. But this is changing. Below we give some indication of the spread of daytime talk shows in the British context. In the (British and German) academic literature the available commentary on talk shows is very largely positive. A key publication here is Livingstone and Lunt (1994). We believe that Livingstone and Lunt's positive view of talk shows in general (including the US imports on terrestrial television, *Donahue* and *Oprah*) is only possible because the writers have not become acquainted with the form and content of *Sally Jessy Raphael*, *Geraldo*, *Ricki Lake*, *Rolonda*, *Jenny Jones* and the rest. Nevertheless, it is important to consider the terms of their positive evaluation, since these are significantly different from those of Ehrenreich's qualified defence, much more concerned with the values of public-service television, public education and political debate, and much less with entertainment and spectacle.

> Throughout this book, our main concern has been with audience discussion programmes as social occasions. We have characterised performance in such programmes as organised around both the expression of diverse voices and legitimation. The two performative modes of the programme are story-telling and debate. Story-telling links a variety of themes: expression of personal experience, the personification of social issues and problems, providing relevance, and giving voice to the various, often marginalised, groupings of the life-world. Debate makes established power accountable to personal experience, providing the opportunity for legitimation through consent together with the danger of discovery. The opposition between these two performances reflects those oppositions between the concrete and the abstract, the disempowered and the powerful, lived-in experience and expertise.
>
> (Livingstone and Lunt 1994: 180)

Thus, what makes it possible for Livingstone and Lunt broadly to approve the content and form of talk shows (and their study includes a substantial amount of audience research along with their textual analysis) has to do with the legitimation of experience, as well as with the presence of a multiplicity of voices, none dominating or containing the rest. There are traces in this account of the feminist critique of Enlightenment rationality (see also Masciarotte 1991; Shattuc 1997, 1998), which we are sympathetic to, in principle. It is important to say that any talk show which did manage these goals would deserve to be considered as a positive development in the conditions for public debate, though not without reservations: no one (it is to be hoped) would want such programming to *replace* forms of TV discussion in which expertise and formal rationality were valued above personal experience. Good talk shows (in Livingstone and Lunt's terms) should supplement other forms of televised political debate, not replace these. But it is also important to say that the new talk shows do not achieve these goals, or even (arguably) try to do so. This is what we shall need to show in the analysis to follow.

By far the best critic and analyst of the new talk shows is Jane Shattuc (Shattuc 1997, 1998; see also Carbaugh 1988; Carpignano *et al.* 1990; Masciarotte 1991). Her perspective is discriminating, as between types of daytime talk show on network TV, and it is historical. It works from a sound appreciation of the conditioning factors which led to the emergence of this cultural form as well as its more recent decline. Shattuc's evaluation seeks to avoid not just the conservatism of the moral-right discourse associated with Bennett and his supporters, but also the simplicities of the 'celebratory' turn which values the openness of the format. Even so, there is some equivocation in her own judgement which cannot be recouped in terms of the texts' 'polysemy'. Polysemy is acknowledged by Shattuc as a property of the genre – an overtly moralistic and judgemental discourse is subverted by camp excesses:

> these newer shows invite a second reading which deconstructs the serious or liberal 'do-good' intentions of 1980s talk shows by inviting an ironic reading. Here the methods of the earlier programmes are so excessively overplayed that they highlight the contradictions of any talk show – particularly the first generation of Oprah Winfrey and Phil Donahue (even Geraldo Rivera) – which unctuously attempts to help disadvantaged people while simultaneously profiting from the act.
>
> (Shattuc 1998: 215)

Our own reading of the talk shows (see below) may be dismissed as *missing* the ironies here; perhaps, as Europeans, our distance from American culture has withheld a layer of meaning from us, and supplied in its place a sense that the programmes' excesses more simply as 'American'. And yet this cannot be the whole story. In the first place, audience *uptake* of irony cannot be guaranteed for any audience, American or otherwise. And, in the second place, the logic which equates excesses with irony, and irony with critical function is flawed, even as counterweight to the moralistic 'naive' readings (one brand of which 'approves' talk shows for adopting normative moral positions and imposing these through the voice and persona of the presenter, while another brand 'disapproves' the allowance of time and space for the performance of 'unacceptable' lives – on exploitative terms?).

The redemptive readings of talk shows place value on the excessiveness therein displayed, *because* it affronts liberal-conservative moral and aesthetic norms. This suggests an audience of political-cultural educated progressives, who enjoy the programmes in an 'eavesdropper' role. They are witnesses of an 'exchange' between the 'outlaw' subjects (to use Shattuc's term) and their opponents, on terms which favour the former. This is a very particular kind of viewing pleasure, especially as it depends on an appreciation of a dialogic relation not fully realised in the text itself. The studio audience engages the outlaws in talk. So does the host. So, sometimes, do 'experts' (therapists of different species). But these co-participants are but a pale shadow of that 'public opinion' (repressive, conservative, paternalistic) which, in this construction, is the real addressee. Even if we allow that this construction does capture something about the viewing relations of one audience segment, it would be a mistake to conceive of the whole audience on these terms – an audience which itself does not need to be outraged by the sins of the subjects, the views they express or the demeanours they adopt through dress style and 'attitude', but conscious of another audience which needs precisely that. For the popular audience, with no *prior* commitment to a progressive politics, the logic of 'camp' and ironic readings does not provide any kind of escape route from the criticisms of voyeurism. As Shattuc herself acknowledges, following Gates (1995):

> If nothing is to be taken seriously, then nothing needs to change ... Not everything is a joke; we need to know about the social logic of this repression [of the American underclass]. The camp aesthetics stops the questioning. This is why the left has reacted so angrily to talk shows.
>
> (Shattuc 1998: 223)

Given this commentary, with which we agree, the final sentence of Shattuc's article bears re-examination: 'But with talk shows, we have only begun to consider how our notions of "good taste" mask power and stop debate' (Shattuc 1998: 224).

The oddity of this is the implication that the 'bad taste' shows had at least begun to expose power and open up debate. But this is textually implausible. The construction and marketing of the shows in question is managed entirely and without regret or compromise on the terms of entertainment television and not at all within the terms of public education/enlightenment from which the concept of 'debate' takes its meaning. Talk shows value the 'spectacular', even if it is not the spectacle of programmes such as *Gladiators*, which make use of the body beautiful and appropriate costumes to glamorise their material. The spectacle in talk shows resides in the emphasis upon display, revelation, shock and confrontation. Not that costuming is altogether irrelevant – for every working-class participant who appears down-at-heel and unkempt, there is another who has chosen much more exotic dress codes: the multicoloured dyed hair, the pierced body, the revealing bustline or hemline, fabrics and forms that would not be out of place on Vivienne Westwood's catwalk.

We can agree to value debate over monologue for certain purposes in television with public-service goals, and not just because the former is more 'entertaining'. But the new talk shows have no such goals: they were made for network television in America and are broadcast on commercial channels in Europe. It is perverse to read their interactive character as a species of 'debate'. The analyses below will seek to demonstrate this.

## The discursive character of the talk shows

The new talk shows attract criticism partly because of their content and partly because of their form. As far as the content is concerned, the issue is the extent to which the case histories exhibit human social/moral conduct of a perverse kind: polygamists; women who marry adolescent boys; people who commit adultery in out-of-the-ordinary ways (with their in-laws or their stepchildren; within a few days of their wedding). The formal point here is that perverse moral conduct should either not be exhibited at all or, if it is exhibited, it should be firmly positioned as unacceptable. Ehrenreich (1995; also see p. 139) and others have pointed out that the behaviour of these perverse human exhibits is evaluated, within the studio discourse, in strongly negative terms. So the issue of perversity does turn more upon exhibition(ism)/voyeurism than upon (lack of) evaluation.

And 'exhibition' is the right term, since, as we have indicated, the format of the show requires the subjects to sit in front of the studio audience and to adopt a 'confessional' mode of discourse in response to questioning from the host and then commentary from the audience. The questioning elicits narratives of self-disclosure from the subjects, with greater or lesser degrees of self-blame according to the degree of remorse the subject is prepared to demonstrate. Sometimes there is no remorse. For Livingstone and Lunt (1994), talk shows are a trans-generic hybrid form combining strands of melodrama, therapy and debate. This particular sub-genre of talk show undoubtedly has eliminated the debate component, while preserving the melodrama and the therapy. In many cases an actual 'therapist' (specialising in TV performances) participates in the show, providing some sort of expert psychological commentary which can be used as a resource within the programme for understanding the conduct of the subjects and perhaps for changing that conduct in a future that will begin after the show has ended.

In our judgement, these shows trade in the exploitation of human weakness for the sake of voyeuristic pleasure. Even the most interesting redemptive readings (see Paglia 1995 – cited on p. 129) do not challenge the terms of the present critique, except in so far as they find virtue in just those qualities we criticise. So let us indulge in some speculation about the possible character of audience response to this material. The 'Otherness' of the subjects in these shows can encourage viewers to watch their exhibition as being without real cause or consequence. The subjects exist in and for the shows where they appear. Their lives outside the show are talked about – since that is the point of the exercise – but those lives are subordinated to the performative character of the show as a media event. The effect is to render those lives *unreal*. Viewers may well suspect that subjects are performing 'inauthentic' selves. They may be led to believe that the perversity demonstrated on the show constitutes all there is to know about these people. They may experience the performers as human freaks, whose world is beyond their understanding in every sense of the term. All of these responses, it might be said, are *dehumanising*, within a format which does very little to uncover common ground between the subjects and the studio audience or the subjects and the broadcast audience, and would justify a critique of voyeurism.

## Talk-show topics

The following list of programme titles for episodes of American talk includes episodes that were not taped for the purposes of data collection, but which were broadcast during the data collection period. They were identified with the help of a listings guide.

- If you're homeless it's your fault
- Newly weds who cheat
- Baby-sitter turns Mom on
- I can't get over my first love
- Wayward fathers reclaim their children
- Why won't you marry me?
- I can't stop cheating
- Get them off the dole or no welfare!
- My husband treats me like a slave
- I lied to you, I'm not pregnant
- Mom wants to dump my baby's father

A common formula for episode titles is the first-person utterance, as if from the mouth of the subject: 'I lied to you, I'm not pregnant'. The formulations in these cases are simple, not to say stark, expressions of moral problems, invoking themes of guilt and innocence, perhaps inviting viewers into a position of conversational exchange with the 'speakers'.

## Talk-show style

To understand the dynamics of these talk shows, it is necessary to take account of their performative character. We can do this by itemising five distinctive characteristics: narratives of self-disclosure; confrontation; audience participation; disclosure effects; and camera work and editing.

## NARRATIVES OF SELF-DISCLOSURE

In the performance of moral guilt by the subjects and moral judgement by the studio audience, a very large part of the airtime has to be devoted to narratives of self-disclosure on the part of the subjects. Such narratives are generally co-constructed by host and subject, inasmuch as it is the questioning of the host which elicits the disclosures of the subject. All participants, host, subjects and audience members collaborate 'knowingly'; that is, they jointly construct a narrative in which the climax is the revelation of a moral offence from the subject which the host's questions are designed to elicit, and which requires an audible collective response from the floor. Often enough, the 'gist' of the moral offence is announced at the outset of the show and may indeed form part of the publicity for it in trailers and listings magazines. But narrative disclosure still has its value:

RAPHAEL: But first I would like you to meet Suzi and Laura. Suzi got married this past May and she has already cheated. Laura says she began her affair just two days on returning from her honeymoon.

Suzi, let's start with you. You've been married, what, three months now. Why did you begin cheating on your new husband?

SUZI: Well, I wasn't married before I started cheating. I had been seeing the man for almost a year and a half and I was living with him at the time. Um.

RAPHAEL: You were living with this man? Then how did you get engaged and get married to another man?

SUZI: Um (*Pause*). I guess you, you kinda look at life in a different light. I have two children from a previous marriage and um I looked for stability and a relationship with someone that I could have the so quote unquote family life for my children.

RAPHAEL: When did you start cheating, and with whom?

SUZI: Um, with a man I worked with, and um I saw him at work and it was sort of, out of a flirtation type of thing, and we went out one night to a ball game.

RAPHAEL: When you'd been married how long?

SUZI: I wasn't married yet.

RAPHAEL: Oh.

SUZI: I was living with my fiancé. And we went out, and I stayed out all night. All night long, and I came back the next morning at six a.m.

RAPHAEL: [?]

SUZI: And I did have a lot of explaining and I guess that's why I thought I could get away with it.

RAPHAEL: Because you did explain it and he bought it?

SUZI: Yes. Exactly.

RAPHAEL: So you got engaged and you got married. When did you meet this
man again?

SUZI: Well, that weekend we spent … His wife was away, to meet, see her family,
and we saw each other for three days. Straight in a row.

RAPHAEL: Does your husband know?

SUZI: No. He has no idea.

RAPHAEL: Does he know now?

SUZI: No.

RAPHAEL: How often has this been going on?

SUZI: I see him on a regular basis about two times a week. Uh, we talk to each
other almost every day. At least once.

RAPHAEL: How do you feel about this?

SUZI: I feel like I lead a separate life. Uh, you try to keep them, when you talk
about them you really think 'God, I can't believe this is really happening to
me'. But at the same time you think, 'Well, there's worse things I could be
doing in life'. You know.

In another example from our collection, a participant tells a story about her
infidelity, anticipated by the host in the following terms: 'I want you to first
meet Sandra. She desperately wants to apologise to her fiancé Gary for cheating
on him almost a year into their relationship.'

We shall refer to this as the 'apology' episode: the show as a whole is built
around four case histories, all different, in which one participant apologises to
someone she or he has hurt. After this introduction, the audience responds
appropriately with audible shock: and Raphael builds upon this response in her
next exchange with Sandra: 'Sandra, see, hear all those "ooohs"?'

Thus, the moral framework is already put into place, and Raphael has given
notice that Sandra is expected to hold herself accountable to it. It is interesting,
then, when Sandra's own narrative reaches its own version of the moral offence.
This version is significantly more low-key, as Sandra seeks verbally to protect
her face:

He came on the boat, talking, and from then on, from then on we kept
talking, and kept talking, and then we got together, and then I told Gary I
was going to see someone else, I was really seeing the other guy before I told
him, and that's the only bad thing.

In terms of the programme's values, the climax of the story is the moment of
infidelity. In Sandra's telling, the moment of infidelity is realised as 'and then
we got together'. Syntactically this moment is 'buried' or, at least, it is down-
played by being cast as one narrative clause in a sequence of these, none
achieving particular prominence through syntax or through intonation. It can
also afford to be protectively vague, euphemistic, since the audience already
knows the essentials. Sandra even seeks mildly to redress the offence:
'… and that's the only bad thing' – telling Gary that she intended to have an

affair when she'd already embarked upon it. The low-key delivery does not inhibit the audience from letting out a reactive 'buzz' of censure as Sandra gets to the point. A buzz of censure is not an audibly distinct *kind* of buzz: it is an indistinct noise made by a number of voices simultaneously, which we hear as a buzz of censure because of the context in which it is produced.

CONFRONTATION

A further performative dimension of talk shows consists in the production of interaction between subjects, of two kinds. One kind consists of interaction between subjects linked within one narrative (e.g. an adulteress and her cuckolded spouse). These will be invited to confront one another, or will do so without invitation. The other kind of interaction consists of confrontation between subjects from different narratives, linked by virtue of their roles. Thus an adulterer in one narrative may be confronted by a cuckold from another narrative.

A condition of confrontation on screen is that subjects be allowed to talk to one another rather than to the host/audience. To understand how subjects enter into interaction with one another, it is useful to look at the forms of footing (Goffman 1981) which occur within the segment and how changes of footing are brought about.

As with all broadcast talk, the talk here is designed for an overhearing audience. There is a studio audience, which is available for direct address, and whose members themselves are allowed to become speakers, under conditions controlled by the programme in the person of the programme host. There is also a domestic, remote TV audience. It too can be the object of direct address, although its members cannot become speakers, except in shows like Granada's *Paul Ross Show*, which take telephone calls as part of the broadcast. The show's host performs a mediating role, and holds the symbol of speaker's power and privilege – not a conch shell, but a hand microphone. The host determines who speaks, for how long, and in what order. Much of this will have been determined before the recording began by the director in consultation with the host, but it is the host who performs the speaker selections and implements the decisions which have been made. There are limits to host control. Flooding out for these participants generally runs to anger rather than grief or happiness, and thus to raised voices and physical gestures rather than tears or laughter. Such flooding out permits the performance of 'breaking out' from the host-controlled rules of engagement, though usually this is brought quickly back under control, since, engaging as it may be, it seriously threatens comprehensibility.

So long as the talk remains under control, it also remains collaborative, though not invariably polite (Table 5). Jones is the host; Lisa and Darlene are mother and daughter. Darlene's first utterance after her mother appears on stage is to challenge what she has just claimed: that she was doing her daughter a favour in going to bed with her husband. The audience reaction shows appropriate degrees of intensity, as indicated in the third column.

*Table 5* Talk-show confrontation

| | | |
|---|---|---|
| Jones | You haven't seen her for a month. Lisa's backstage. Lisa, come on out. | |
| *(Music: Lisa walks on stage and over to chair on stage. Loud applause, cat calls, boos, etc. from audience)* | | |
| Jones | Well, Lisa. You really… | |
| Darlene | Doing me a favour? | |
| Lisa | Yes. | |
| Jones | You really… | |
| Darlene | Doing me a… | |
| Jones | How did you, how did you think you were helping your daughter by sleeping with her husband? | |
| Lisa | Because he treats her like a [whore].* | Oooh! |
| Darlene | Excuse me, he treats me like…Oh, that's [?] | *(Loud, prolonged* |
| Lisa | Yes he does Darlene. | *over three* |
| Darlene | No he does not. You don't [know]. | *turns)* |
| Lisa | Yes he does. | |
| Darlene | He does not. | |
| Jones | Lisa, how was that supposed to help her? | |
| Lisa | I figured if I'd be his [whore] maybe he'd treat her like a lady. | Oooh! *(Very loud,* |
| Darlene | Excuse me, so what does that make you? | *prolonged over three* |
| Lisa | I don't care what it makes me. | *turns)* |
| Darlene | Mmm hmm. | |

The conventions of interaction require host control over relations of *footing* (Goffman 1981). In the 'apology' episode already referred to (see p. 135), the footing arrangements develop as follows: host/audience; host/Sandra; host/Gary; Gary/Sandra; Gary/host; Len/host; Gary/Len; Gary/host; Len/host; Sandra/host; Len/host; Gary/host; Sandra/host; Gary/host; Sandra/host; host/audience member; audience member/Sandra; host/audience member. The audience is a ratified participant throughout, but Len and Gary are not: they are held backstage until required to appear on stage. The following sequence is of interest because it suggests that the 'lay' participants have a less secure sense than the host of this genre's performance structure in respect of its footing requirements. The script for the show requires Sandra to apologise *to* Gary – i.e. to initiate a new footing, Gary/Sandra, with the host and the audience as ratified participants beyond the dyad:

R *to* G:   Wait, wait wait. Hold on. She wanted to apologise to you.
R *to* S:   Go ahead. First ask him for forgiveness.
S *to* ?:   I'm sorry for what I did but …
R *to* S:   No, not to me. I haven't, you haven't done anything to me.
S *to* R:   I'm sorry for what I did, but … There's something else I want to do. I want to bring Len out here.

The 'unacceptable' utterance is Sandra's first attempt at the apology. Raphael chooses to construe this as 'wrongly addressed' – addressed to her and not to Gary. It is not obvious that Raphael's interpretation is correct, though there are no Gary-directed address terms and her gaze is not towards Gary. But it is not clearly towards Raphael, either. The salient point is that Sandra has not understood how important to this show it is that its 'apologies' are performed directly between the participants involved for witnessing by the studio and TV audience.

AUDIENCE PARTICIPATION

We have already mentioned the function of the audience in collectively acknowledging the revelation of moral offence, when it occurs – offering sympathy for victims and censure for sinners, as in the extract shown above. Beyond this and related *collective* speech acts, members of the studio audience may be drawn into individual participation when invited by the host to address comments or questions to the subjects. Their own relation to the type of narrative is rarely an issue here, so they are rarely asked if *they* are involved in adulterous relationships, for example. They produce attacks upon offending subjects; and sympathy and advice for the victims. The 'speaking position' is overwhelmingly from inside normative morality, though some issues do find it harder than others to articulate normative morality (notably where sexual preference and race are involved). Here is another extract from the show involving adulterous newlyweds:

RAPHAEL:   Suzi and Laura, we have heard of the seven-year itch, but it is a little unusual to hear of a newlywed cheating. May I ask why you got married in the first place?
SUZI:   Stability.
LAURA:   Yes, yes, stability. Stability.
        (*Audience applause*)
LAURA:   I have something to say, Sally. Everyone here in the audience, you know, you're like, 'Oh, wow!'
RAPHAEL:   Right.
LAURA:   You know. But, you know, you don't walk in our shoes, you don't live our life, you don't know, you don't know, you don't know the whole story.
        (*Laura above is talking over very loud crowd noise*)
AUDIENCE MEMBER:   I can understand what you're saying, nobody's walked in

your shoes. But look, but you're making the road that you're going down, and you're going down a dead-end.

SUZI: That's right, that's right, bravo. It's not yours, it's *my* road.

AUDIENCE MEMBER: What about your husband, what about him, if you married him what about him, don't ... If you have feelings to get married ...

LAURA: If my husband treated me the way I should be treated I wouldn't have to [?]

SUZI: ...then we wouldn't have to go. We wouldn't have to go.

AUDIENCE MEMBER: You should have checked it out before you got married.

LAURA: That's right, that's right, but ...

AUDIENCE MEMBER: You don't just get married for the sake of getting married today. That's why, that's why you're in the boat you're in. You should have checked it out first, you should have stood with him, longer than you did.

SUZI: We're doing the best we can do now.

RAPHAEL: I think you can ex ... you can understand that the audience is a bit upset and ...

SUZI: I can understand, but, too, I was put here for me, and you were put here for you.

LAURA: I'm not here to please anybody else in this audience except myself.

SUZI: I'm not here to judge you, you're not here to judge me.

RAPHAEL: The answer ... Wait, wait ... The answer, then, is this is what's right for you.

LAURA: Yes.

GENIE: Yes.

SUZI: Yes.

This is the first of several interactive sequences in this episode where the audience and the subjects come into noisy confrontation. The transcription above is barely adequate to convey the confrontational style. It pays no attention to the body language which is picked up by the camera: bodies sitting well forward on chairs, eyes focused hard forward towards challengers, energetic hand gestures. Nor does it fully convey the extent of the overlapping talk. These are the obvious features of the conflict talk, but one or two less obvious points can also be made. First, there is evidence of an element within the studio audience more sympathetic to Laura and Suzi than the majority. Why else would there be applause when both women gave 'stability', not 'love' as their reason for marrying their cuckolded spouses? Raphael orchestrates the majority response, 'you can understand that the audience is a bit upset and...', and gives no talk opportunities to audience members with a more supportive moral perspective. The tone adopted by 'Suzi', in replying to the first audience speaker, pushes the latter into a sharper critical tone than she began with.

Second, although between the audience and the subjects the interaction comes across as conflict talk, between the three women on stage there is considerable solidarity: the women don't just agree with one another and signify agreement with nods and verbal response tokens. They also build upon one another's utterances, exchange supportive looks, and use 'We ...' formulations. There is even a hint of *sotto voce* talk between them not meant for the studio audience of the microphones.

## DISCLOSURE EFFECTS

The shock value of every episode depends not only upon the choice of topic, but also upon more local mechanisms employed for the production of disclosure effects within the diegesis, as narratives and exchanges unfold in real time. True, there is a considerable amount of 'pre-disclosure' – 'Today you're going to meet ...' – to hook viewers into watching. But once they are watching, the release of information is controlled by the conventions of the show and the skill of the production crew in deploying those conventions. Things are pre-planned with disclosure effects in mind, and edited after performance to the same end. And the shows involve not only disclosure to the studio and television audience – disclosure often takes place also between participants within the same narrative.

Spatial relations are important to these disclosures, and especially the control of on-stage/backstage space. On stage is space directly in front of a studio audience; off-screen space is elsewhere in the building, accessible to the studio audience only via closed-circuit cameras. Disclosure effects are managed by keeping participants apart until the development of the story requires them to encounter one another. One version of these arrangements has cameras focused upon an 'off-stage' participant – the cuckolded husband or boyfriend, for example, who does not see or hear what is happening on stage, although he can be seen by the studio audience on monitors and on the TV screen by cutting between shots on stage and shots in the 'green room' or other space where he is being held. In the 'apology' episode, Gary is treated in this way. When he does appear on stage, he learns of the infidelity as new information, simultaneously receiving Sandra's apology.

The other type of disclosure arrangement is similar, except that the off-stage participant does witness the on-stage events, via monitors in the off-stage arena. This participant is unavailable for direct address revelation from the co-partici-pant, who is telling her story to the studio audience. The off-screen participant learns of the 'offence' as a third-party observer of a speech event in which he takes no part. More accurately, perhaps, he is 'addressed' in the same way that the domestic audience is addressed, hearing himself referred to in the third person. In the apology episode, Len is treated in just this way. Len, while he witnesses on-screen events, is himself witnessed by the television audience (and, on monitors, by the studio audience). His experience of the event to that point is more 'private', cameras notwithstanding, than the experience of Sandra, the 'confessing'/'disclosing' participant, out in front of the studio audi-ence. In both types of disclosure arrangements, the off-stage 'disclosee' is presumably aware that there are cameras trained upon him, using his facial expressions and demeanour (though not his voice) to achieve televisual effects.

Talk shows are a cheap form of television. Yet, as we have begun to see, there is much more to their construction than just talk. No analysis would be complete without some attention to the visual character of these shows, and to a consideration of what is done to the raw video material after filming and before transmission.

One much-used device in talk shows is the split screen. The usual convention with split-screen sequences is that they represent scenes of action in different locations. This is the convention followed, for example, in the 'apology' episode. While Sandra is alone on stage, talking to the host, the split-screen device is used three times to show Sandra and Gary simultaneously, and once to show Sandra and Mike (the 'other man') simultaneously. But there is an additional use of the split-screen technique that we should mention. In the apology episode, after Gary moves from off stage to on stage, he and Sandra are co-present with the host and the audience. Indeed, they are sitting on adjacent chairs, facing the audience. It is not necessary to use a split screen in order to show them both at the same time. And initially the director is happy with a two-shot for this purpose. But then comes the emotional 'moment of truth': Sandra apologises to Gary and asks if Len can come out on stage. Now both Sandra and Gary are at their most emotionally vulnerable. Both faces, simultaneously, are in tight close-up. Only a split screen can produce this effect – a two-shot is too remote for the purpose.

In these shows there is undoubtedly the feeling of 'fresh talk' in Goffman's (1981) sense. This is partly because the narratives are elicited under questioning from the host; partly because emotions are frequently running high (passion = spontaneity); partly because of the extent of the disfluencies typical of fresh talk, as well as the overlaps when different speakers are competing for the floor; and, finally, partly because of the presence and participation of a studio audience.

The fresh-talk effect may or may not be genuinely achieved. You could be forgiven for thinking that performances had been rehearsed before filming. However, it is also the case that the television shows are edited constructions designed to enhance certain aspects of the talk, notably the disclosures and the confrontations. We have talked about the use of a split screen; other aspects of the production which contribute are: the regular cutting between audience and subjects; the shots of 'backstage' as well as 'on-stage' participants; and the variable-speed editing for different phases of the encounters. After the 'event' has taken place, there is an opportunity to edit the material to produce a finished version ready for transmission. Of all the series currently being aired on European English-language channels, the one which makes the most use of studio editing tools to craft a specifically televisual version of the event is *Jerry Springer*. We have seen episodes of this show where a substantial amount of airtime is taken up with material filmed 'after the show', as the subjects continue to discuss their affairs in the 'green room' away from the eyes and ears of a studio audience (although still in the presence of cameras). Springer also gets groups of people from the audience to speak on camera away from the studio and separately from the show-as-performed. These speakers will, in chorus, say things like 'We've come all the way from [town] to see *Jerry Springer*' (but do they mean the man, or the show, or both?). These sequences are edited into the tape, to be aired just before the closing credits. The beginning of the show features a montage of edited highlights to whet our appetite for what is to follow. Extensive amounts of the spoken dialogue are 'bleeped out' rather noisily with cuckoo-clock-type sounds, occasionally accompanied by visual aids in the form of cartoon-style speech balloons, saying 'Oops' or similar. Bleeping is for bad language, but also for references to proper names which the show thinks it is better to conceal. Springer likes to close the show with some explicit moral-ising, delivered to camera, based upon the shared experience of the case histories as performed in his studio. *Jerry Springer* also goes one stage further than other shows of its type in its celebration of the host as hero. The effect is constructed of a phenomenal Springer fan club, and part of this effect is due to the above-mentioned use of extracts with members of the audience. When they chorus 'We've come all the way from …', they round off their performance with loud cheering. The other celebratory device is the use of applause, of standing-ovation type, as Springer enters 'his' studio for the start of another show. The audience is seen from the side, standing, as this takes place, and the noise levels from their voices, their clapping hands, and their stomping feet, is very high. Springer thanks the audience for their enthusiasm. 'Greeting the host' no doubt occurs in the studios of other presenters too, but it is not at all usual to retain these greeting sequences as part of the broadcast text.

# 8 European high culture – arts discourse in the new regime

The new TV environment in Europe is clearly not reducible to the delivery of cheap entertainment to mass audiences. Across the whole spectrum of satellite or cable channels, there are many which offer a more demanding diet of programmes. The aims and origins of these channels differ: they may be terrestrial publicly funded channels which now also transmit on satellite, such as the formerly regional third channels in Germany – sometimes called educational channels (Bildungskanäle), or 3 SAT, a compilation of quality programmes from all public-service terrestrial channels; or the compilation channel of French-speaking nations, TV5. Apart from the bilingual cultural channel ARTE, which we will focus on in this chapter, there are channels specialising on relaying live artistic performances (e.g. the Performance channel), and many generic channels geared towards education, infotainment and current affairs broadcasting, channels such as Discovery, which specialises in documentaries, and public-service or commercial round-the-clock news channels, including the multilingual EuroNews for a transnational European audience.

We have already shown in Chapter 4 how EuroNews in particular addresses an audience assumed to be interested in, and mobile across, different European countries. We argued that EuroNews is most at ease when it moves away from news proper into the cultural sphere, reporting about artistic events – music, theatre, painting, etc. For cultural events, EuroNews does not need to construct an imaginary European, but can rely on the shared artistic pleasures and interests of transnational audiences.

However, this availability of what may arguably be called quality programming does not mean a return to a traditional bifurcation into high versus popular art. EuroNews distinctly addresses cultural phenomena which embrace all categories or which in themselves cut across such a fuzzy divide. Such hybridity is a typical phenomenon in late twentieth-century cultural production and reception in general. The tastes of cultural elites incorporate popular genres as well as high-culture ones, just as traditionally high culture is increasingly consumed by mass audiences.

Advertisements for the mass audience, for example, use classical musical themes; works of art are mass-produced as posters and in product packaging; Pavarotti is associated with football, and the three tenors Pavarotti, Domingo and Carreras fill football stadiums for their concerts made up of opera arias as well as traditional folk and popular music. Melvyn Bragg, long-running presenter of the *South Bank Show*,[1] and himself an author of novels, discusses the pop star Madonna or the popular British TV satire *Spitting Image* as readily as art cinema or exhibitions; the Greek classical historian Herodotus has hit the best-seller list of paperbacks with a front cover featuring a scene from the Oscar-winning Hollywood film *The English Patient*; and former Beatle Paul McCartney writes classical symphonic orchestra pieces as well as rock and pop music. Production and consumption of culture in the late twentieth century is post-modern in its mixes of every possible kind of symbolic material.

Does this fuzziness in the division of popular and high art forms render the pursuit of culture more egalitarian and democratic? Or is it more likely that the appropriation of a wide spectrum of cultural content by cultural elites is gauged in forms which retain the divide by other means? And how does television, the most egalitarian of modes for delivering cultural material, respond to these challenges?

In the previous chapter we explored this question in relation to forms which are widely perceived as the lowest of bad-taste TV. We would now like to turn to the other end of the scale, and look at ARTE, a channel accused of elitism and cultural ghettoisation (see p. 146). We will investigate whether the hybridisation of cultural forms is also reflected in ARTE's programming and, if so, whether this in itself is a defence against the charge of catering only for elites.

ARTE describes itself as a cultural channel (or rather, in German, as a 'Kulturkanal'; in French as a 'chane culturelle'. Such translations already beg the question of linguistic equivalence (see, for example, Baker 1992). As Raymond Williams (1976) has famously shown for the etymology and contemporary use of the English term, the term 'culture' itself has deeply ambivalent connotations, ranging from traditional associations of middle-class tastes (e.g. high culture) to those which embrace ordinary everyday-life pursuits (popular culture) (see also McCabe 1986; Collins 1989). In its rendering as French 'culture' or German 'Kultur', a bold equivalence is asserted between the French and the German which is not at all self-evident if one takes the different connotations into account; the French pointing more towards high culture and the German towards the more inclusive meaning (see also Emanuel 1993, 1995).[2] Note in this connection the difficulty of translating the English term 'popular culture' into German – 'Populärkultur' is not a widely used term and usually brought in to capture the British-derived academic debate in this area.[3]

Given this difficulty with the term, the only way to find out what it means to be a cultural channel will be to look at what a cultural channel does and how it defines itself through its discourses of and about culture.

ARTE was set up in Strasbourg in 1991 as a collaboration between the French La Sept ARTE (headquarters in Paris) and Germany, ARTE Deutschland TV GmBH (headquarters in Baden Baden). The bilingual channel started transmitting on cable and satellite in May 1992. In France it was also granted a terrestrial frequency in September of the same year. Different frequencies allow viewers to select the French or the German version. The name of the channel ARTE suggests art, but it is in fact a cunning acronym for 'Association Relative à la Télévision Européenne'. At present, three-quarters of ARTE's programming is delivered in equal parts by its French and German branch, each in turn collaborative public-service organisations. Since its foundation, ARTE has struck up deals with Belgium (Radio-Television Belge de la Communauté Française/RTBF), Switzerland (Schweizerische Rundfunk- und Fernsehgesell-schaft/SRG) and Spain (Television Española/TVE) who deliver the remaining programmes.

To create a publicly funded cultural channel at a time of privatisation and commercialisation of much of the European media was bound to attract criticism; not only because it seemed to be running against the tide of the times, but also because it appeared to favour the exclusive tastes of a small minority audience over the general public. On the other hand, given the huge and continuing expansion of available channels, many of a generic type, targeting specific viewer groups, an argument can be made in favour of a channel which simply targets a further taste segment – a channel specifically designed for the culture experience of trans-national audiences. From that latter point of view, the venture of a culture channel as such deserves no criticism, except perhaps for the fact that it is publicly funded and not by advertising revenue. But ARTE does not wish to restrict itself to a minority niche audience; it wishes to become 'the leading European TV channel'. What kind of culture, then, does ARTE represent?

Susan Emanuel, in two highly critical articles (1993, 1995), sees the creation of a cultural channel – by France in particular – as a defensive move against the perceived threat of Americanisation. She argues that: 'ARTE is symptomatic of a lingering anti-Americanism of the European intelligentsia, traceable back to figures like Sartre and Pirandello, and of the consequent bifurcation of television offering into high and mass culture' (1995: 170). Only by appealing to the elitist tastes of Europe's trans-national cultural elites, which have always shared a taste for high culture – music, literature, painting, independent cinema (cinéma d'auteur/Autorenfilm) – has ARTE in her view found its – albeit minimal – audience.

> The creation and maintenance of a cultural channel devoted to European cultural heritage, and its inclusion of certain forms from avant-garde, youth and peripheral cultures, will have the effect of amplifying cultural stratification ... while the masses are abandoned to a diet of so-called global kitsch provided by the commercial channels.
>
> (Emanuel 1995: 174)

Emanuel finds little to recommend in the channel's efforts to attract European audiences. While not denying that ARTE, like Channel 4 in Britain, is making attempts to reach wider audiences, its isolation from market pressures will, in her opinion, keep it in an artistic ghetto apart from mainstream TV culture. ARTE, then, is caught up in more than one of the dilemmas of TV production in the late twentieth century: it is a public-service channel within an increasingly commercial environment, it defines itself as distinctly European staking claims for quality and good-taste television in opposition to low-cost, low-quality, low-taste productions – the latter often unfairly identified with American-style TV.

Emanuel's essays were published in 1993 and 1995. Since then, ARTE's audience figures have grown, possibly in response to a more mixed diet and more publicity in the scheduling magazines, but its essential characteristics as a publicly funded culture channel have remained in place. Indeed, one of the programmes targeted by Emanuel for its high tone and aloofness, *Histoire Parallèle* or in its German title, 'The Week 50 Years Ago', continues in its prime-time slot of 7.45 to 8.30 p.m., every Saturday. What we will do in this chapter is investigate how the cultural mission of ARTE and the channel's desire to produce quality TV is realised in three related quality discourses.

First of all we will investigate what ARTE has to say about itself. To do this we will discuss ARTE's own Web pages, still in celebratory mood because of the channel's fifth anniversary in 1997. Second, we will look at how ARTE's mission translates itself into its weekly programme schedules, by looking in particular at the programming of one week in September 1997, with some comparative glances at other weeks. Third, and most important for our argument, we will investigate in close detail two programmes which could be said to come from the opposite end of the taste spectrum, but which both belong very typically to ARTE. The first section below is concerned with *Histoire Parallèle*, where we discuss a single episode, broadcast in May 1997, where newsreels from the first week of May 1947 are shown and discussed by the historian Marc Ferro and his studio guest. We will then look at a run of programmes from a thematic evening, in this instance one that dealt with the popular end of the spectrum, an evening about soap operas, 'Soap Around the World'.

## ARTE about ARTE

That there is a tension between the aim to produce quality TV on the one hand and yet be accessible for wider audiences becomes very obvious if one looks at the way ARTE presents itself on its Web pages. Below are three passages from an address by Jérôme Clément, president of ARTE, apropos of the channel's fifth anniversary, which waver between stressing the openness for all viewers (see Example 1), while at the same time also insisting on how special and demanding it is (see Example 2). In some cases the contradictions are built into the same passage, such as below, in the somewhat idealist assertion that quality and favourable audience ratings go hand in hand.

### Example 1: *the wider audience argument*

ARTE has been stigmatised as cultural ghetto, in some cases even before it started transmitting. ARTE has no desire to favour the creation of isolated elites, but on the contrary has become an extraordinary channel that shows openness towards Europe and the world, its people, their ideas and fantasies, their hopes and fears, but without denying itself. Furthermore: the more the channel follows its own criteria, the more it is likely to be accepted and the higher will be the audience quotas.

Five years since its foundation, ARTE's aims remain clear and not too high-brow. Acceptance by viewers must be strengthened and everything must be done to make ARTE the European channel of the next millennium.

### Example 2: the special audience argument

Against global competition where TV companies are more and more forced to adopt shared norms until the television system has become completely uniform, ARTE by contrast is able to retain the values of public service television, and be demanding and full of respect towards its viewers, but also demanding of itself, be pluralistic and close to the citizens.

On a further Web page, where ARTE defines its (actual and target) viewers, this tension resolves into a clear definition of the above average viewer. Apart from one statement that ARTE programmes have become more versatile and more accessible to wider audiences, the Web page's ideal viewer clearly belongs to a cosmopolitan cultured elite. This is borne out in the way ARTE viewers are said to watch TV:

- They treat the medium of TV in a self-aware sense.
- They select with deliberation one or more programmes per week and follow these with great attentiveness.

It is also borne out in their alleged interests and hobbies, their attitude about travel, their skills in languages and, by implication, their socioeconomic status:

ARTE viewers are Europeans with highly developed cultural interests.... According to a study in March 95 (by IPSOS in France and GFM-Getas in Germany) ARTE viewers are similar in both countries in many respects: they are convinced Europeans, for whom TV plays an important role in making peoples of different nations closer to each other. They travel abroad more often and their knowledge of foreign languages is above average. They are also very interested in culture. They are enthusiastic readers and go more often to operas, theaters, museums, exhibitions or concerts than the national average of each respective population.

For these taste-defined audiences, ARTE provides a welcome and much-appreciated service:

The same poll shows that more than two thirds of the respondents in both countries think of ARTE as the 'TV channel of the future'. 90 percent liked in particular 'the different ways of looking at things', which they thought was typical for ARTE. 85% in France and 84% in Germany are convinced by the high quality of the programmes. For those who watch a programme at least once a week, ARTE is one of the most innovative channels. For those respondents, ARTE counts in both countries as one of the channels from which there is most to be learned.

Overall, the impression on the Web pages is of a channel proud of its success with highly cultured audiences, of its success with critics who give prizes to many of its productions and its trans-national appeal to these segments; but it also comes across as extremely self-conscious about its need to be seen to be addressing wider audiences, the classical dilemma of public-service channels that try to educate as well as entertain.

## ARTE scheduling

*The week of 20–27 September 1997*

To tease out whether the tension in ARTE's self-description might be borne out in the programmes as well, we would now like to look more closely at what a typical ARTE schedule offers its viewers.

ARTE transmits from 7.00 p.m. until about 2.00 a.m. During the day its German and French frequencies are occupied by the German Children Channel (Kinderkanal) and the French Fifth Channel (La Cinquième). ARTE runs on weekly schedules, with each day of the week devoted to a mix of programme types. Perhaps the most distinctive feature of this scheduling can be found in the thematic evenings, of which there are three each week on Sundays, Tuesdays and Thursdays.

These thematic evenings, which according to Emanuel were particularly favoured by the Germans, against a French preference for horizontal programming (Emanuel 1995), devote most of one whole evening to a single topic, usually presented as a mixture of film, TV drama, documentary and discussion.

Each of these thematic evenings comes with a different emphasis. Thematic evenings on Sunday, starting at 8.45 p.m. and lasting until after midnight, are meant to be on an 'entertaining' topic. According to ARTE's own Web pages, thematic evenings on Sundays are entertaining, dealing with popular heroes and myths – for example, extraterrestrials, wolves, Brigitte Bardot. True to this description, ARTE's thematic evening on Sunday 21 September had vampires as its topic. Under the umbrella title, 'Dracula, the Kiss of Death', the evening began with a German–French co-production from 1978, a remake of Murnau's famous silent film *Nosferatu* by German film-maker Werner Herzog, with Klaus Kinski in the lead part. This was followed at 10.30 p.m. by three documentaries: one about Bram Stoker, the Irish author of Dracula (*Master of Immortality*); another at 11.30 p.m. (*The Count at Your Neck*) about contemporary obsessions with vampires (*Vampirismus*) with text extracts from advertising and films, and a third between 11.45 p.m. and 00.30 a.m. about the reasons why people enjoy horror (*Die Lust am Gruseln* – 'The Pleasure of the Scary').

*Nosferatu*, a film noir made by one of the representatives of the New German Cinema is of course not a mainstream vampire film, but 'cinéma d'auteur' (Autorenfilm). Many of the films chosen for this Sunday slot are sophisticated independent cinema of this kind, though not restricted to French or German art cinema. This is in line with ARTE's declared support for European and worldwide independent cinema. A recent thematic evening on Joseph Conrad, for example, opened with the screening of Francis Coppola's *Apocalypse Now*, an anti-Vietnam War film based on Conrad's story *Heart of Darkness* (transmitted on 2 November 1997). Another had as its topic 'the Mediterranean', and opened with a 1977 Italian comedy *Viva Italia*. But not all thematic evenings include feature films, as we will show below when we discuss the thematic evening 'Soap Around the World'.

Thematic evenings on Tuesdays starting at the later time of 9.45 p.m. have cultural topics, according to the ARTE Web page. 'Literature, art, portraits of celebrities (living or dead), surrealism, erotic stories.' On Tuesday 23 September, the topic was TV itself. Under the umbrella title 'TV Families, or the Dream of Viewing', the evening consisted of two documentaries about the history of TV, first from a French and then a German perspective, each introduced by TV producers and presenters and their families. The French programme featured a popular TV presenter, himself a son of two French TV personalities; the German focused on a producer of a popular children's programme (*Die Sendung mit der Maus*), and father of two children who also became involved with TV – hence the title 'TV Families'. This was followed by various short films, including some by students of film and TV. Another typical Tuesday introduced independent black cinema through the portrait of one of its pioneers, Melvin van Peebles (4 November 1997); another thematized American writer Tennessee Williams (11 November 1997).

Thematic evenings on Thursdays focus on 'important social events, history, politics, economy, society, such as for example AIDS, oil, Stalin Dollar'. On 25 September 1997 this brought us an evening about sex. ('Sex Without Frontiers – The Billion Dollar Business'), again realised through a mixture of TV film and documentary. Another Thursday was devoted entirely to the war in Algeria (6 November 1997); another on youth and violence included comparative studies from different European countries, and round-table discussions (13 November 1997).

This brief look at the scheduling arrangements of the three thematic evenings each week, and the range of material typically transmitted gives an indication of what ARTE means by its claim to be a European cultural channel. It clearly does not wish to be seen as a niche for high art, the TV equivalent to what Radio Three does for classical music. Nor is it a channel that relays primarily live performances from the world of art to TV audiences (as the Performance channel does), though these are included from time to time. A recording of the Mozart opera *Die Entführung aus dem Serail* from the Salzburg Festival of that year was shown on the Wednesday of the week in question (24 September 1997). Other programmes deal with jazz and rock performances as well. There is the already mentioned emphasis on independent cinema which also receives regular Monday slots for films from across Europe, often shown in the original with subtitles.[4] But even here it would be difficult to assign labels such as high versus popular art to what is being shown: on 22 September the choices were for a 1979 French tragicomedy by François Truffaut, *Domicil Conjugal*, 8.45–10.20 p.m., and a 1993 Japanese film by Kurosawa (*Madadayo*), 10.50 p.m.–1.00 a.m., the two films only separated by a short French film and a film magazine. But this is as much part of ARTE's commitment to international rather than national programming as it is about high art.

We can illustrate the character of the channel's hybridity with reference to the programming on a fairly standard Saturday. On 20 September 1997 transmissions started at 19.00 with *KYTV* a British comedy series from 1992 consisting of 'spoof' TV broadcasting from an imaginary low-budget channel, followed by *Histoire Parallèle*, followed by David Lynch's cult thriller serial *Wild Palms* (US 1993), followed by a portrait about female rock and roll bands *Rockladies*, a German TV thriller (*Children of the Devil*) and *Cartoon Factory*. The day closed with a visit to *Documenta* X, the 10th quintennial festival of contemporary visual art – unashamedly elitist – in the German town of Kassel.

There is, of course, an absence of some of the most frequent TV genres from commercial TV – there are no game shows, no commercials and no regular soap. But it is not exclusively high art, either. ARTE, in its scheduling of different programme contents, actually exemplifies the late twentieth-century hybridisation of (TV) culture.

We would, however, like to go beyond the observation that a cultural channel such as ARTE is a hybrid, which it undoubtedly is. What makes ARTE's programming policy different from most other channels is not just its hybridity, but – and this may underlie the impression of a certain elitism – its way of embedding individual programmes inside longer schedules, so that texts appear in contexts lasting several hours. Whether this is the result of an under-lying assumption that ARTE viewers are loyal across a whole evening, or whether the range of provisions is there to allow a range of choices, is hard to tell. In its self-description on the Web page, ARTE defines as a regular ARTE viewer someone who sees one of its programmes at least once per week – a rather modest requirement, given the average viewing hours of TV audiences. But, if loyalty across a whole evening may be too much to ask for, as a viewing experience ARTE viewing is most certainly meant to be the result of careful selection, concentrated viewing, and no zapping while it lasts.

Perhaps, then, the accusation of elitism may lie not so much in the actual range of ARTE programmes and their content, but in the way programmes address the viewer within the context of individual programmes or across a whole thematic evening. In spite of its declared openness to different and varied cultural contents, ARTE may nevertheless help to reproduce a continuing ambivalence about culture and taste. It is not, yet, comfortable with the loss of privilege that the old 'high' culture has succumbed to. While refraining from an exclusive focus upon high art content, its use of scheduling, discourse structures and tone mediate a particular relation to culture which will be more congenial to the educated classes than to the less educated. ARTE, we argue, does not wish to appeal by privileging a particular aesthetic sensibility which takes pleasure in certain exclusive forms with cultural capital attached, such as opera or classical theatre (cf. Bourdieu 1986, 1990, 1997). Rather, its appeal is based upon a kind of 'epistephilia' (Nichols 1991: 31), the pleasure of knowingness, of expertise. 'Knowingness', of course, is not the privilege of the educated classes. There are subject-specific forms of expertise surrounding most social and leisure activities – soccer, rock music, film, motorbikes. But ARTE seeks to extend the principle of expertise across the range of its offerings. As such, it is both egalitarian and elitist at the same time. It is egalitarian in that it allows all tastes to be taken seriously, so that any topic – soap opera, vampires, Maria Callas or the war in Algeria – can be equally worthy of having not just one programme, but a whole thematic evening, dedicated to it. And then it is elitist in that the pleasure of engaging with these tastes is itself framed within a metadiscourse about the cultural phenomenon in question. These metadiscourses can take different forms. On the one hand, there are the conventional verbal strategies: expositions, arguments and analyses of what it means to know. On the other hand, there is the 'craft' of television production: the techniques of sound and image juxtaposition achieved through editing and camera work. In either case the common factor is the serious, in-depth engagement with the topic.

Let us now discuss this in detail by focusing on two exemplary instances which present us with different styles of metadiscourses. With the first programme – one Saturday evening episode of *Histoire Parallèle* – we will show how verbalised metadiscourses of expertise are employed in a series which deals seriously with the very demanding topic of history and world politics. With the second – a thematic evening, 'Soap Around the World' – we will show how equal attention is paid to a very popular form of light entertainment, employing production techniques to create very specific judgemental framings.

## Metadiscourses of expertise: Histoire Parallèle

Generically *Histoire Parallèle* (*HP*) could be called a historical documentary focusing on what happened 50 years ago, realised in the format of old newsreels, embedded in a dialogue between two experts. But *HP* is not a classical documentary, where the point of what is being shown is usually clearly signalled either by a voice-over to the footage which explains what is being shown, or by a fly-on-the-wall technique where what is being shown will speak for itself, or some other related means of combining commentary and documentary footage (cf. Nichols 1991; Corner 1996). *HP* is more ambitious and strenuous in what it expects of its viewers, not only in the way the film extracts are employed, but also in the way the dialogue partners frame these filmic extracts.

The point of selecting extracts from old newsreels is the illustration of a particular historical moment as it was presented at the time. By showing several extracts from more than one country on a related theme, a comparative frame is already built in just by looking at the film footage. But the point of the programme is not primarily the comparative viewing of old film, but the historical analysis of events which may or may not be demonstrated by the newsreels. This historical analysis is provided by Marc Ferro, a well-known French historian, who leads a discussion with one invited guest with special knowledge about the events to be discussed. He or she may be an eyewitness of these events, but usually the guests are fellow historians or academics from related disciplines, writers or journalists. The discussion before and after each clip subjects the themes addressed by the newsreels to the analysis of the academic historian with a very different historical context to offer than the one implicit in the footage. Very often the point of the discussion is that the newsreels ignored the events of the time – a major crisis in the country, an impending strike, a threat of war, etc. – in favour of a more propagandist and upbeat version of events. The significance of producing the original footage is thus as much for what *is not* as for what *is* shown. The corrective is provided to some extent by the comparative footage, but most importantly by the historians' analysis of the historical and political context to the events shown.

Let us now look at this in more detail by focusing on the different programme segments of HP: the introductory sequences, the clips proper and the discussion between the experts. To focus our discussion we have selected one programme from the first week of May 1997; that is, a programme which discussed the events of the first week of May 1947.

*History in sepia: framing the past (introductory sequences)*

The transition from preceding programmes to *Histoire Parallèle* is set by three moves, which take the viewer from a glossy artistic colourful image to the black-and-white sequences from the past. The initial programme ident – ARTE does not have studio announcers but a range of special templates – is of a deep-blue sky with stars, where the world appears as a ball as seen from outer space. A man rolls it around on his shoulders and finally whirls it on his fingertips. Here, along with a possible allusion to Atlas carrying the world on his shoulder, there is a playful touch: I have the world on my fingertips – all made possible by advanced computer graphics. The voice-over to this sequence also suggests movement and viewing from a distance. Below are two examples from two different programme announcements:

> What moved the world 50 years ago, moves us now – with Marc Ferro.
> Resurrected/returned from the archives – the week 50 years ago.[5]

This ident then gives way to *Histoire Parallèle*'s introductory sequences. A rapid sequence of black-and-white footage again suggests movement. We see a diver jumping from a high board, turning in the air and disappearing in the water; we see waves roaring up against the side of a steamer; miners descending in a cage, pit-head wheels turning, etc. This set of black-and-white images is accompanied by a strangely reverberating, hollow sound sequence reminiscent of noises heard under water, followed by a sombre cello. The images are not particularly refer- ential, but symbolic of the past. Together with the music, they work aesthetically by setting the mood: we are now entering a past that is moving and turning, but also mysterious, remote, even gloomy. An inset box is then superimposed upon this footage, and the box is used to introduce that week's programme, with images taken from the newsreels of 50 years ago, in sepia tones, lending them the patina of a time long gone. A voice-over introduces the episode's themes.

In the first week of May 1997/1947, this episode-specific lead-in comprised references at once suggestive and elusive.

*Images*
May procession in Moscow
Pictures of Stalin and other members of Politburo carried by the marchers
Close-up on picture of Tito
Three men walking out of a building
A group of photographers
Berlin Brandenburger Gate with pictures from German 1 May. Marchers carrying banners reading 'Arbeit u. Brot für Alle' (Work and Bread for Everyone)
*Text*
On 1 May 1947 communism has reached the climax of its power. The Soviet Union holds parades and refuses any agreements about Germany. It controls Bulgaria and Poland.
Tito goes further still. He finds it too opportunistic that Thorez remains in the three party regime. As far as the two German parties are concerned, they are already on collision course.[6]

If these announcements are to give the viewers a specific idea of what they are to see, then their success depends on a high level of historical knowledge on the viewer's part. Although the comment about the power of communism and the Soviet Union are clear enough, the reference to Tito (Tito – then president of Yugoslavia – what does it mean that Tito goes further – with what?) and his connection to Thorez (a member of the French Communists – but who would know this?), and two German parties (which parties?), are far too vague and obscure, and one can only assume that the main point of the lead-in is again atmospheric mood setting rather than referentiality.

*Scopic pleasures: viewing the past*

During the programme about the first week of May 1947, the following clips from newsreels appear in this order:

- Newsreel from the Soviet Union (SU)
- Newsreel from the Western-Anglo-American zones of Germany (WG)
- Newsreel from the Soviet zone of Germany (EG)
- Newsreel from France (F)
- A documentary about the history of trade unions made from the point of view of the Left (DOC).

These films provide a fascinating contrast in their use of images, music and news text since in each case they support very different ideological positions. Just to compare the opening lines of each shows this clearly:

SU: Celebrations about May the first in the USSR and abroad. With enthusiasm the Soviet people celebrated the first of May, the international festival of the working people ... The heroic city of Leningrad, cradle of the October Revolution ... [7]

WG: May celebrations everywhere. As everywhere in the world, so in Germany too, the first of May was celebrated as the festival of the working people and the day of peace for all people.[8]

EG: On the morning of the first of May, the great assembly of all working people begins in town and country.[9]

F: The first of May, festival of the workers, of the may-bells and, theoretically at least, of the first warm days, intimately mixes poetry with trade union demands and makes a clear definition impossible. But, whichever it is, every year on the first of May we find the same atmosphere ... closed shops, empty squares and streets. The students complain: this year the holiday fell on a Thursday where schools were closed in any case. What a shame. 'Dear Minister, if the first of May falls on a Thursday couldn't you please move it to an ordinary school day ... '[10]

These opening lines are indicative of what is to follow in each case. The SU newsreel stresses the heroic victory of workers and military by homing in on parades of soldiers, tanks, etc. in front of politicians and generals, moving from heroic Leningrad, to the Navy and the warships in the Black Sea, to Kiev and to Minsk, before moving abroad to Bulgaria and Czechoslovakia, and finally back home to Moscow. It closes with the triumphant lines: 'Under the banner of Lenin and Stalin the people showed that they are fighting for the eventual victory of communism in our country. Praised be Stalin.'[11] This heroic discourse is further strengthened by the appropriately heroic music.

The WG newsreel, by contrast, shows thousands of ordinary people marching in the street, with banners proclaiming their lack of food. Here, too, the newsreel covers different (West German) cities – Hamburg, Munich, Essen and Berlin (which in these pre-Berlin Wall days was of course still accessible from the East and the West). But it also stresses the folk tradition of May:

In thousands of little towns and villages there was a May celebration of the traditional kind. Here in Ebenhausen in Bavaria, after the procession the dancing around the maypole completes the festival of all working people.[12]

The East German newsreel is more similar in its triumphant tone to the one from the SU than to its WG counterpart. It reports the same demonstration and meeting in the Berlin Lustgarten as was shown in the WG clip, but here the socialist hymn, the *Internationale*, is playing in the background. As the quote by one of the speakers demonstrates, the celebration is in the service of socialism: 'Hermann Schimmel appealed to the audience to commit all their strength so that through unity we achieve peace, through unity we overcome hunger and misery, through unity we achieve socialism.'[13]

And finally the French newsreel insists on the pleasures of May, and down-plays any possible tension: 'The May days when buses were set aflame gave way to more peaceful but equally interesting demonstrations. Today one thinks more about how to make windows rather than how to break them.'[14]

In each case, the images – parades of weapons, soldiers, ordinary workers, people in local costume, bunches of may-bell flowers, etc. – and the music soundtrack confirm the tone of what is being said, from triumphant heroism, appeal to solidarity of workers and socialism, to the pleasures of spring.

By juxtaposing original newsreel footage from different sources, viewers are to some extent able to judge for themselves some of the differences in the reporting that went on in the different military zones of postwar Germany (East versus West) and contrast these in turn with an Eastern (e.g. SU) and a Western (French) version of events. But since these were newsreels targeting audiences 50 years ago in different countries, many of the visual and textual references remain elusive, since viewers may or may not have knowledge about the events as shown from other personal or historical sources. Younger viewers may not recognise any of the images, whereas for older viewers the footage may generate nostalgic pleasures irrespective of content. During the showing no further explanations are provided, with the exception of subtitles in French or German where the soundtrack is in another language. But the point of showing these extracts is not to understand the newsreels as such, but the historical interpretation of this period 50 years ago by the experts in the studio. This may or may not be anchored in what the newsreels show. Much, then, depends on how the experts mediate the newsreels to the viewers.

## Overhearing the experts

The dialogues between Marc Ferro and his guest usually take place in a televi-sion studio, with the two partners sitting opposite each other at a round table (occasionally Ferro meets his guest at other locations, but the set-up is always the same face-to-face mode). In the studio, a large screen behind them is set for screening the film, title captions, and some still frames.

During the discussions only a very limited range of camera angles are employed: the dialogue partners are either shown facing each other across the table, or more often we get an oblique close-up shot of the speaker looking slightly past the camera, so it is obvious that the eye contact is with the addressee in the studio, not the listener at home. Regular reverse shots show the addressee, to gauge his or her response to the speaker. This positions the viewer at home in the role of the privileged overhearer/bystander. The atmosphere thus created is of serious concentration, where nothing deflects from the dialogue between the two interlocutors.

## Expert talk

The viewer's marginal role as bystander rather than addressee is not just constructed by visual means through camera angles, but affects every aspect of the discussion.

### ADDRESSING THE EXPERT

Apart from the closing sequence, Ferro only once addresses the viewer directly: at the beginning of the programme when he introduces his guest in the third person. This third-person introduction serves to establish his visitor's expert role. As his expert interlocutor in the May programme, Ferro introduces Pierre Broué, as a former Trotskyist who has written about historical events. His expert credentials are thus established by both being a participant in as well as eyewitness of a particular historical movement – he was a Trotskyist and a trade unionist – and by having written about historical events and movements. This double expertise is referred to several times during the programme. Once his expert credentials are thus established Ferro switches to the pronoun of direct address, sometimes reinforced by adding his name.

FERRO:  In order to talk about the first of May 1947 I welcome Pierre Broué who
    has written about the Bolshevik Party, about the Spanish Civil War and
    about the German revolution. He was a Trotskyist, and I therefore want to
    ask him: You, the Trotskyists were already able to imagine that the SU
    might disintegrate...[15]

FERRO:  Pierre Broué, what does this first of May in West Germany tell you...[16]

### DISPLAYING MUTUAL KNOWLEDGE

In the discussion between Ferro and his guest, many of the references depend on mutual knowledge between the discussants about the events or the personalities involved. This takes different forms:

•   referring to facts known to the discussants, such as names or acronyms of
    personalities, organisations, places which are simply mentioned without
    further explanation;

- looking back at the events from a vantage point in the future, showing with-hindsight knowledge, with the discussants in the role of omniscient narrators; and
- judging and interpreting history on the basis of shared historical knowledge.

*Known facts, not explained by the context*  Consider the references here to CGTFO, Demargie, Thorez, the Kominform.

BROUÉ:  .... For some, the starting point of the CGTFO ...

FERRO:  in any case, Demargie wants to exclude them ...

BROUÉ:  And so Thorez says, we are in favour of wage increases ...

FERRO:  And later the Kominform gets together and criticises Thorez because of his conciliatory politics.

*Omniscient narrator*  Notice how Broué anticipates the future behaviour of the German trade unions, and Ferro anticipates the future formation of the GDR:

FERRO:  And the German trade unions, what is their role?

BROUÉ:  At this moment, they are still agitating. But later they gradually realise their advantages and make a nice apparatus for themselves, nicely oiled, nicely integrated into the new state...

FERRO:  And now let us look how Eastern Germany, which will soon be a new state, celebrates the first of May.[17]

*Interpretation and judgement*  The presenter and the expert both allow themselves to speculate about the purposes of the Communists.

FERRO:  And the Communists believed that they were regaining their power by other means?

BROUÉ:  The Communists think this is only an intermezzo, and when Stalin reassures them that their demonstrations are pushing back the imperialism in the colonies, that they're pushing back the Marshall Plan initiative, etc., they figure that they are still somewhere part of the government. They reaffirm this all the time, even when they get persecuted. Their hand remains stretched out, stretched out towards the government.

FERRO:  And they're waiting until the Mitterrand era arrives.

BROUÉ:  Yes, one might say that.[18]

The paragraph below combines all these modes successively. The emphasis in the discussion is not on what the French newsreel shows – for example, what has just been seen and heard by the discussants and the viewers alike (capital letters, lines 1–3) – but what it hides, with the experts dismissing the film as propaganda. Known facts, not explained by context, are shown in bold print;

the underlined sequences represent the omniscient narrator; interpretation and judgement is given in italics:

FERRO: Pierre Broué, THIS NEWSREEL IS BEING PRESENTED IN THE WELL-KNOWN, SUPPOSEDLY RELAXED AND DISTANCED VOICE OF THE CHRONICLER. *But it is deceptive to present things in this way.* If there was one stormy first of May for the political and trade union organisations, then that first of May 1947 was it. This is the moment when **Daniel Manière** and the socialists are booed. They are in government when the communists are nearly split over the question, should they continue with the government or not. And one is supposed to believe that everything was fine. That will change in a few months.

BROUÉ: *Yes it's the classical propaganda myth,* because now, at the start of 1947, we find extreme tension everywhere: in the dissolution of the governing coalition in the East and in the West, but also in the dissolution of the Communist Party. We experience this split in Italy but also in France. There we have the tension between the workers and the **CGT**, between the workers and the leaders of the Communist Party, partly also within the Party and the **CGT**. The strike at **Renault**'s is therefore no accident. There you have for the first time a confrontation where the majority of the workers turn against the trade unions and criticise them. It's a decisive event which explains the speed and force of the change around in France.

FERRO: And we know what will happen in a few months.

BROUÉ: Of course.

FERRO: But the newsreels won't let us guess any of these events. Basically *this is pure disinformation.*

BROUÉ: Certainly.[19]


NARRATING PERSONAL EXPERIENCE

A different strategy for establishing expert talk is the use of anecdotal personal experience. Broué, in the extract below, authenticates his present-day assessment of past events by his direct personal participation in the events then, here made even more convincing by his admitting to having been mistaken at the time.

BROUÉ: Yes, and then there was this strike at Renault's which I could follow very closely because I was a member of the GCI, a Trotskyist youth organisation. Our General Secretary was Daniel Renard, a superb guy, a young Parisian worker, without fear, expressive, a brilliant public speaker and agitator ... And Daniel worked for Renault ... I became the bodyguard of our friend Daniel Renard, I slept on his doormat. But in fact, we were wrong, things had advanced much further than we thought. Those who really needed protection were those responsible in the trade unions and in the Party ...[20]

USING FILM AS EVIDENCE

Of all the strategies used to establish expert knowledge, the one that is least used by either of the discussants is the one most familiar from documentary film; namely the use of film as evidence. Given the amount of time that *HP* spends with showing newsreels (at least one half of the programme is devoted to them), it is surprisingly rare that the discussants refer to these directly. Below is one example where this does happen in relation to the West German newsreel, where the observation about what the historian sees in the reels (in capital letters) is then tied in with the interpretation of the event.

FERRO: Pierre Broué what does this first of May in West Germany tell you...?
BROUÉ: I AM SURPRISED ABOUT THE MASSES OF THE WORKERS; THEY ARE THERE, DETERMINED, POOR, BADLY DRESSED, UNDERNOURISHED. ALL HAVE THE FACES OF PEOPLE WHO HAVE JUST EXPERIENCED A TERRIBLE WAR AND POSTWAR PERIOD. GERMANY IS STARVING AT THAT TIME. In Germany we have a social time bomb. If our topic were the Marshall Plan, here we would find one of the reasons for this plan, since at all costs Germany had to be made stable.[21]

This passage shows vividly how well a reading of the film clip which was just seen by experts and viewers alike can be integrated with a discussion of the events. It certainly allows the viewer more ready access to what is being said, as well as giving them more opportunities to share in the reconstruction of events by the experts. That *HP* ignores so much of this more user-friendly strategy, privileging instead the more distancing devices of displaying shared knowledge between the discussants, may well be connected on the one hand with their suspicion about the propagandist nature of the newsreels in question. But it does make the viewer overdependent on expert talk and marginalises their own media literacy and expertise. The programme could be made more accessible if attempts were made to mediate difficult concepts, provide subtitles giving proper names of historical figures, trade unions, places, etc., and if more detailed references were given to what is being shown, before and after the showing.[22]

The impression one gets is that in *Histoire Parallèle* it is not really the viewers' own judgement that is appealed to, but viewers on the margins are allowed to listen in to the discussion of experts. As such it is undoubtedly interesting, but more could be done to involve the viewers. Even for an educated audience the programme takes too much for granted. This is not to deny this fascinating and informative programme its place, but it does explain the critique levelled against it – and, since this is one of ARTE's longest-running programmes – against ARTE's perceived elitism.

Overall, the juxtaposition of newsreels with such different emphases provides extraordinary documentary material for anyone interested in the way the media presented events half a century ago; gives memorable images of historical significance; and an intelligent, if hard-to-follow, debate about a period in history seen from the double perspectives of past and present. It celebrates the pleasure in knowing and the pleasure of rational debate and reasoning.

### 'Soap Around the World'

Any TV producer can safely assume that there are niche audiences to whom the engagement with serious metadiscourses, the language of expertise, rational debate and the quest for knowledge is pleasurable in itself. Discussions about serious topics, such as history and world politics, are often couched in formats like the one employed by *HP*. But, as we will show, ARTE sets a similar value upon expertise when the topic comes from the other end of the cultural spectrum – in talking about soap operas. In fact, in its combination of interviews with experts on the one hand and extracts from original footage on the other, the thematic evening 'Soap Around the World' (SAW) is not totally different from *HP*, except that here the original footage is supplied by extracts from past and contemporary soap operas, and the experts are those who market, produce, write, act in and – importantly – view the soaps. Where it does differ substantially from *HP* is in its style of editing, and its address to the viewers.

Like *HP*, SAW also works by contrasting different instances of original footage – in this case the different sub-genres of soap operas as produced in different parts of the world – and different expert voices from these countries. During the evening, we are shown six documentaries organised by country of origin:

- US/American glossy/melodramatic soap
- Mexico and US: glossy/melodramatic telenovelas
- Britain: social realist tradition (*Coronation Street*)
- Kasakhstan: social realist, British-inspired and -funded (*Crossroads*)
- Germany: social realist, British-inspired (*Lindenstraße*)
- Nigeria: satirical (*Basi and Company*)

In each of these documentaries, we are shown extracts from soap operas, interspersed with interviews with the experts, e.g. the soap professionals and the viewers.

In between the showing of each of these six films from SAW, three further film segments are interspersed as part of a trilogy of the title *My Life is a Soap Opera*. These short film segments feature three women talking about their lives. The first, a trained actor and a psychotherapist, includes among her clients former soap stars suffering from depression. One of the topics that she addresses is the difficulties that arise when fantasy worlds and reality merge. The two other parts of the trilogy are demonstrations of exactly that, in that both involve the imitation of TV stars. In one case, a rather heavy German woman totally hooked on soap operas and TV in general, declares her admiration for her role model, the American comedian Roseanne, and follows her path all the way to California. In the other case a viewer copies slim blonde Pamela Anderson from the US series *Baywatch* in her looks and style of dress.

All film segments provide contrasts between themselves: sentimental Mexican telenovelas contrast with the daily-life concerns of *Crossroads* in Kasakhstan; amused and critical viewers of Mexican telenovelas contrast with the Pamela Anderson clone, and the psychoanalyst in the trilogy provides an implicit critical commentary on the lives of the two other women. But internal to each film sequence further contrasts are achieved by the way different expert voices are edited against each other. This is where SAW differs from HP. Whereas *Histoire Parallèle* relied on the academic metacommentary delivered by the two studio discussants, SAW's metaposition emerges as a result of the different expert voices and illustrative extracts from the films juxtaposed to one another by editorial cuts. Although not directly referring to each other's arguments, the way these cuts are made positions the experts in confrontation with each other. The assessment of their credibility, negative judgements about whether they are gullible, vain, avaricious, manipulative, etc., or positive judgements about their imagination, inventiveness, truthfulness, is thus directed by the editorial control, inviting the viewer at home to share the implicit critique and ironic stance of the editorial arrangement. The interpolated extracts from various soap operas and other documentary shots are hereby used as evidence in favour of, or against, the positions taken by the experts: in many cases they undercut the authority of the speakers rather than illustrating or confirming their positions. This is, of course, a well-known technique in television documentaries in general. Walker (1993: 157) in his analysis of Channel 4's prestigious art series from 1987, *State of the Art*, describes a similar style of presentation as a Brechtian quotational technique, concluding (as we do) that the lack of a single author or point of view in the traditional sense does not prevent a series through selection, arrangement and editing of voices from taking an ideological stance. Meinhof (1994) takes a more critical stance in her analysis of Channel 4's *Media Show*, arguing that the technique was used to prompt misleading inferences between positions, as does van Leeuwen (1991). There is, of course, no reason to assume that actual viewers will respond accordingly (Richardson 1994).

We would now like to illustrate our argument by selecting passages from the film about telenovelas.

### Telenovelas

Below are transcriptions of the different voices used in this programme, thematically ordered and numbered, and taken in isolation from the argumentative context produced by the editing.

The commercial argument for producing and selling telenovelas is made by showing the commercial produced by the production company Grupo Televisa. Although it does mention talent as one of the advantages, the main emphasis is on its cost-effectiveness:

Commercial for Televisa

RESOURCES:  We have the talent and the studios, the equipment and the personnel; our library contains more than 115,000 half-hours of programming

COST EFFECTIVENESS:  Televisa's enormous value and economies of scale make us one of the most cost-efficient production companies in the world. And today we further expand our audience by producing telenovelas simultaneously in Spanish and English. Our dual-language production is cost-effective, because we use the same scripts, sets and technicians.

The strength of the company is confirmed by the director of export, Pedro Font, who is featured behind his desk in a New York office, smoking a thick cigar, gold-beringed, and sipping tea from a gold-rimmed cup. He speaks in Spanglish, i.e. a mixture of English and Spanish words, rendered more coherent by the subtitles.[23]

PEDRO FONT:  We're producing telenovelas, today 22 novellas in Spanish and 5 novellas in English, that makes 27 novellas, new ones, per year. Beside that, Televisa is a company with 3.5 billion dollars; the company has five channels in Mexico, and the company controls more than 87 per cent of the rating in Mexico; and the company is all around South America, is a very strong power company.

But he subordinates the financial arguments to the pleasure of soap operas for its viewers, which he describes in the following rather contradictory fashion:

PLEASURE-IN-ROMANCE

PEDRO FONT:  *Televisa novella* is similar to a book. You are starting a book, you enjoy the book, you finish the book and you buy another book. In the novellas or soap operas, the American, it's the same script, the same history year after year. We have only 100 hours, three months, one book, and you enjoy it, then it's finished, you cry, oh poor girl, or you're happy, you're extremely happy, and you get another. Life is romantic ...

PEDRO FONT:  People are looking for something; many people are full of illusions, full of dreams, the dreams they have but cannot fulfil. The telenovelas represent part of these dreams. They represent the boyfriend you never had and now you can have. And you like to remember that. You see, we have taken out all the dreams you have inside of you, and this way we go inside, we grab the inside of people; that's the power of the telenovelas.

PLEASURE-IN-REALITY

PEDRO FONT:  ... life is reality, life is the family, and life is the day-to-day happening for any human being. These are telenovelas ...

PEDRO FONT:  ... Never politics, we try to be very neutral; we like to be entertainment, life in the day-to-day working, we like to show the life in Mexico, the life in whole of South America, the life in America, the life in reality, OK politics is also a reality, but we like to be outside politics, how people suffer, how they love, how they work, how they dream.

UNIVERSAL PLEASURE

PEDRO FONT: It's unbelievable; it's unbelievable, in an Arabian country, it's unbelievable in European countries, it's unbelievable in Asian countries, and even in China, it's unbelievable, people love the novellas.

PEDRO FONT: Any human being has 40 or 50 per cent in common; the rest is history or education, or country or age, but with these 40 per cent you can make a big audience.

Against these commercial voices, the Barragan family, six women of Mexican descent living in California assembled together in front of a TV screen where one telenovela is playing, come over as refreshingly intelligent, media-literate and humorous. They provide a stark contrast to the two portraits given in the trilogy, and are more in tune with what Geraghty, Fiske and many others since have claimed; namely, that viewers of soap operas play, rather than identify, with soap narratives and heroes (Geraghty 1991; Fiske 1987). The arguments of the Barragan women for and against soap operas are anchored in their everyday life experience and their critical perception of the function which soap operas fulfil in different peoples' lives. Below are some illustrative extracts from their comments:

PERSONAL BONDING

VIEWER 1: People that live in Los Angeles or in California or in the United States – that's the only bond or connection they have to the country that they're no longer in. And they watch it and they feel like the telenovela family is part of their family, their faraway family, their Mexican family.

VIEWER 2: You go to Mexico and your family in the US is watching the same novella as you are in Mexico; and you could go over there and you could talk to your cousin about the novella, what happened in the novella and everybody feels like oh yeah, oh yeah, we have some connection with each other still something we have in common.

AMUSED DISTANCE

VIEWER 1: It's just something that they do in the soap operas or in the telenovelas that we wouldn't do in real life, but we look at it and we laugh at it and say I'd never do that.

VIEWER 2: I'm not addicted.

OTHERS (*LAUGHING*):  Oh yes you are.

VIEWER 2:  OK I like them when I watch them, but for me it's just a form of entertainment, you know, I don't dream that I want to be like them.

INTERVIEWER:  Do you think that life is a soap opera?

VIEWER 3  (*LAUGHING, MAKING FUN OF THE INTERVIEWER*): I hope it is.

CRITICAL DISTANCE

VIEWER 4:  Definitely it's a cover-up; because you know there's crisis in Mexico, economical crisis and political crisis, is very hard and very deep. And people is very like unhappy; you can see it in the news and you can read it in the newspapers. And you see the people who come here to LA, when they come here you can tell … that they come as refuge from poverty. They can't take it any more, they are angry.

VIEWER 2:  … And that's the way for the government or big corporations to keep the population happy, to make them feel, on TV it's not that bad. But one day, you know, reality is gonna get too close and TV is not going to be enough to keep them happy.

CUTS AS MEANS OF ARGUMENTATION

By interlacing clips and quotes from these different sources, sharp contrasts emerge between them, which position the different voices as being sentimental, credible, critical, hypocritical, cynical or manipulative:

- *Soap as seen*: extracts from various telenovelas stress their melodramatic, hugely sentimental nature as well as their cross-cultural popularity. Some extracts are collages made up of snapshots from different telenovelas, creating rapid sequences of different people kissing, or collapsing on the floor, and violent scenes. Longer extracts are shown where a marriage declaration is made in front of a party, another where a pauper girl roams the empty streets, etc. Apart from their Spanish and American versions, there are also clips from the same soap opera dubbed into Thai, Russian and Turkish, etc.
- *Producing and marketing soap*: voices representing the interests of producing and marketing soap stress financial rather than artistic merits, represented by clips from commercials for Grupo Televisa, one of the leading soap-producing companies. Set against he words of Pedro Font, the company's director of export, his attempts at putting a different gloss on his company's output makes him appear manipulative and hypocritical, and the commercials in turn exploitative and cynical.
- *Viewing soap*: voices representing groups of viewers who, by sharp contrast to Pedro Font's claims, are not at all taken in but produce more discerning arguments which combine a personal validation of what soap means to them and their families with a critical reading of its reality-suppressing narratives.

Below is just one brief example of some extracts, as above, but here in the actual order of broadcasting:

(*Collage of different clips from telenovelas*)

PEDRO FONT: ...People are looking for something; many people are full of illusions, full of dreams, the dreams they have but cannot fulfil. The telenovelas represent part of these dreams. They represent the boyfriend you never had and now you can have. And you like to remember that. You see, we have taken out all the dreams you have inside of you, and this way we go inside, we grab the inside of people; that's the power of the telenovelas.

> (*Cut to Barragan women sitting in front of a TV screen and laughing at what they see.*)

VIEWER 1 (*POINTING TO THE SCREEN*): I like that guy.

VIEWER 1: It's just something that they do in the soap operas or in the telenovelas that we wouldn't do in real life, but we look at it and we laugh at it and say I'd never do that.

VIEWER 2: I'm not addicted.

OTHERS (*LAUGHING*): Oh yes you are.

VIEWER 2: OK I like them when I watch them, but for me it's just a form of entertainment, you know, I don't dream that I want to be like them.

INTERVIEWER: Do you think that life is a soap opera?

VIEWER 3 (*LAUGHING, MAKING FUN OF THE INTERVIEWER*): I hope it is.

COMMERCIAL FOR TELEVISA: Televisa's enormous value and economies of scale make us one of the most cost-efficient production companies in the world.

PEDRO FONT: We're producing telenovelas, today 22 novellas in Spanish and 5 novellas in English, that makes 27 novellas, new ones, per year. Beside that, Televisa is a company with 3.5 billion dollars; the company has five channels in Mexico, and the company controls more than 87 per cent of the rating in Mexico; and the company is all around South America, is a very strong power company.

COMMERCIAL FOR TELEVISA: We have the talent and the studios, the equipment and the personnel; our library contains more than 115,000 half-hours of programming.

PEDRO FONT: Well, we'd say, welcome, come back, come in and see the novellas, they're enjoyable.

COMMERCIAL FOR TELEVISA: And today we further expand our audience by producing telenovelas simultaneously in Spanish and English. Our dual language production is cost-effective, because we use the same scripts, sets and technicians.

As can be seen by the above illustrative example, the programme on telenovelas uses editorial cuts as a means of presenting a meta-position which undercuts the authority of some of the experts in the film, i.e. the 'promotional voice' of the commercials and of Pedro Font. The filmic evidence, in this case a mixture of

very brief melodramatic, sentimental images from telenovelas, makes the statements by the production company's own commercials, and especially the claims
by the export director seem completely ludicrous. The latter is further undercut
by the women viewers, who show a more mature and critical attitude to the
programmes they are watching. The viewers at home are thus offered positive
identification figures through the voices of the viewer experts, against which
the telenovelas themselves, and those who produce and market them, come
across as cynical and manipulative. At no point are these positions spelled out
by a metacommentary.

The telenovela programme is not the only place in SAW where judgements
are conveyed through editorial practices. Another programme, about the
making of a soap in Kasakhstan, works in a similar (but less stark) way. The soap
is called *Crossroads* and it is noteworthy for two reasons. First, it has an 'educational' project – to introduce the citizens of Kasakhstan to the ways of
enterprise culture and capitalism in general. Second, British 'experts' employed
by the Know-How fund, a Western aid programme, have been recruited to give
professional advice. From our point of view the most interesting element of the
production, which, like the Telenovela programme, gives a range of voices, is
the conflict it reveals between the various perspectives. Certainly there is a
conflict between the goals of good entertainment and the didactic goals. But as
well there is an *aesthetic* conflict. Extracts from some of the most celebrated art
cinema in the world – notably by Eisenstein, the master of Soviet montage – are
cut against statements by the artistic team in Alma-Ata. They tell the viewers
how they had to relearn their craft from English teachers who favoured surface
over depth, speed of production over quality, and showed insufficient sensitivity
towards local customs. Undoubtedly the material has been cut to produce an
ironic stance towards the *Crossroads* project.

## In conclusion

This chapter investigated the attempts by the bilingual channel ARTE to
produce cultural television for the next millennium. Two programmes were
looked at in close detail to see how far the ambivalences which mark out the
channel's self-declared mission are registered in ARTE's scheduling policy and
in its style of programme making. With *Histoire Parallèle*, ARTE has adopted a
programme style which relies heavily on expert discourses about history from
which many viewers will feel excluded. In the thematic evening 'Soap Around
the World', on the other hand, ARTE shows that serious engagement with a
very popular genre can be equally rewarding. During the thematic evening
SAW, hardly any metacommentary was employed. Instead editorial cuts juxtaposed voices and filmic extracts in such a way that an argumentative chain
emerged which positioned the different experts in opposition to one another,
inviting an ironic and distanced view on what is being shown. One could thus
argue, on the one hand, that SAW adopts a more open, democratic and partici-
patory format by involving the viewers directly and appealing to their media

literacy, whereas *HP*'s style is more authoritarian and elitist. On the other hand, however, *HP* is very open and uncompromising in its demands on the viewers' attention, and does not disguise the fact that the programme presents experts with distinct opinions about historical events and their significance. By contrast, one could argue that SAW disguises its editorial control. There is no authorial signature behind the ironic collage of voices, though attempts to influence viewers by these editorial decisions can be clearly seen through the detailed analysis of the texts in their final edits.

Within a mushrooming media world, the ARTE offer of quality TV – be it in the form of the highly demanding *HP* or in the more viewer-friendly and hybrid forms and contents of thematic evenings – clearly has a role to play, though it is doubtful whether it will ever be able to attract a huge audience share. It may be that some compromise has to be found which allows ARTE to continue its special programming without relying entirely on public finances. Other than in Britain, where the terrestrial BBC channels are prevented from seeking advertising revenue by law, the public-service German (as well as many other European) channels are dually financed by licence fees and advertising. The cultural commitment to more demanding television, so welcome to ARTE's regular viewers, would in the current climate be far less vulnerable to criticism if ARTE accepted its role as a specialist channel catering for particular transnational segments of the population, a population group undoubtedly less well served by the global media. Successful commercial channels such as the British Channel 4 have shown that an appeal to different specialist audiences can indeed attract substantial advertising revenue, especially if they are as economically strong as ARTE's key audiences undoubtedly are. Whether the same can be said for transnational audience segments remains to be seen. But, in contrast to the self-conscious construction of Europeanness in EuroNews, ARTE's cultural concerns make it a more obvious candidate for successful trans-national European programming.

# Worlds in common? Conclusions

In this short concluding chapter we will draw threads together from previous discussions and offer some more general observations regarding the characteristics of European television at the end of the twentieth century. We will aim first to assess the kind of 'television research' which is on offer in the book; second to examine the extent of the novelty which has been made possible by the coming of the multi-channel environment; and third to reflect on the view of 'Europe' which emerges from our consideration of some of its television production.

## Industry, texts and experience

Dahlgren (1995), struggling with the polymorphous character of the television phenomenon, invites us to think of it as a kind of prism with three faces: one industrial, one textual and one focused on sociocultural experience. The industrial perspective emphasises economic and political forces which act on the medium's scope of operations intra- and internationally. The textual perspective emphasises the construction of meaning in audiovisual productions, including the role of audiences in that construction. The sociocultural perspective emphasises the links between television and the larger symbolic orders of social and political lives. These distinctions are necessary if we are to do justice to the complexity of the realities within which television operates. As in an actual prism, a certain refraction occurs when one or other perspective is adopted. Sociocultural and textual phenomena do not disappear in the context of an industrial point of view; nor does a sociocultural angle of vision eliminate industrial or textual matters. Distortions occur: 'content analysis', for example, is still employed as a methodology in studies with an industrial (policy) focus, although it is less than useful as a way of exploring textual phenomena in their own right, since it is so little concerned with the construction of meaning.

The prism metaphor also offers an apt characterisation of existing television research. Most studies tend to concentrate pre-eminently on one or other of these perspectives; or, like Barker (1997) adopt an approach which allows them to develop more or less distinct but complementary strands of research, corresponding to the faces of the prism.

The present volume takes the industrial context as a background, a set of conditions which has given rise to a new television environment in Europe. Our task has been to characterise that new environment, in terms of the range of audiovisual texts which constitute it; foregrounding always the implications of textual characteristics for the sociocultural experiences of European viewers at the start of the third age of broadcasting. It is thus the interface of these two faces of the prism – the textual and the sociocultural – with which we have been principally concerned.

As for the industrial context itself, this must be understood as a component within 'the inherently globalizing nature of modernity' (C. Barker 1997: 4). Barker's account is consonant with the theoretical perspectives of such writers as Harvey (1989), Giddens (1994) and Lash and Urry (1994). Modernity is characterised by time/space compression at every level – economic, political, social and cultural. Modern capitalism possesses a high degree of flexibility and mobility: investments are not tied to place to the same extent as before, and computerised information technology makes financial transfers instantaneous. Labour markets are chosen, rather than given in particular national contexts, while industry increasingly makes use of post-Fordist modes of production, and information has itself become a market commodity. All of this has consequences for the operation of television as an industry, and makes television ineluctably a part of the globalisation process. In consequence:

> television is a global phenomenon on an institutional level involving both national systems and the development of transnational television. Advances in television technology have created new distribution mechanisms which, allied to political and industrial support for market solutions, has weakened national regulatory environments. New transnational commercial corporations have entered into the global television market creating serious competition for public service broadcasters which, while they continue to survive, have lost part of their audience to their competitors. There has been a rise in transnational and monopoly ownership circumventing national regulation, so that global television is dominated by commercial multinational corporations.
>
> (C. Barker 1997: 6–7)

This is a good characterisation of what is happening to television as a result of changing economic conditions, along with regulatory frameworks where considerations other than the purely economic are still relevant. Media policy is not exclusively about the maximising of markets; it can still be about cultural protectionism, public-service and ethically justifiable restraints upon freedom of speech. Yet such characterisations as Barker's do not have much to say about the consequences of these changes for the nature of broadcast output, nor about the ways in which television is experienced by viewers as consumers, citizens and possessors of distinct cultural identities. Hence the need for complementary accounts which do attend to these phenomena, and for the necessary move to *specific* programming tendencies which result from the conditions thus described in general terms.

Dahlgren's discussion of the textual focus in media research is one which understands texts as constructions of *meaning* or, more accurately, as contributions to the process of meaning-construction which have to be completed by active viewers, making sense of what they see and hear. He is nevertheless wary of exaggerating the scope of textual polysemy, and suspicious of research which, in its eagerness to recognise the role of the audience, ignores or eliminates considerations of textual form:

> This populist proclivity is understandable as a reaction to some earlier strands of research which overemphasised the unilateral power of media messages. Yet this excessive underscoring of the multivalence of televisual texts ignores the repetitive and formulaic nature of most television output, the relative stability of most social frames of perception and the cultural familiarity with televisual discourses and genres – all of which contribute to delimit, though by no means ever eliminate, polysemic meaning.
>
> (Dahlgren 1995: 31)

This reflection upon textuality is one which questions the emphasis on polysemy and audience power in terms of the specific character of *television* texts and genres, i.e. their formulaic properties and their familiarity, and it is in these terms that it is worth further comment. The coming of the multi-channel environment means some destabilisation of cultural familiarity with televisual discourses and genres, and thus some increase in the potential for variant interpretations of television programming. At the same time it also, as we have shown, means the introduction of new formulae, and a potential restabilisation on different terms from those of the terrestrial era.

The third face in Dahlgren's prism is that of sociocultural experience:

> What appears on the screen is encountered and interpreted by viewers, and then enters into their social worlds through social interaction, being reinterpreted and inserted in a vast array of discourses. Moreover, television and elements of its output – modes of discourse, themes, topics, forms of humour, etc. – are then intertextually circulated through other media. Television is a part of our daily lived reality, penetrating into the microcosms of our social world. It also serves to organise and structure that world, both in terms of daily schedule and interaction within the household and in offering frameworks of collective perception: television links the everyday world to the larger symbolic orders of social and political life.
>
> (Dahlgren 1995: 39)

The interface of the textual and the sociocultural is profound, since sociocultural experience enters into the very construction of the text. This, too, is relevant to the analyses which we have provided in the present volume. The aspects of textual form that we have concentrated on have been those with the potential to penetrate into the microcosms of our social world in significant ways, because they carry meanings which are constitutive of very fundamental aspects of the social. This emphasis is important for arguments about the temporal and spatial organising properties of television discourse. These organising properties in terrestrial-era broadcasting, it would seem, operated in ways which cut across social and cultural differences between audience members. The cultural tendency of television and radio was, at a certain level of operation, a unifying one, at least as regards the consumption of material for the national audience to which the programming was directed. Diverse, divergent 'decodings' were demonstrable (see Morley 1980; Lewis 1985; Corner *et al.* 1990), yet such decodings generally concerned the *substantives* of programme material, rather than the unspoken assumptions about membership in national society and temporal synchronicity (the carrying of a shared present). The question mark in this book's title reflects our understanding that the new conditions of broadcasting pose a challenge to those assumptions.

## Novelty and familiarity

Although the case studies for this book were all conducted in the late 1990s, they exemplify forms of programming which we expect to continue into the next decade and perhaps beyond. It is appropriate to end this book by using those case studies to reflect on the extent of the novelty in the new era.

There is a deliberate bias towards the novel in the selection of case study material. Twenty-four-hour news channels, 'European' channels, shopping channels are all relatively new and not yet universally available across the continent. Yet this prima facie case for change is one that needs to be supported by more careful examination of the textual evidence. The risk here is that the bias in our selection will lead us to 'talk up' the differences between the old TV and the new more than is warranted; we may be in danger of underestimating the continuities because these have not been in the forefront of analysis. And yet we have been very careful to approach the new channels and programmes so as to recognise how they build on established conventions of address and of scheduling, even while they modify those conventions for new viewing conditions.

'Talk shows' are a case in point. The viewing conditions which led to the emergence of the new talk shows developed not in Europe, but in the United States of America. They were experienced as 'new' in Europe several years after the format had become common on the other side of the Atlantic. Shock value attended their introduction. In Britain the moment of greatest impact came, not in 1996–7, when the talk shows first started transmission over the European audiovisual space, but many months later in early 1998, when Jerry Springer made the transition from cable/satellite stations to terrestrial television. This was a moment attended by much media hype, since the star himself decided to visit Britain at that point and to undertake the usual circuit of media appearances to promote the show. Meanwhile, in the United States ratings were falling, and some 'toning down' was in process. *Jerry Springer, Rolonda, Sally Jessy Raphael et al.* have to be differentiated from other shows which fall under the general rubric of 'talk show'. This is not hard to do: the distinctiveness is real enough. Yet they do represent a modification of existing conventions, not a wholly new form. It is because of this that they can be comprehended by the viewing audience.

Or take the case of rolling news. Rolling TV news has been around now for more than a decade, though it still deserves to be treated as new by comparison with fixed-point news programming. It is a bandwagon upon which national broadcasters are keen to jump. The BBC did so in 1998 – controversially, since the funding for its news channel came principally from the licence fee, even though terrestrial viewers were unable to receive it.

A case can be made that there is very little about 24-hour news which is innovatory. After CNN had proved itself, it was as if 24-hour news was something that viewers had always wanted and only technological limitations had prevented the fulfilment of this desire. There is something about the nature of 'news', as our societies conceive it, that is likely to foster just such a prospect. The world is a constantly changing place and only a 24-hour rolling news channel can truly keep pace with that change. Viewers know what they are getting when they tune in to CNN, n.tv, Sky News, etc. Once they could only get it at fixed schedule points, but now it is constantly available. To push the point a little further, 24-hour news is even less different from fixed-point news than its own rhetoric suggests. The scheduling on these channels still involves fixed point delivery, though the delivery points come around much more quickly than on other channels, and the schedule can more easily make room for breaking news and updates. Clearly, differences of this kind can be talked up or talked down according to the argument at hand. It is fair to say that the rolling news channels have been conservative in their appropriation of the existing conventions for news production and delivery – in comparison to the forms employed by Euronews or by Live TV.

Is rolling news, then, different from fixed-point news only in degree and not in kind? Some critics fear that the logic of 'liveness' will encourage the 24-hour channels to develop their capacity to show at the expense of a commitment to explain. Indeed, EuroNews already runs one regular feature, entitled *No Comment*, which shows 'raw footage' without any soundtrack other than the sounds on scene. Our account has focused upon the *constancy* of rolling news. Even though scheduling is cyclical, and cyclicity was developed on the older channels before it was adopted by the newer ones, there is something about the short news cycle which gives rolling news an intensity that is significantly different. This intensity, this unremitting news delivery, fosters a belief in the viewer that the broadcasters cannot possibly *miss* anything. Their presence at news events, their fidelity to running stories, and their frequent opportunities to pass on what they know, underpin this viewing orientation, and it is this which constitutes the novelty of the new approach.

The multi-channel experience is itself a novelty for European viewers. It is a novelty which quickly wears off once the technology is installed, especially as the viewer quickly discovers, for example, that rolling news channels can be very similar to one another; that the same trailers and commercials can be found on different channels; that repeats of terrestrial-era programming make up a large part of the diet, and so on. After that, the promise of the new technology depends on the desirability of the particular offerings, rather than the multi-channel experience as such. Certainly there is a market for particular kinds of broadcasting, notably sport, movies and pornography, and these are the services for which a premium can be charged. The novelty effect in fact is likely to diminish rather than increase in the immediate future. The scope for innovation in a crowded marketplace is less, even if there are still niche markets to be discovered. There have been predictions of less nationally shared television in the future. This is a prediction that must be treated with considerable caution. We discuss the European dimension below. It may be that the 'Did you see … ' conversations of the past will become less common in the future. People will not have watched the same shows at the same time, and will not be able to cement their interpersonal relations with friends and colleagues with talk which builds on this particular kind of shared experience. And yet popular series can get around the erosion of the shared experiential moment through extensive repetition, if they can afford the repeat fees to performers. As for the news – if the news gatekeepers working for different institutions continue to share the same news values, then the national audience will continue to have broadly comparable news experiences whichever (national) channel they watch.

Live broadcasting will continue, especially on sports channels. These will retain, even when recycled, a certain inherent, authentic relation to an originary moment, through deictic features of language and in other ways. But it is probable that a much clearer separation will emerge between programmes of this kind and those designed for portability between times and places, bearing in mind right from inception the range of contexts (markets) within which the text will be consumed. Viewers whose TV lives revolve around programmes of the latter type will have little reason to assent to the idea of TV as a medium which brings them into a shared spatiotemporal reality.

## Television in a changing Europe

In our discussion of the changing face of the European media world, we have concentrated on those channels which attempt to address viewers across national boundaries, and are searching for innovatory ways to overcome the difficulty caused by the enormous linguistic and cultural variation between different European countries – a search which is not necessarily successful. Both EuroNews and ARTE in their different ways follow an agenda which is explicitly bi- or multilingual, explicitly trans-national, explicitly European.

EuroNews, with its close links to the European Union, follows a political agenda in trying to construct a degree of European subjectivity as part of the wider task of creating a united Europe. In our case study of the forms in which it operates and the rhetoric it employs, we came to the – possibly unfortunate, possibly overpessimistic – conclusion that, for the present at least, the channel is unsuccessful in constructing or appealing to a shared European experience. The minuscule audience share it receives across Europe underlines in sociological terms what we have shown in our analysis of the linguistic and semiotic forms within which it manoeuvres.

ARTE, on the other hand, has a distinctly cultural agenda – one which prefigures to some extent the political construction of Europe in that there were always well-travelled, multilingual elite groups with an appetite for transnational high culture outside television. In that sense, the channel finds it easier to find a minority TV audience whose tastes coincide with the public-service ethos of education and the serious rational engagement with topics as a form of entertainment – 'Bildung' and 'Kultur' experienced as joyful or otherwise rewarding. However, in our case study it became clear that ARTE is uneasy about the minority appeal to these cultural elites who live mainly in France, where ARTE has a terrestrial frequency; to a lesser degree in Germany, where it is only receivable via satellite or cable; and to a minute degree across Europe in general, where it is in principle receivable via the Astra satellite in many homes. ARTE would instead like to imagine itself as a Europe-wide channel of culture. This attempt to construct a Europe-wide experience of culture, where culture means transnational pleasure in knowing and expertise for more than a small niche audience, is less likely to succeed, and we have shown through the channel's confused rhetoric about itself that ARTE itself is not clear what this would imply. On the level of programming, a wider appeal even for a more general, trans-national, educated audience would require a radical rethinking of some of the elite forms through which it operates, epitomised by programmes such as the unrelentingly demanding *Histoire Parallèle*. However, as a channel for a trans-national minority audience, ARTE clearly has found its niche in a much more comfortable way than EuroNews.

By concentrating on these two channels, we have focused on what is innovatory in the European TV world rather than on what is the old and the same, but in much greater quantity.[1] Certainly, the majority of new channels receivable across Europe via DBS either follow the pattern of Sky and offer various generic and light-entertainment channels encrypted in the national language of the main target group; or they follow the German pattern, where mixed programming is still the norm for private and public channels; or they offer mixed channels alongside generic ones. The most popular channels, whether terrestrial, satellite or (as in the German case) both, address national audiences in their national languages, paid for by advertisers who target national consumers, often in ways highly specific to those audiences. These channels survive on extensive repetition, with a large percentage of US imported material, and an emphasis on light entertainment.[2] No 'lingua franca' unites European television viewers in front of their screens, and if there is a media 'cultura franca', it is based on American-style popular entertainment forms – soaps, game shows, talk shows, hospital and detective series – but preferably with nationally specific themes and settings. There are some licensed game-show formats such as the ubiquitous *Wheel of Fortune* or *Jeopardy*, which allow interesting intra-European comparisons in this respect (Skovmand 1992; Meinhof 1998: Chapter 3). It is likely that the new digital age will provide the viewers Europe-wide with more of this kind of national/international-type programming, possibly in the direction of more generic channels replacing the current mixed-entertainment ones.

A tiny (and elite) audience segment uses DBS technology to participate in a kind of armchair tourism. DBS (but not cable) allows channel hopping across a Europe of many different televisual experiences, from the Italian Rai Uno to the French TV5, to the Spanish TVE, to the German ARD, or any of the other huge number of national channels, including many new Eastern European ones. For these viewers, DBS has created a unique and extraordinary opportunity to bring the multilingual, multicultural, multi-perspectival Europe of many nations and regions into their living rooms. Perhaps the Europe of the future will be able to nourish more such citizens, able to construct and negotiate their regional national and European identities in multiple overlapping ways through what is likely to continue to be the most popular medium of our times. No one should expect to see programming *designed* for the neighbours to (over)hear. These sophisticated neighbours don't want such a concession, nor does their market value warrant it.

Yet the possibility of such an audience returns us again to the complexities in the cultural dynamics of the new programming patterns. National solidarity is the key. At one level, national solidarity as constituted through forms of programming is offered here as a characterisation of the *past*. It has been undermined by the multiplicity of alternatives to the televisually shared moment across the nation – undermined by CNN, by EuroNews, by channel hopping, by endless repeats, by Liverpool Live. Yet, at a different level, it is in national solidarity that we find the major *resistance* to the emergence of Europe as a new 'World in Common' on the model of the earlier national worlds. There is no paradox here, since the constituents of national solidarity at the first level are different from those which constitute the second level. At the national level there is some (albeit qualified) credibility to the notion of unity-in-diversity, thanks to the broad and overlapping bases for shared knowledge and experience underpinned by institutional structures. Europe, like the world, is all diversity; its Others (Jews, Muslims, immigrants, the black-skinned) as much within as without. Satellite tourism after all is not confined to *European* countries, except to the extent that technology prohibits more geographically ambitious ventures.

# Notes

## Introduction

1 In fact, Straubhaar's seven major geocultural markets are not 'unified by language' in the sense that they are monolingual entities. But even nations are not unified in this sense. Most countries are multilingual, though many, like Britain, have one language which is clearly dominant (see Gifreu 1996).

2 This perspective, of course, does not in itself do much to illuminate the causal relations between the wider socioeconomic and political conditions within which television operates, and the forms of programming which result from those conditions. The reality of those causal relations in general terms is beyond dispute; their operation in specific cases is worthy of further study which attends, much more than our own, to considerations of textual *production* in the new regimes of broadcasting. A case in point would be that of the Shopping Channel. It is impossible to understand the distinctive forms of audiovisual discourse produced therein without reference to the necessity of studio-based production as a means of maintaining very low production costs, and the channel's position as the 'owner' of the commodities on offer – apparently a necessary device for ensuring that its promotion of those commodities does not count as 'advertising' in the terms of the relevant national and European legislation which (still) ration the amount of airtime during which commercials can be screened.

## 1 Regularity and change in 24-hour news

1 The toddlers' truce was an interval between 6.00 p.m. and 8.00 p.m. during which no programming was broadcast, allowing parents to put their children to bed.

2 Notice that this description of true televisual 'flow' equates it with the absence of structure, discontinuity, refusal of coherence. This is not consistent with the notion of 'flow' as a superordinate level of coherence, planned (perhaps) but covert, which other theorists have employed. Corner (forthcoming) discusses such contradictions in the use of the term in media scholarship.

## 2 Timeliness: textual form and the beef crisis story

1 The exception was the 10.00 a.m. cycle, when the beef story was displaced from lead position by a report on the trial of Yitzhak Rabin's assassin. Recency seems to determine this order of priorities. The trial report allows the newsroom to lead on an item featuring actual events (the verdict and the sentence) closer to the moment of broadcasting than the beef story allows at that time of day. What's more, there is actual courtroom footage to show.

2 Times in this section are Brussels times – one hour ahead of London times as given in the discussion of Sky News. When it is important, the corresponding London time will also be indicated.

### 3 Liveness as synchronicity and liveness as aesthetic

1 It is worth noting that on 14 May 1997, the day of the first Queen's Speech following Tony Blair's General Election triumph, it was possible to watch the same (live) footage from the House of Lords simultaneously on three different British channels. Sky News transmitted it, BBC2 transmitted it and the Parliament Channel transmitted it. Of course the event itself obtained even more coverage eventually as it worked its way into the news bulletins of all channels with any kind of claim to a news content – not only the five terrestrial channels, but also the three rolling-news channels (Sky News, EuroNews and CNN) – to say nothing of the foreign-language channels available to viewers in the UK. But it is presumably the international (as against the merely national) interest which accounts for this saturation coverage. It is not really a counterexample to the argument concerning television's retreat from a role in the maintaining of national ceremonial and identity.

2 Of course, most dialogue on television is scripted: all dramatic material, in films, plays, series, serials, documentary dramas, provides 'lines' for performers to exchange. Scripted dialogue, strictly speaking, lacks the property of *emergence* which is so important to liveness (see Marriott 1997). Instead of composing the talk in real time, whole conversations are crafted with a particular plan in mind, before they are delivered. But the point of drama dialogue is that it is mimetic of emergence: the characters don't know what happens next, and neither do viewers (canonically), whose mode of engagement is required to respect that virtual emergence.

### 4 Constructing Europe

1 But even MTV has felt the need to diversify its pan-European schedules. MTV now provides four regional services, which target specifically viewers in different parts of Europe: MTV in the UK, MTV Central (Germany, Austria and Switzerland), MTV Italy, and MTV pan-Northern (basically all the rest of Europe, as well as some other countries such as Egypt and South Africa). In Germany, where several music channels have copied the style of MTV while catering more specifically for their home audiences by using the native language and by including more home-grown music from other European countries, the uncrypted Viva (audience share in January 1998: 0.5 per cent), in particular, has become more popular than MTV (audience share: 0.2 per cent).

2 Billig does not differentiate between relational and absolute deixis, but his thesis is based on the use of the more context-dependent relational forms (for a discussion of this distinction, see Chapter 3, and Fillmore 1975).

3 Since no audience research is included in our study, we are making no claims about the actual meanings which viewers make out when watching these programmes. Our analysis is of the textual phenomena of EuroNews from which one can infer the constructed or implied audience of EN. For a critical discussion of the issues in audience research and its relationship to textual analysis, see Corner (1991).

4 It is too early to speculate whether the arrival of digital television will restore these choices to cable users as well.

5 It is not known whether, or how many, viewers make use of this multilingual facility for other purposes than just news-watching, such as boosting their foreign-language skills; it is to be assumed that at least some of the elite market sector targeted by EN – that is, those 'upper and middle-class younger audiences, … who have an interest

in international affairs' (Schlesinger 1994: 42) – have caught on to this almost unique opportunity for instantaneous translation (Meinhof 1990).
6 We owe that information to one of Ulrike Hanna Meinhof's Finnish students, Hanna Kaisa Rintanen.

## 5 Narrowcasting

1 In the original German language:

| | |
|---|---|
| *Moderator (M):* | Wie war denn das zu der DDR Zeit? Konnten Sie da loslegen, wie sie wollten? |
| *Uschi Brüning (UB):* | Nein, nein, durchaus nicht. Da gabs dann die Verordnung 60 zu 40, oder umgekehrt. |
| *Ernst-Ludwig Petrowski (EP):* | Es gab da den Begriff VE. |
| M: | Und der stand für? |
| EP: | Das ist nicht der Anfangsbuchstabe oder der Buchstabe für VEB, sondern für verbotene Einfuhr und da konnte man sogar in dem erlaubten Bereich 60 Prozent Ost sein. |
| UB: | ja 60 Prozent |
| EP: | und 40 West, aber wenn man dort Verbotenes in die Westmischung hineintat. |
| UB: | Dann kams zum Berufsverbot |
| EP: | Genau |
| UB: | Das gabs alles |
| M: | Das war ja jetzt total interessant. Könnten Sie aus der Kalten etwas Verbotenes von damals spielen und etwas nicht-Verbotenes, aber nur mal so anklingen, daß man einen Unterschied hört, oder hört man den gar nicht? |
| EP: | Wir würden den nicht mehr hören. Da wurde dann hineininterpretiert menschenverachtende, dekadente, oder friedensgefahr- dende Thematik in der Musik, und da konnte man {je nach dem} |
| M: | {In den} Texten, oder auch selbst wenn nur {Saxophon} |
| UB: | {Entscheidend} war zunachst mal die Herkunft … {des Stuckes } |
| M: | {Ach so} |
| UB: | {und dann} |
| EP: | {Ich erinnere}mich wir hatten den *River Kwai Marsch*. Wir hatten eine Besetzung mit einer legendaren sachsischen Band, ubrigens, Eberhard Weise, da hatten wir immer drei-vier Posaunen, es war ein posaunenlastiges Unternehmen, und mit diesem Stuck sehr viel Erfolg, und wir wurden mit ihm auch verboten, und gingen dann sozusagen *River-Kwai* spielend unter. |

## 6 Spatial relations and sociability

1 However, these innovations have largely disappeared for some of the new regional services. MTV Germany, with its German moderators and its regular replay of the German hit parade, is no longer considered a trendsetter but rather in competition with the more successful home-grown channel viva (audience share: 0.5 per cent) with its ad slogan 'viva loves you' (the channel, of course, speaks German all the

time). Whether the recent reshuffle of the top personnel will make any difference in reclaiming some innovatory energy for MTV remains to be seen.

## Part III  Trash and quality

1 But one particular afternoon talk show, *Arabella Kiesbauer* on Pro 7, became the focus of a great deal of debate in the German media in spring 1998. With titles such as 'Schafft die Huren ab' (Get Rid of the Whores) and 'Nackte Tatsachen – ich kenne keine Scham' (Naked Facts – I Know no Modesty), Kiesbauer's show was attacked by the media, including the participants of one other talk show (*Sabine Christiansen*) devoted to the topic. As in the USA, the perceived excesses of such shows, and their transmission time in the early afternoon, are currently leading to pressure on all channels to reconsider their afternoon programmes, with more protection for young viewers. Pro 7 was even threatened with a withdrawal of its terrestrial licence, which it holds in many federal states, unless it agrees either to clean up these shows or move them to an evening slot.

## 7  Bad television?

1 We disagree with Schröder (1992), whose anti-elitist line – that quality is in the mind of the beholder – cannot entertain the possibility that there may be dangers behind the validation of audience satisfaction. For certain viewers, pornography would get the 'quality' seal of approval on Schröder's terms – but not on ours.

## 8  European high culture – arts discourse in the new regime

1 See also Meinhof and Smith (forthcoming) for a discussion of the *South Bank Show*'s appropriation of the popular.
2 See, for example, the derivations of the word: a 'cultured' person in English still implies someone of refined tastes; the German equivalent would be a 'gebildete Person'; an event can be described as 'kulturell', but this does not make it specifically high culture; 'kultiviert', a derivative of 'Kultur', has 'cultivated' as a false friend, and stresses the sense of having been carefully nurtured. As a characteristic of a person, it has slightly snobbish associations in modern German. French has no difficulty with 'l'homme culturel', clearly a well-educated intellectual with high artistic tastes – no snobbery intended.
3 There is, however, the judgemental term 'Trivialliteratur' for popular, i.e. trivial, literature.
4 European audiences are divided in their preferences for viewing foreign films with subtitles or dubbed into their own language. In France and the UK, imported 'art' films are almost always subtitled; in Scandinavian countries this is true for most imported film, including imported US TV drama. This finds little favour with German mainstream TV audiences, who prefer dubbed versions. ARTE's German partner therefore usually shows dubbed versions where available and transmits subtitled versions only where they are not.
5 Was die Welt vor 50 Jahren bewegt hat, bewegt uns heute mit Marc Ferro
Auferstanden aus Archiven – die Woche vor fünfzig Jahren
6 Am 1 Mai 1947 ist der Kommunismus auf dem Höhepunkt seiner Macht. Die UDSSR hält Paraden ab und verweigert jede Vereinbarungen zu Deutschland. Sie kontrolliert Bulgarien und Polen.
Dabei wird sie noch von Tito überboten, der Thorez in Frankreich wegen seines Verbleibens in einer Dreiparteienregierung zu opportunistisch findet. Was beide Parteien in Deutschland betrifft, so sind sie bereits auf Konfrontationskurs.

7  Feierlichkeiten zum 1. Mai in der UDSSR und im Ausland. Begeistert beging das Sowjetvolk den 1. Mai, den internationalen Feiertag der Werktätigen. (Panorama shot of Leningrad with river/pictures of May parade/Now spoken voice-over – Russian – with German subtitle captions and music) Die Heldenstadt Leningrad, Wiege der Oktoberrevolution …

8  Maifeiern überall. (Pictures of people marching through Brandenburger Gate) Wie überall in der Welt wurde auch in Deutschland der 1. Mai wieder als Festtag der Werktätigen und Tag der Völkerversöhnung gefeiert.

9  Am Morgen des 1. Mai beginnt in Stadt und Land die große Kundgebung der Werktätigen.

10  Der 1. Mai, Fest der Arbeiter, der Maiglöckchen und – nach der Theorie – der ersten warmen Tage vermischt aufs innigste Poesie und Gewerkschaftsanforderungen und macht eine eindeutige Definition unmöglich. Wie dem auch sei, jedes Jahr herrscht am 1. Mai die gleiche Stimmung: geschlossene Geschäfte, verlassene Plätze und Straßen. Die Schüler beklagen sich: der Feiertag fiel dieses Jahr auf ihren freien Donnerstag. So ein Pech. 'Lieber Herr Minister, ist der 1. Mai ein Donnerstag, legen Sie ihn doch bitte auf einen Schultag … '

11  Das Volk brachte zum Ausdruck, daß es unter Lenins und Stalins Banner den endgültigen Sieg des Kommunismus in unserem Land anstrebt. Gerühmt sei Stalin.

12  In Tausenden von kleinen Orten und Dörfern gab es eine Maifeier nach alt herge-brachter Art. Hier in Ebenhauen in Bayern. Nach dem Umzug durch den Ort beschließt der Tanz unter dem Maibaum den Festtag aller Werktätigen.

13  Herrmann Schimmel mahnte die Versammelten alles einzusetzen, damit wir durch Einheit zum Frieden, durch Einheit zur Überwindung von Hunger und Not, durch Einheit zum Sozialismus gelangen.

14  Die Maifeiertage, an denen Busse angezündet wurden, wichen friedlicheren, ebenso interessanten Demonstrationen. Heute denkt man eher daran, fenster herzustellen, als Scheiben zu zerschlagen.

15  Zum Gespräch über diesen 1. Mai 1947 begrüße ich Pierre Broué der über die bolschewistische Partei geschrieben hat, über den spanischen Bürgerkrieg und über die deutsche Revolution. Er war Trotzkyist und ich frage ihn deshalb: Sie, die Trotzkyisten konnten sich damals bereits den Zerfall des Sowjetregimes vorstellen…

16  Pierre Broué was sagt ihnen dieser 1. Mai in Westddeutschland…?

17  Nun wie Ostdeutschland, das bald ein neuer Staat sein wird, den ersten Mai feiert.

18  *Ferro:*   Und die Kommunisten glaubten, die Macht auf eine andere Weise wiederzubekommen?

   *Broué:*   Die Kommunisten halten das alles für ein Zwischenspiel, und als Stalin versichert, daß ihre Demonstrationen den Imperialismus in den Kolonien zurückdrängen, die Marshallplaninititative zurückdrängen, usw sagen sie, wir sind immer noch irgendwo Teil der Regierung. Das beteuern sie unaufhörlich, selbst, als man sie verfolgt. Es bleibt stets die ausgestreckte Hand, die ausgestreckte Hand in Richtung Regierung.

   *Ferro:*   Und sie warten bis zur Ära Mitterrand.

   *Broué:*   Ja, so ungefähr.

19  *Ferro:*   Pierre Broué, dieser Wochenschaubeitrag wird in dem bekannten, angeblich stets lässigen und distanzierten Tonfall des Chronisten vorgetragen. Aber es ist irreführend, die Dinge so darzustellen [discourse of judgement]. Wenn es einen stürmischen 1. Mai innerhalb der politsichen und gewerkschaftlichen Organisationen gegeben hat, dann ist es der 1. Mai 1947. Es ist der Zeitpunkt, an dem Daniel Manière und die Sozialisten ausgepfiffen werden, Sie sind an der Regierung, als die Kommunisten sich beinahe spalten mit der Frage, weiter mit der Regierung, oder nicht. Und man will glauben machen, es sei alles in Ordnung. Das wird sich in einigen Monaten ändern.

*Broué:* Ja, es ist das übliche Propagandamärchen, denn gerade jetzt, Anfang 1947 kommt es zu einer extremen Spannung, die sich überall bemerkbar macht. In der Auflösung der Regierungskoalitionen im Osten wie im Westen, aber auch in der Auflösung der kommunistischen Partei. Zum Beispiel erleben wir in Italien die Spaltung und in Frankreich. Dort haben wir die Spannung zwischen den Arbeitern und der CJT, zwischen den Arbeitern und den Führern der kommunistischen Partei, teilweise auch innerhalb der Partei und der CJT. Der Streik bei Renault ist daher kein Zufall. Wo man zum ersten mal eine Konfrontation erlebt, wo sich die Mehrheit der Arbeiter gegen die Gewerkschaften wendet und sie kritisiert. Es ist ein entscheidendes Ereignis, das die Schnelligkeit und Heftigkeit der Wende in Frankreich erklärt.

*Ferro:* Und wir wissen, was sich in einigen Monaten abspielt.

*Broué:* Natürlich.

*Ferro:* Aber die Wochenschau läßt von solchen Ereignissen nichts ahnen. Im Grunde ist das reine Desinformation.

*Broué:* Ganz sicher.

20 Ja. Und dann kam es zum Streik bei Renault. Den Streik bei Renault habe ich aus nächster Nähe verfolgt, weil ich zur GCI gehärte, dem trotzkyistischen Jugendverband. Unser Generalsekretär hieß Daniel Renart, ein toller Kerl, ein junger Pariser Arbeiter, unerschrocken, ausdrucksstark, ein begnadeter Redner und Agitator. Und Daniel arbeitete bei Renault ... Ich war Leibwächter unseres Freundes Daniel Renart, ich schlief auf seiner Fußmatte. In Wirklichkeit hatten wir uns getäuscht, die Dinge waren weiter fortgeschritten, als wir glaubten ...

21 *Ferro:* Pierre Broué was sagt ihnen dieser 1. Mai in Westddeutschland?

*Broué:* Ich bin erstaunt über die Arbeitermassen, sie waren da, entschlossen, arm, armselig gekleidet, mager. Alle zeigten Gesichter von Menschen, die eine schreckliche Kriegs- und Nachkriegszeit erlebt haben. Deutschland hungert damals. In Deutschland gibt es eine soziale Zeitbombe. Wenn unser Thema der assessment Marshallplan wäre, fänden wir hier eine der Ursachen für diesen Plan, da Europa um jeden Preis stabilisieren wollte.

22 A further difficulty for German viewers of the programme is that the dialogue between the experts is held in French, with a German simultaneous translation spoken over a still audible French soundtrack. The German translation is far from perfect with often cumbersome phrasing and non-standard grammar. Again, help could be given by supporting subtitles, at the very least a written display of the proper names that are referred to.

23 Our transcription stays as close to his original speech as is possible, but in some of the most incomprehensible instances we have re-translated his speech from the French and German subtitles provided by ARTE.

## Worlds in common? Conclusion

1 For an analysis of the cross-cultural differences and continuities in TV advertising, see Pitcher (1989), Myers (1994), Kelly-Holmes (1996), Meinhof (in press: Chapter 5) and Meinhof (forthcoming).

2 Many of the new commercial channels do not meet the quota set by the EEC regulations of October 1989, which requires a majority proportion of broadcasting time for European productions (see Commission of the European Communities 1984: Article 4; also Commission of the European Communities 1994, and the regular reports published by the EU).

# References

Note: The World-Wide Web addresses given here were correct as of December 1997. However, the Web is a fluid environment: addresses change; sites, and pages, disappear. Hard copies of works cited are in the possession of the authors.

Allen, Robert C. (1992) 'Audience oriented criticism'. In *Channels of discourse, reassembled*, Allen, R.C., London: Routledge, pp. 101–37.
Anderson, Benedict (1991) *Imagined communities*, London: Verso.
Ang, I. (1985) *Watching 'Dallas': soap opera and the melodramatic imagination*, London: Methuen.
Bachmair, B. (1996) *Fernsehkultur: Subjektivität in einer Welt bewegter Bilder*, Opladen: Westdeutscher Verlag.
Bachmair, B. and Kress, G. (1996) *Höllen-Inszenierung Wrestling: Beiträge zur pädagogischen Genre-Forschung*, Opladen: Leske and Budrich.
Baker, Mona (1992) *In other words*, London: Routledge.
Barker, Chris (1997) *Global television: an introduction*, Oxford: Blackwell.
Barker, Martin (1997) 'Taking the extreme case: understanding a fascist fan of Judge Dredd'. In *Trash aesthetics: popular culture and its audience*, Cartmell, D., Hunter, I.Q., Kaye, H. and Whelehan, I., London: Pluto, pp. 14–30.
Bell, Alan (1991) *The language of news media*, London: Blackwell.
Bell, Alan and Garrett, Peter (1998) *New approaches to media discourse*, London: Blackwell.
Bennett, W.J. (1995) 'Statement by William J Bennett, announcing a public campaign against select day-time television talk shows', 26 October, http://www.heritage.org/empower/pr1026a.html: Bennett
Berger, Peter Ludwig and Luckmannn, Thomas (1967) *The social construction of knowledge: a treatise in the sociology of knowledge*, London: Allen Lane.
Billig, Michael (1995) *Banal nationalism*, London: Sage.
Bourdieu, Perre (1986) *Signs of distinction: a social critique of the judgement of taste*, London: Routledge.
——(1990) 'The aristocracy of culture'. In *Media, Culture and Society* 12: 225–54.
——(1997) 'L'économie des échanges linguistiques'. In *Langue Française* May: 17–34.
Boyd-Bowman, Susan (1985) 'The MTM phenomenon: the company, the book, the programme'. In *Screen* 26(6): 75–87.
Brunsdon, Charlotte (1990) 'Problems with quality'. In *Screen* 31(1): 67–90.
——(1991) 'Satellite dishes and the landscapes of taste'. In *New Formations* 15. Reprinted in Brunsdon, C. (1997) *Screen tastes*, London: Routledge, pp. 148–64.

Caldwell, J. (1995) *Televisuality: style, crisis and authority in American television*, New Brunswick, NJ: Rutgers University Press.

Carbaugh, D. (1988) *Talking American: cultural discourses on Donahue*, Norwood, NJ: Ablex.

Carpignano, P., Andreson, B., Aronowitz, S. and Difiazio, W. (1990) 'Chatter in the age of electronic reproduction: television and the "public mind"'. In *Social Text* 25/26: 33–55.

Caughie, J. (1990) 'Playing at being American: games and tactics'. In *Logics of television: essays in cultural criticism*, Mellencamp, P., Bloomington, IN: Indiana University Press, pp. 54–65.

Coates, Jennifer (1996) *Women talk*, Oxford: Blackwell.

Cohen, A., Levy, M., Roeh, I. and Gurevitch, M. (1996) *Global newsrooms, local audiences: a study of the Eurovision news exchange*, London: John Libbey.

Cohen, Robin (1994) *Frontiers of Identity: the British and the others*, London: Longman.

Coleman, James and Rollet, Brigitte (1997) *Television in Europe*, Exeter: Intellect.

Collins, Jim (1989) *Uncommon cultures*, London: Routledge.

Collins, Richard (1992) *Satellite television in Western Europe*, London: John Libbey.

——(1994) *Broadcasting and audio-visual policy in the European single market*, London: John Libbey.

Commission of the European Communities (1984) *Television without frontiers*, Luxembourg: Commission of the European Communities.

——(1994) *Communication from the Commission to the Council and the European Parliament on the application of Articles 4 and 5 of Directive 89/552/EEC television without frontiers*.

Corner, John (1991) 'Meaning, genre and context: the problematics of "public knowledge" in the new audience studies'. In *Mass media and society*, Curran, J. and Gurevitch, M., London: Edward Arnold.

——(1995) *Television form and public address*, London: Edward Arnold.

——(1996) *The art of record*, Manchester: Manchester University Press.

——(1997) ' "Quality" and television: histories and contexts'. In, *Quality television*, Eide, M., Gentikow, B. and Helland, B., Report no. 30, Department of Media Studies, University of Bergen, 49–66.

——(in press) 'Flow'. In *Critical ideas in television studies*, Corner, J., London: Oxford University Press.

Corner, John, Harvey, S. and Lury, K. (1993) 'British television and the "quality" issue'. In *Media Information Australia* 68: 78–86.

Corner, John, Richardson, K. and Fenton, N. (1990) *Nuclear reactions: form and response in public issue television*, London: John Libbey.

Cunningham, Stuart and Jacka, Elizabeth (1996) *Australian television and international mediascapes*, London: Cambridge University Press.

Dahlgren, Peter (1995) *Television and the public sphere: citizenship, democracy and the media*, London: Sage.

Doohan, D. (1995) 'Skeptical about the skeptics: reaction to "The TV Talk Shows", Gene Emery's article for *The Skeptical Inquirer*'. In *The Skeptical Inquirer* 9 July.

Ehrenreich, B. (1995) 'In defense of talk shows', In *Time Magazine* 4 December (146): 23.

Eide, Martin, Gentikow, Barbara and Helland, Knut (1997) *Quality Television*, Bergen, Norway: Department of Media Studies, University of Bergen.

Ellis, John (1982) *Visible fictions*, London: Routledge.

Emanuel, Susan (1992) 'Culture in space: the European cultural channel'. In *Media, Culture and Society* 14: 128–99.

——(1993) 'Cultural television: Western Europe and the United States'. In *European Journal of Communication* 18: 131–47.

——(1995) 'A community of culture? The European television channel'. In *History of European Ideas* 12(2): 169–76.

Fairclough, N. (1994) 'Conversationalisation of public discourse and the authority of the consumer'. In *The authority of the consumer*, Keat, R., Whiteley, N. and Abercombie, N., London: Routledge.

——(1995) *Media discourse*, London: Edward Arnold.

Featherstone, M. (1990) *Global culture, nationalism, globalisation and modernity*, London: Sage.

——(1992) *Cultural theory and cultural change*, London: Sage.

Ferguson, Marjorie (1990) 'The mythology about globalisation'. In *European Journal of Communication* 7: 69–93.

——(1992) 'Electronic media and the redefining of time and space'. In *Public communication: the new imperatives*, Ferguson, M., London: Sage, pp. 152–72.

Feuer, Jane (1983) 'The concept of "live television": ontology vs. ideology'. In *Regarding television*, Kaplan, E.A., Los Angeles: American Film Institute/University Publications of America, pp. 12–22.

Filion, Michel (1996) 'Broadcasting and cultural identity: the Canadian experience'. In *Media, Culture and Society* 18(3): 447–67.

Fillmore, C. (1975) *Santa Cruz lectures on deixis, 1971*, Bloomington, IN: Indiana Linguistics Club.

Fiske, John (1987) *Television culture*, London: Methuen.

Fowler, Roger (1991) *Language in the news: discourse and ideology in the press*, London: Routledge.

Gates, Henry Louis (1995) 'Thirteen ways at looking at a black man'. In *New Yorker* 23 October: 60.

Geertz, C. (1960) *The religion of Java*, Chicago: University of Chicago Press.

Geraghty, C. (1991) *Women and soap opera: a study of prime time soaps*, Cambridge: Polity Press.

Giddens, Anthony (1990) *The consequences of modernity*, Cambridge: Polity Press.

——(1994) 'Living in a post-traditional society'. In *Reflexive modernisation*, Beck, U., Giddens, A. and Lash, C., Cambridge: Polity Press.

Gifreu, Josep (1996) 'Linguistic order and spaces of communication in post-Maastricht Europe'. In *Media, Culture and Society* 18: 127–39.

Goffman, E. (1981) *Forms of talk*, Oxford: Blackwell.

Goodwin, Andrew (1993) *Dancing in the distraction factory*, London: Routledge.

Gray, Ann (1987) 'Behind closed doors: video recorders in the home'. In *Boxed in: women and television*, Baehr, H. and Dyer, G., London: Pandora Press. pp. 38–54.

Gresser, Charis (1996) 'Kelvin seeks gravitas with bouncing dwarfs'. In *Electronic Telegraph* 14 September (479).

Gripsrud, J. (1995) *The 'Dynasty' years: Hollywood television and critical media studies*, London: Routledge.

Gurevitch, M., Levy, M. and Roeh, I. (1991) 'The global newsroom: convergence and diversities in the globalisation of television news'. In *Communication and citizenship*, Dahlgren, P. and Sparks, C., London and New York: Routledge.

Habermas, Jurgen (1989/1962) *Structural transformation of the public sphere*, Cambridge: Polity Press.

Hall, Amanda (1996) 'Three-way talks on single channel'. In *Electronic Telegraph* 8 September (473).

Hannerz, U. (1992) *Cultural complexity: studies in the social organisation of meaning*, New York: Columbia University Press.

Harvey, David (1989) *The condition of postmodernity*, Oxford: Blackwell.

Horton, D. and Wohl, R. (1993) 'Mass communication as para-social interaction: observations on intimacy at a distance'. In *Psychiatry* 19: 215–29.

Humphreys, P. (1990) *Media and media policy in West Germany: the press and broadcasting since 1945*, New York: Berg.

Hunter, I.Q. and Kaye, H. (1997) 'Introduction'. In *Trash aesthetics: popular culture and its audience*, Cartmell, D., Hunter, I.Q., Kaye, H. and Whelehan, I., London: Pluto, pp. 1–13.

Hutchinson, John and Smith, Anthony (1996) *Nationalism*, Oxford: Oxford University Press.

Jensen, K.B. (1995) *The social semiotics of mass communication*, London: Sage.

Kelly-Holmes, H. (1996) 'Cultural convergence and national stereotyping: the future of advertising in the United Europe'. In *Conceiving of Europe: Diversity in Unity*, Musolff, A., Schaffner, C. and Townson, M., Aldershot: Dartmouth, pp. 97–107.

Larsen, Peter (1992) 'More than just images: the whole picture. News in the multi-channel universe'. In *Media cultures: reappraising transnational media*, Skovmand, M. and Schröder, K.C., London: Routledge, pp. 124–41.

Lash, S. and Urry, J. (1994) *Economies of signs and space*, Newbury Park and London: Sage.

Levinson, S. (1983) *Pragmatics*, Cambridge: Cambridge University Press.

Lewis, J (1985) 'Decoding television news'. In *Television in transition*, Drummond, P. and Paterson, R., London: British Film Institute.

Lieberman, J. (1995) 'Statement of Senator Joe Lieberman, Talk show campaign news conference' 26 October, http://www.heritage.org/empower/pr1026b.html: Lieberman

Liebes, T. and Katz, E. (1989) 'On the critical abilities of television viewers'. In *Remote control*, Seiter, E., Borchers, H., Kreutzner, G. and Warth, Eva-Marie, London: Routledge, pp. 204–22.

Liebscher, Grit (1997) 'Unified Germany? Processes of identifying, redefining and negotiating in interactions between East and West Germans'. In *Proceedings of the fourth annual symposium about language and society*, Chu, A., Guerra, A.P. and Tetreault, C., Austin, TX: Department of Linguistics.

Livingstone, Sonia and Lunt, Peter (1994) *Talk on television*, London: Routledge.

Lury, Karen (1997) Cynicism and enchantment: British youth television in the 1980s and 1990s, unpublished Ph.D., University of Liverpool.

Lyons, J. (1977) *Semantics*, 2 vols, Cambridge: Cambridge University Press.

McCabe, Colin (1986) *High theory/low culture*, Manchester: Manchester University Press.

MacGregor, Brent (1997) *Live, direct and biased: making television news in the satellite age*, London: Edward Arnold.

McLellan, J (1993) 'Down the tube'. In *Face* 54: 48–53.

Marriott, S. (1996) 'Time and time again: live television and the construction of replay talk'. In *Media, culture and society* 18(1): pp. 69–86.

——(1997) 'The emergence of live television talk'. In *Text* 17(2): 181–98.

Masciarotte, Gloria-Jean (1991) 'C'mon girl: Oprah Winfrey and the discourse of feminine talk'. In *Genders* 11: 81–110.

Meinhof, Ulrike H. (1994) 'Breadline Britain'. In *Text, discourse and context: representations of poverty in Britain*, Meinhof, U. and Richardson, K., London: Longman, pp. 67–92.

——(1998) *Language learning in the age of satellite television*, Oxford: Oxford University Press.

——(forthcoming) 'Italian Longings: British TV commercials and the myth of the south'. In *Media, culture and the social world*, Bachmair, B., Kress, G. and Scalamonti, C.

Meinholf, Ulrike H. and Smith, J. (forthcoming) *Intertextuality and the Media: From Genre to Everyday Life*, Manchester, Manchester University Press.

Mellencamp, P. (1990) 'Beyond the pleasure principle'. In *The logics of telvision: essays in cultural criticism*, Mellencamp, P., London: British Film Institute, pp. 240–65.

Moores, Shaun (1996) *Satellite television and everyday life*, London: John Libbey.

Morley, D. (1980) *The nationwide audience*, London: British Film Institute.

——(1986) *Family television*, London: Comedia.

Morley, D. and Robins, K. (1995) *Spaces of identity: global media, electronic landscapes and cultural boundaries*, London: Routledge.

Morrison, D. (1992) *Television and the gulf war*, London: John Libbey.

Mowlana, Hamid (1997) *Global information and world communication*, 2nd edition, London: Sage.

Mulgan, Geoff (1997) 'Television's holy grail: seven types of quality'. In *Quality television*, Eide, M., Gentikow, B. and Helland, K., Bergen, Norway: Department of Media Studies, University of Bergen, pp. 13–48.

Myers, G. (1994) *Words in ads*, London: Edward Arnold.

Negrine, Ralph and Papathanassopoulos, S. (1991) 'The internationalisation of television'. In *European Journal of Communication* 6: 9–32.

Nichols, B. (1991) *Representing reality*, Bloomington, IN: Bloomington University Press.

Noam, Eli (1991) *Television in Europe*, Oxford: Oxford University Press.

Paglia, C. (1995) 'Talking trash: in defence of TV talk shows'. In *Salon Internet* 12 November (1), http://www.salon1999.com/12nov1995/feature/paglia.html: Salon Internet

Parker, Richard (1995) *Mixed signals: the prospects for global television news*, New York: Twentieth Century Fund.

Paterson, Christopher (1997) 'Global television news services'. In *Media in global context: a reader*, Sreberny-Mohammadi, A., Winseck, D., McKenna, J. and Boyd-Barrett, O., London: Edward Arnold, pp. 145–60.

Pitcher, F. (1989) 'Searching for European cultural identity: vivent les differences'. In *Intermedia* 17(6).

Postman, N. (1985) *Amusing ourselves to death*, London: Methuen.

Price, Monroe (1995) *Television, the public sphere and national identity*, Oxford: Oxford University Press.

Richardson, Kay (1994) 'Interpreting Breadline Britain.' In *Text discourse and context: representations of poverty in Britain*, Meinhof, U. H. and Richardson, K., London: Longman, pp. 93–104.

——(1997) 'Twenty first century commerce: the case of QVC'. In *Text* 17(2): 199–224.

Robertson, R. (1995) 'Globalisation: time–space and homogeneity–heterogeneity'. In *Global modernities*, Featherstone, M., Lash, S. and Robertson, R., London: Sage pp. 25–44.

Rustin, M. (1989) 'Post-Kleinian psychoanalysis and the postmodern'. In *New Left Review* 173: 107–28.

Sandford, John (1997) 'Television in Germany'. In *Television in Europe*, Coleman, James and Rollet, Brigitte, Exeter: Intellect, pp. 49–60.

Scannell, P. (1988) 'Radio times: the temporal arrangements of broadcasting in the modern world'. In *Television and its audience*, Drummond, P. and Patterson, R., London: British Film Institute, pp. 15–29.

——(1996) *Radio, television and modern life*, London: Blackwell.

Scannell, P. and Cardiff, D. (1991) *A social history of british broadcasting: serving the nation, 1923–1939*, Oxford: Basil Blackwell.

Schlesinger, P. (1992) 'Europeanness: a new cultural battlefield?'. In *Innovation* 5(1): 12–22.

——(1993) 'Wishful thinking: cultural politics, media and collective identities in Europe'. In *Journal of Communication* 43(2).

Schlesinger, P. (1994) 'Europe's contradictory communicative space.' *Daedalus*, Spring.

——(1997) 'From cultural defence to political culture: media, politics and collective identity in the European Union'. In *Media, Culture and Society* 19: 369–91.

Schröder, Kim Christian (1992) 'Cultural quality: search for a phantom'. In *Media cultures: reappraising transnational media*, Skovmand, M. and Schröder, K.C., London: Routledge, pp. 199–219.

Shattuc, J. (1997) *The talking cure: women and talk shows*, London: Routledge.

——(1998) '"Go Ricki": politics, perversion and pleasure in the 1990s'. In *The television studies book*, Geraghty, C and Lusted, D., London: Edward Arnold, pp. 212–25.

Silverstone, Roger (1992) *Consuming technologies: media and information in domestic spaces*, London: Routledge.

——(1993) 'Television, ontological security and the transitional object'. In *Media, Culture and Society* 15: 573–98.

——(1994) *Television and everyday life*, London: Routledge.

Sreberny-Mohammadi, Annabelle, Winseck, Dwayne, McKenna, Jim and Boyd-Barrett, Oliver (1997) *Media in global context: a reader*, London: Edward Arnold.

Straubhaar, Joseph D. (1997) 'Distinguishing the global, regional and national levels of world television'. In *Media in global context: a reader*, Sreberny-Mohammadi, A., Winseck, D., McKenna, J., Boyd-Barrett, O., London: Edward Arnold, pp. 284–98.

Swales, Valerie (1997) 'Television in the United Kingdom'. In *Television in Europe*, Coleman, James and Rollet, Brigitte, Exeter: Intellect, pp. 21–34.

Tetzlaff, D. (1986) 'MTV and the politics of postmodern pop'. In *Journal of Communication Inquiry* 10(1).

——(1995)'Anecdotal television'. In *Screen* 26(2): 18–27.

——(1996a) *Mediations: text and discourse in media studies*, London: Edward Arnold.

——(1996b) 'Televised chat and the synthetic personality'. In *Media studies: a reader*, Marris, P. and Thornham, S., Edinburgh: Edinburgh University Press, pp. 189–97.

Tomlinson, A. (1991) *Cultural imperialism*, London: Pinter Publications.

van Dijk, Teun (1988) *News as discourse*, New York: Erlbaum.

van Leeuwen, Theo (1991) 'The consumer, the producer and the state: analysis of a television news item'. In *Language, semiotics, ideology*, Threadgold, T., Grosz, E.A., Kress, G. and Halliday, M.A.K., Sydney: Pathfinder Press, pp. 203–25.

Venturelli, Shalini (1993) 'The imagined transnational public sphere in the European Community's broadcast philosophy: implications for democracy.' In *European Journal of Communication* 8: 491–518.

Vincent, R. (1992) 'CNN: elites talking to elites'. In *Triumph of the image: the media's war in the Persian Gulf*, Mowlana, H., Gerbner, G. and Schiller, H., Boulder, CO: Westview Press.

Walker, John (1993) *Arts TV: a history of arts television in Britain*, London: John Libbey.

Wenham, B. (1982) *The third age of broadcasting*, London: Faber and Faber.

Weymouth, Tony and Lamizet, Bernard (1996) *Markets and myths: forces for change in the European media*, Harlow: Addison Wesley Longman.

Williams, Raymond (1974) *Television: technology and cultural form*, London: Fontana.

——(1976) *Keywords*, London: Fontana.

# Index